THE LIFE AND DEATH
OF COLONEL ALBERT JENNINGS FOUNTAIN

*

THE LIFE
AND DEATH
OF COLONEL ALBERT
JENNINGS FOUNTAIN

by A. M. Gibson

*

UNIVERSITY OF OKLAHOMA PRESS
NORMAN AND LONDON

By A. M. GIBSON
The Kickapoos: Lords of the Middle Border (Norman, 1963)
The Life and Death of Colonel Albert Jennings Fountain
(Norman, 1965)
Fort Smith: Little Gibraltar on the Arkansas (with Edwin C. Bearss)
(Norman, 1969)
The Chickasaws (Norman, 1971)
*Wilderness Bonanza: The Tri-State District of Missouri, Kansas,
and Oklahoma* (Norman, 1972)

For
ARTHUR McANALLY AND DICK GRISSO

ISBN: 0-8061-1231-X

Library of Congress Catalog Card Number: 65-11229

4 5 6 7 8 9 10 11 12 13 14 15 16 17 18 19 20 21 22 23 24 25

ACKNOWLEDGMENTS

Many persons and institutions were of great help in bringing together the Fountain story and deserve a word of appreciation for their splendid efforts. Members of the National Archives staff went beyond the call of duty to help me trace the career of Colonel Fountain as a soldier and as a special prosecutor for the Department of Justice. University libraries, including the University of New Mexico Library at Albuquerque and New Mexico State University Library at Las Cruces, were fruitful sources of information on my subject, and the staff members at these institutions were remarkably co-operative and helpful. I am also indebted to the New Mexico Museum Library and New Mexico State Records Center, both at Santa Fe, for Fountain material. The Texas State Library at Austin was a gold mine for material on Colonel Fountain during the Texas period.

Individuals who were exceedingly helpful include: Alvin Stanchos, Mrs. Fisher Osburn, and James Day of the Texas State Library staff; Dr. Myra Jenkins of the New Mexico State Records Center; Ruth Rambo, New Mexico Museum Library; Cecil L. Chase, University of California Library; Dorothy Firebaugh, Sonora, California; Allan R. Ottley, California State Library; Hiram Dow, Roswell; W. C. Whatley, Las Cruces; Margaret Behringer, Oklahoma City; Dr. Thurman Wilkins, New York City; Michael A. Otero, Jr., Santa Fe; A. B. Carpenter, Roswell; Helen W. Platt, Sierra County; Chester Linschied, Las Cruces.

I am especially indebted to C. L. Sonnichsen, El Paso, and Elizabeth Fountain Armendariz, Albert Fountain, and Henry Fountain of Mesilla, New Mexico.

A. M. GIBSON

Norman, Oklahoma

Colonel Fountain

*"By 1880 he ruled Republicans in that region [Doña Ana County]
with an iron hand."*

CONTENTS

ILLUSTRATIONS

THE LIFE AND DEATH
OF COLONEL ALBERT JENNINGS FOUNTAIN

Major Albert Jennings Fountain

"While as a general rule, Fountain was affable and gentle, he was never known to go out of his way to avoid a fight; he was at his best in conflict."

CHAPTER I

The Man of Mystery

IT WAS A COLD, GLOOMY DAY, that Saturday in February, 1896. Low-hanging leaden clouds, covering the sky from horizon to horizon, added to the ominous setting. A buckboard rattled over the rutted Tularosa–Las Cruces highway. The driver bent his powerful body to shield the small boy beside him from the chilling wind and urged the horses to greater speed. Now and then he turned to study the road and the rolling plains on either side. His stalkers were still there, keeping their distance as if to avoid recognition, but always in sight. This had been going on for days. When he left Lincoln court on Thursday, two riders followed him. Friday a solitary horseman rode the horizon; by midday there were two again; and today there were three, one of them mounted on a mighty white horse.

The man stopped at Pellman's Well on the rim of the White Sands to water and rest the team. As he fixed the boy a quick dinner, he looked for his stalkers. There they were. On a hill to the northwest the three remote figures had pulled up, ominously patient, waiting for him to start again.

Turning back to the main road, the driver forced his team and by three that afternoon they were approaching the long cut through Chalk Hill. Just beyond lay the rise which led into San Augustin Pass; from there it was downhill into Las Cruces and home. Three miles from Chalk Hill he met Saturnino Barela, the stage driver. As they visited in the road, Barela saw the three stalkers reined up on the rim of a hill and pointed them out. The man told Barela that he had been followed since leaving Lincoln, and Barela encouraged him to ride back to Luna's Well, spend the night with him at the stage station, and then they could ride together into Las Cruces next morning. The man thought this over and thanked Barela but declined, explaining that the boy had caught a cold and needed his mother's care. For some time Barela watched the pair move down the road toward Chalk Hill before he turned on toward Luna's Well.

It was getting colder. The man wrapped the child in an Indian blanket and stuffed a quilt under the seat and around the boy's legs, buttoned his heavy overcoat and pulled his wide-brimmed hat down over his forehead to check the icy blast. Then he turned in all directions searching for the outriders. They had disappeared. He had not been too concerned as long as he could see them, but as he entered the Chalk Hill cut, he reached for his Winchester, flexed his chilled hands, and jacked a shell into the chamber. Holding the stock against his hip with one hand, he urged the team to a faster gait with the other. On the approach to the west side of the hill his eye caught a movement in a clump of weeds bordering the rutted road. In the gathering dusk he strained his eyes into focus; alert, ready, his fighter's sense aroused. He told the boy to lie flat under the spring seat. Just as the child cuddled beneath him, a burst of fire erupted from the weed patch. A staccato roar filled his ears. Before he could whip the Winchester into line, heavy slugs tore through his thick chest, into his heart and vitals. The old fighter's last sensation was that of hopelessness, the boy's shrill scream, and the surge of the runaway team tearing wildly down the sandy trace.

The Chalk Hill ambush cut down Colonel Albert Jennings Fountain, a leading citizen of New Mexico Territory, and brought to a close one of the most colorful and amazing careers in the history of the American West. Appropriately, death came in a dramatic, carefully staged performance to match the exciting life the Colonel had lived. Mystery shrouded his death just as it had his living past.

What was the origin of this man of splendid courage, great energy, and many talents? Until 1861 his life is folklore—family tales. Only two shreds of documentary evidence are known for that period. After 1861 he left a clear trail.

The folklore seems wild and exaggerated on first reading. But his later life, which can be documented and which, too, at times seems impossible and improbable and yet is true, lends credence to the tales of the early years. One as versatile and prominent as Colonel Fountain could be expected to become the subject of a rich—and possibly embroidered—epic among admiring family members.

Between his reported birth date in 1838 and 1861, there are twenty-three years—a time span in which a man's life is hardly begun. Yet, if family tradition can be trusted, this man did more in twenty-three years than most men do in several lifetimes. The only way to account for the accomplishments of his early years, for which there is no known proof, is the rare combination of native genius, abundant talent, excessive ambition and energy, and great physical strength plus an equally sensitive and powerful ego which Fountain had in later years—years for which his achievements can be documented.

According to family tradition he was born Albert Jennings on Staten Island, New York, in 1838. Here begins the mystery. Reportedly he was born into an Episcopalian family, yet no ecclesiastical record can be found in the Staten Island area of his birth or of his affiliation (either as a Jennings or a Fountain or a Fontaine) in any way with this religious group.

Colonel Fountain's father was Solomon Jennings, a sea captain. His mother was descended from the colonial Huguenot family of Fontaine. Even his name has an aura of mystery. If he was born Albert Jennings, why would he take the surname of Fountain? One family-history expert reported that a mysterious murder in the Jennings family caused many members to take other names.[1]

Fountain reportedly was educated in local schools and colleges. Although there is no record of his enrollment or attendance at any educational institutions, Fountain's published speeches, his histrionic ability, his talents as an artist and a playwright, his letters,

---

[1] Letter to the author from New York Genealogical and Biographical Society, New York City, November 28, 1961.

and his scholarly interests show a polish and erudition which only formal training could produce.[2]

Until 1861 there are only pieces of proof of Colonel Fountain's existence.[3] In the Fountain Papers is a letter sent from San Francisco in 1857 bearing the signature "Albert Jennings." There is a Sacramento directory list for Albert J. Fountain, but there is no one explanation for his presence in California.

One family story is that his father planned for his son to become an Episcopalian clergyman and that Fountain ran away from home to escape this fate, making the overland trek to the West Coast with an uncle.[4]

Another story is that his father's ship went down in the Orient, and that Fountain went to search for him. The youth's search reportedly was fruitless, but his travels brought him eventually to California where he remained. There is an official notice that a Solomon Jennings of New York went down at sea on January 28, 1854.[5] However, the 1857 letter signed "Albert Jennings" was addressed to his father, Solomon Jennings.[6]

Yet another account is that Fountain as a student at Columbia went on a world tour with five other adventure-seeking youths. Their itinerary included the chief ports of Europe and from there to Cape Town, Calcutta, and Hong Kong. After various escapades on the China coast, Fountain and his companions went on to San Francisco. The others returned to their homes in the East, but Fountain remained in California.[7]

If Fountain arrived in California about 1854, he cast about for seven restless years searching for gold, freighting supplies to the upper camps (the Albert Jennings letter of 1857 tells of his work-

[2] Letter to the author from Dr. Thurman Wilkins, New York City, March 3, 1962.

[3] Albert Jennings to Solomon Jennings, San Francisco, August 18, 1857. Fountain Papers, University of Oklahoma Library.

[4] Interview with Albert Fountain, Mesilla, New Mexico, August 10, 1961.

[5] Letter to the author from New York Historical Society, New York City, April 20, 1962.

[6] Albert Jennings to Solomon Jennings, San Francisco, August 18, 1857. Fountain Papers, University of Oklahoma Library.

[7] Interview with Henry Fountain, Mesilla, New Mexico, August 11, 1961.

ing for a Mr. Wherry who planned "to go home to purchase goods to the amount of $20,000" for distribution among the camps of upper California), and working as a reporter for the Sacramento *Union*.[8]

Fountain's adventures as a roving correspondent for the *Union* reportedly took him to Nicaragua where he covered the Walker expedition. When the notorious filibusterer announced plans to establish a slave-holding republic in Nicaragua, Fountain sent his editor reports of Walker's plans. This exposure led to Fountain's arrest and to a summary order of execution by Walker's firing squad. The resourceful Fountain claimed he disguised himself in woman's attire, slipped away, and eventually returned to California. The *Union* had a representative covering the Walker expedition, but his reports to the *Union* carried no by-line except "Notices from our Special Correspondent in Nicaragua."[9]

What manner of man did this youth become? In 1870 when Fountain was president of the Texas senate, the Austin *State Journal*, puffed up with pride over Fountain's rising political star, published a word portrait to introduce its readers to the "dashing young Senator from El Paso." The *Journal* declared that "it is no disparagement to the other Senators to say that in familiarity with details, readiness of resource and capacity to grasp and grapple with any emergency, he has no superior in the Senate. Senator Fountain is affirmative in character, positive in his convictions, emphatic in his political views, and singularly devoted in his friendships. He is a gentleman of great courtesy and demeanor, extensive reading, varied requirements and scholarly tastes, well fitted by his gentlemanly characteristics for any society, while his positive and unquestioned courage naturally make him a favorite on the frontier. In personal appearance, Senator Fountain is rather above than below the average size, being about five feet nine inches in height, and weighing we suppose, about one hundred

[8] Albert Jennings to Solomon Jennings, San Francisco, August 18, 1857. Fountain Papers, University of Oklahoma Library.

[9] Letter to the author from Cecil L. Chase, Berkeley, California, August 2, 1961, and letter to the author from Dorothy Firebaugh, Sonora, California, October 27, 1961.

7

and sixty-five. Is of light complexion, pleasing features, and face closely shaven with the exception of a moustache. . . . We predict for Senator Fountain a brilliant future career, and it is no vain compliment to say that he would do honor to any office in the gift of this or any other state."[10]

As a youth at Sacramento, the capital of the new state of California, Fountain must have been impressed by the importance of lawyers, not only because of their positions as legislators and officeholders, but also because of the private influence they exerted over legislation and general affairs of the state and because of their relatively favorable economic position. Convinced that only through this profession could he enjoy the prestige, power, and social position which his aggressive nature demanded, Fountain decided to study law.

In Sacramento lived N. Greene Curtis, one of the leading attorneys on the West Coast. Curtis had arrived in California soon after the initial gold discovery when Sacramento was a typical rough-and-tumble mining camp. The local forces for law-and-order arranged his appointment as town magistrate, and in no time at all Curtis' stern judgments tamed the raw community. Because Curtis was described by the western legal fraternity as possessed of a "comprehensive knowledge of the law's ramifications" equalled by few attorneys, every aspiring lawyer in northern California sought his patronage. Thus it was a stroke of good fortune for Fountain that, when he applied to Curtis, the judge thought enough of the youth's prospects to take him into his office. Fountain served as Curtis' law clerk for two years. Besides imparting a thorough knowledge of the law, Curtis also stamped Fountain's character with his obsession for law and order.[11]

By the summer of 1861, Curtis' tutelage had prepared the youth for the state bar, but before Fountain could be certified,[12] an anxious Union government, faced with a Confederate thrust at the

[10] Austin *State Journal*, July 2, 1870.

[11] "Greene Curtis Biography," *Sacramento California Directory for 1859*, Bancroft Library, University of California, Berkeley.

[12] Letter to the author from California Bar Association, San Francisco, July 19, 1961.

very gates of Washington, sent out a call to the loyal states and territories for volunteers. When army recruiters appeared in Sacramento during August, 1861, Fountain enlisted and was assigned to Company E, First California Infantry Volunteers. Thus, at the age of twenty-three, Albert Jennings Fountain launched a military career which carried him through the ranks from private to colonel in less than twenty years.[13]

[13] Service Record of Albert J. Fountain (1861–66), National Archives.

CHAPTER II

The Apache Hunter

PRIVATE FOUNTAIN TRAINED at Camp Downey near Oakland. The routines of military life fitted well with his views on order and duty. He disdained the petty gripes of his fellow soldiers, was conspicuously proper in military drill, and won company honors in marksmanship. Fountain's excellence as a soldier came to the attention of the commander of Company E, Captain Thomas L. Roberts, and before the end of basic training the youth had won his corporal's stripes.[1]

Camp Downey was a rumor factory concerning the assignment awaiting the First California Infantry Volunteers: they were to defend Washington against Confederate armies; to protect the Overland Mail route near Salt Lake; to tame the restive Indian tribes of the Pacific Northwest; and to serve as a home guard to discourage an alleged Confederate conspiracy in southern California, where, according to Union newspapers, "treason stalked abroad."

Apparently some official credence was given this threat, for the commander of the First Infantry Volunteers, Colonel James H. Carleton, a professional army veteran with twenty years' frontier service, assigned his men to southern California, ostensibly to continue training, but really to guard against the rumored cabal. Company E, one of the first units ordered south, was transported aboard the steamer *Active* from San Francisco to Camp San Pedro, arriving at the new post on September 18, 1861.

Corporal Fountain's company remained at Camp San Pedro less than two weeks, spending long days on the drill field improving march and skirmish exercises, ever ready to quell Con-

[1] Service Record of Albert J. Fountain (1861–66), National Archives.

federate uprisings. On September 30, Company E moved to Camp Latham, near Los Angeles, reportedly for additional training in an area where marching patrols watched around the clock for subversion in the "infected district."[2]

After nearly a month's surveillance of San Bernardino and Los Angeles counties by the California First, the West Coast high command, confident that the Confederate conspiracy would not materialize, reassigned the volunteer army. Most regular United States Army units on the West Coast had been ordered to New York. The First California Infantry Volunteers were directed to relieve the regulars at Fort Yuma and San Diego.

Beginning on October 14, Carleton sent six companies east, three to Fort Yuma on the Colorado River, California's most forward defensive bastion, and three, including Corporal Fountain's Company E, to a point where the San Diego and Los Angeles highways united to form the Butterfield Mail road. At this junction, a 140-mile march from Camp Latham, an intermediate post was to be established; its purpose was to serve as a supply depot for Yuma and as an operating base for patrols to watch the approaches to southern California towns.

Carleton warned the men to be alert for Confederate agents attempting to slip through their lines. "If you use circumspection you can never be surprised. . . . All persons passing into Sonora or to Arizona from California must take the oath of allegiance before they pass; so must all coming into California by the route overland via Yuma. Do not hesitate to hold in confinement any person or persons in that vicinity, or who may attempt to pass to or from California, who are avowed enemies of the Government, or who will not submit to the oath of allegiance. Keep an exact record of name, place of residence, age, occupation, and whence he came and whither he is to go, of each person passing the river to or from California." The garrison at Yuma was directed to "seize all the ferryboats, large and small upon the River Colorado. All the crossings of the river must be done at one point under the guns of the fort."[3]

---

[2] *War of Rebellion*, Series I, Vol. L, 136.   [3] *Ibid.*, 711.

Corporal Fountain arrived at the Butterfield road junction on October 23. The 140-mile march, routed through Lagunita, San Jose, Chino Ranch, Greenwade's Station, and Temecula, was the longest stint yet for Carleton's troopers, each carried a forty-pound pack and an eight-pound Sharps carbine.

At Warner's Ranch, just off the Butterfield road, Captain Roberts selected the site for the new military station. His choice was ideal—abundant water, forage, wood, and a commanding location. The footsore infantrymen went to work erecting tents and constructing ammunition dumps and storage buildings for quartermaster supplies. In a week they had established a tidy post, which Colonel Carleton named Camp Wright in honor of General George Wright, commander of the Department of the Pacific.

Goaded by Carleton, Fountain and other noncommissioned officers were constantly in the field watching for Confederate agents or leading details into the desert for the purpose of cleaning sand and debris from every well and spring between Camp Wright and Fort Yuma. For fear the troops might still have idle moments, Carleton directed that each company increase its skirmish practice and that the officers and noncoms "recite their [Hardee] tactics, commencing at the beginning of the first volume and going through seriatim, both volumes. Report at the end of each month the progress you have made."[4]

Corporal Fountain excelled in all of this, and by the first of the year he had passed successively through the noncommissioned grades to first sergeant. Company E, rated as the crack unit of the First California, was rewarded for sustained high performance. Captain Roberts' troopers were sent to San Diego to relieve a company of the Fourth United States Infantry embarking for New York. This was a timely move, for Company E escaped the rigors of winter at Camp Wright.

While Fountain and his comrades basked in the mild, sun-bathed coastal climate, the California First companies at highland Camp Wright suffered a miserable three months of snow, freezing temperatures, and wind. According to the garrison at

4 *Ibid.,* 672.

Wright, this wind was not a moderate breeze but a "perfect gale" which blew more than half the time, driving dust in clouds, blinding the eyes of every one, and infiltrating into every coffee pot, camp kettle, and water bucket. It was claimed that on some days the wind blew so hard that the chilled infantrymen could not even make a fire for cooking.[5]

Whether at San Diego, Camp Wright, or Fort Yuma, Carleton's men became weary of home guard duty, and itched for an opportunity to meet the enemy in combat. As the spring of 1862 approached, ominous tidings from New Mexico Territory improved their chances for realizing this. To Carleton's headquarters came intelligence that during early March, 1862, a Confederate Texan army under General Henry H. Sibley had smashed Union defenses on the Río Grande and captured Albuquerque and Santa Fe. In addition, it was reported that General Earl Van Dorn was organizing a Confederate army in Texas for the purpose of driving through to California and that already his vanguard under Captain R. S. Hunter had entered Arizona and occupied Tucson.

Carleton offered his California volunteer army to check this threat, claiming that with certain re-enforcements he would have the capability not only of driving the Confederates from Arizona, but, in addition, of marching to the Río Grande to contest Sibley's Rebel brigade. The West Coast high command received Carleton's proposal favorably, and at once he instructed his officers at San Diego, Camp Wright, and Fort Yuma to prepare for the expedition by having their men "in fighting order all the time, night or day. Keep me advised of all you do. Much is expected of you . . . . Drill, drill, drill until your men become perfect as soldiers, as skirmishers, as marksmen. Keep the command in good health . . . . Have a drill at the target, three shots per man a day for ten days, commencing at 100 yards and increasing ten yards each day. Have also two hours' skirmish drill. Make a tabular report of every shot to me."[6]

During the spring of 1862, the re-enforcements Carleton had

[5] *Ibid.*, 704.
[6] *Ibid.*, 700, 773.

requested began arriving at Camp Wright and Fort Yuma—the Fifth California Infantry under Colonel George Bowie, Captain John C. Cremony's Second California Cavalry, and a light battery from the Third United States Artillery commanded by Lieutenant John B. Shinn. With his own First California Infantry and Cavalry as a core, Carleton now had a fighting force of over fifteen hundred men; the combined units he designated the California Column.

Sergeant Fountain's company returned to Camp Wright in February and served as the supply company—supervising and collecting and issuing of rations, arms, and equipment in preparation for the overland march. Camp Wright and Fort Yuma bulged with mountains of commissary stores and equipment—flour, sugar, rice, beans, salt, pork, coffee, and beef (over ten thousand pounds of jerked meat plus a ninety-day supply of cattle to be driven with the expedition and slaughtered as needed), artillery, rifle, and revolver ammunition, riflemen's knives, and three hundred six-gallon water kegs.

Each of the 150 wagons distributed to the companies of the Column was loaded and weighed under the watchful eye of Captain Roberts. By Carleton's order, no wagon was to make the crossing with more than one thousand pounds of cargo, and to assure maximum space for provisions and ammunition, no officer from Carleton down was permitted baggage to exceed eighty pounds. Since the officers and men were expected to sleep in the open, the only shelters loaded were hospital tents.

By March 31, seven companies of the California Column had been equipped and provisioned for the overland march, and Carleton ordered Colonel Joseph R. West to lead this vanguard force on Tucson. Successive units were readied and by mid-April only Sergeant Fountain's company remained at Camp Wright as a caretaker force.

The California Column approached Tucson by companies; the marches spaced a day apart to allow wells and springs to fill along the route. Carleton's army, meeting only light resistance on the approaches to Tucson, occupied the city on May 20, 1862. The previous week, Captain Hunter's Confederate force had retreated toward the Río Grande, and many civilian Rebel sympathizers had crossed into Sonora. The United States flag was raised over Tucson with appropriate ceremonies, and Carleton, now a brigadier general, divided his time between establishing a military government for Arizona Territory and readying his Californians for the long march to the Río Grande.[7]

Tucson, midway between Fort Yuma and the Río Grande, bustled with military activity. Infantry and cavalry companies drilled daily under the scorching Arizona sun, sharpening their combat tactics. Supplies, especially grain and beef, were gathered from the Pima villages and Sonora. When not on the drill field, the troopers were divided into details, some to guard the horse and mule herds as the animals grazed on the sparse Gila grass in the canyons about Tucson; others were assigned to repair the wagons. The grinding march from Wright had loosened the beds, and the heat and dryness had shrunk the wagon wheels, which had to be cut and refitted.[8]

Captain Roberts' Company E was the last unit of the California Column to reach Tucson. Sergeant Fountain and other troopers of this, the acknowledged top outfit of the First Infantry Volunteers, were disgruntled over missing the conquest of Tucson; but little did they know an assignment awaited them which would surpass in danger and excitement anything yet experienced by the California Column. During June, General Carleton learned of Sibley's disastrous defeat at Glorieta by combined New Mexico and Colorado volunteer forces. Hopeful of intercepting the limping Confederate Army before it reached Texas, Carleton ordered Colonel Edward E. Eyre with 140 men from the First California Cavalry to make a forced reconnaissance to the Río Grande. This was to be a lightning thrust, and the mounted squadron traveled with only thirty days' rations, ammunition, and weapons. To support Eyre's squadron, Carleton called on Company E to proceed by forced marches to the Río Grande. Sergeant Fountain and

[7] *Ibid.*, Series I, Vol. IX, 553.
[8] *Ibid.*, Series I, Vol. L, 1147.

his comrades, thirsting for combat, rushed preparations for the expedition.[9]

Besides his company of riflemen, Roberts' train contained twenty-two supply wagons loaded with provisions and ammunition, a two-howitzer battery, and a cavalry escort furnished by Captain John C. Cremony's Second California. Departing Tucson at 4:30 on the morning of July 10, the support column marched over the Butterfield Mail road, a route which twisted through mesquite thickets and sand-floored canyons. Powdery alkali dust on the lowland roadbed, stirred up by the moving column, spread "out over the country on either hand like a lake," and remained in suspension for some time after the train of mules, horses, wagons, and foot soldiers had passed. The infantry, by preceding the wagons, avoided most of the discomfort from the dust, but the hapless teamsters suffered "greatly with inflamed eyes and with coughs," and at times were so engulfed with the whitish pall that they could not see their lead mules.[10]

The heat became so intense that Roberts changed to extended night marches using light marches interspersed with rest periods during the day. Arriving at the San Pedro River on July 13, Roberts, slowed by the supply train and anxious for contact with Eyre, decided to divide his command. Leaving the wagon train with Cremony, Roberts selected Sergeant Fountain and sixty sharpshooters, the howitzer battery, and eight cavalrymen. This reduced force left San Pedro Crossing for Dragoon Springs at one o'clock on the morning of July 14. Two days of forced marches brought Roberts' column, by now out of water, into the Chiricahua mountain range to the western approach of the famous Apache Pass. About four miles long at 4,800 feet elevation, the defile was midway between Tucson and the Río Grande. The Butterfield Stage Company had constructed a station in the pass near a spring. The sharp cliffs and rocks overlooking both sides of the road made Apache Pass an ideal ambush site. In the rough country about the pass ranged the Great Mountain People, the

[9] *Ibid.*, 98.
[10] *Ibid.*, 99.

Chiricahua Apaches led by Cochise and the fierce Mimbreño Apaches of Mangas Coloradas. Unknown to Roberts, both Cochise and Mangas Coloradas awaited his entry into the pass with four hundred well-armed Apache warriors hidden in the rocks on either side of the defile.[11]

As the weary, thirsty column approached the mouth of Apache Pass, the men quickened their pace and joked and sang for the old stone station was in sight, the march nearly ended, and water, food, and rest were at hand to compensate for the long march. The head of the straggling column had nearly reached the station, the rear was half a mile distant. Then from both sides of the narrow canyon there exploded a wave of flame as the hiding Apaches poured a deafening volley into the unsuspecting column at short range. The men darted like rabbits for cover behind the huge boulders lining the pass road, and fired into the ramparts at a foe they could not see. Above the din of battle came the voice of Captain Roberts: "Fall in men! Fall in! Form as skirmishers! Keep cool! We'll whip hell out of them yet! Fall in!"

Screened by huge boulders, the column retrieved the wounded and worked down the pass road out of range. According to Sergeant Fountain, Roberts' next move was to order him "to take a platoon of infantry and deploy as skirmishers and make a dash for the spring and try to hold it until we could obtain sufficient water for our immediate necessities. The second platoon supported the howitzer whose commander was directed to throw shells over our heads beyond the spring where it was certain a large number of Indians were lying in ambush to defend the water. Our line dashed forward, and advanced under a continuous and galling fire from both sides of the cañon until we reached a point within fifty yards of the spring. As it came into sight the men cheered. There it lay, water and life, a beautiful pool of limpid water, only a few yards from us. Then from the rocks and willows above the spring came a sheet of flame, three hundred rifles sent a hail of hissing bullets into our faces. Private Barr . . . fell shot through

[11] Richard Y. Murray, "Apache Pass—Most Formidable of Gorges," *Corral Dust*, Vol. VI (June, 1961), 18.

the head. I saw a number of our men stagger back wounded. From the fortifications on the summits of the hills to our right and left came a rapid and scathing fire, which could not be effectually returned. The first platoon was in danger of annihilation when, Roberts perceiving our danger, sounded the re-call, and we fell back, taking with us our dead and wounded, but no water.

"It did not require the exultant yells of the victorious savages to stir our men to madness; they wept; they raved; they hurled back fierce and brutal curses from cracked lips and swollen tongues; they called upon Roberts to lead them to water—or to death.

"The howitzers were brought up and an attempt was made to shell the enemy out of his fortifications on the hills above the spring, which we considered the key to his position, but the elevation was too great. The trails of both pieces were broken, and they were temporarily put out of action.

"Roberts looked intently at the highest hill, to the left of the spring, then, turning to me he said: 'We must have that hill, and you must take it; it can be done. Take twenty men and storm it.' I called for volunteers and immediately had the entire command to pick from. I detailed the first twenty, and deployed them as skirmishers. They were ordered to advance alternately, that is, ten men would dash ten or twelve yards to the front, lie down, and cover the other ten as they made a dash, and so on. We pushed slowly up the hill in the face of a galling fire. Below stood our comrades watching our effort, and prepared to make a dash on the spring should we succeed in carrying the hill."

Just below the crest Fountain ordered his men to fix bayonets and charge en masse on the summit. "As we emerged, fifty rifle shots came from the breastworks. They overshot us, and the next moment we were over a rough stone wall and on the inside of a circular fortification some thirty feet in diameter; fifty or more Indians were going out and down the hill on the opposite side. Then thirst, hunger, and fatigue were forgotten, the men became demons; with savage yells and curses they hurled themselves upon the flying foe and slaked their vengeance in blood."

18

"As we carried the hill a cheer came from below; as our comrades dashed to the spring with camp kettles and canteens, fire was opened upon them from the opposite hill, but we turned a plunging fire upon the enemy, and they were soon in full flight. The howitzers were again brought into action, and from our elevated position we could see hundreds of Indians scampering to the hills to escape the bursting shells."[12]

By a vigorous, sustained offense, Captain Roberts' small force had defeated a well-armed foe, large in number. Capturing the Apache Pass spring had cost the Californians two killed and five wounded. Sixty-six Apache warriors reportedly were slain in the six-hour engagement. After the exhausted, thirsty troopers had slaked their thirst and filled their canteens from the contested spring, Roberts, fearful that the retreating Indians might attack Cremony and the supply train, had Fountain select twenty-eight riflemen and marched them fifteen miles to Cremony's camp.[13]

Finding the train safe, Roberts deployed his infantry and Cremony's cavalry about the wagons in a tight defensive cordon and moved toward the pass. A small Apache force had returned to the heights during the early morning hours and threatened to contest Roberts' passage. The howitzers were placed in front of the train, and after a few twelve-pound cannister shells were lobbed into the rocks, the attackers withdrew, and the Californians moved through the pass.[14]

Roberts marched the column sixteen miles beyond the pass to San Simon Station. After sending couriers ahead to the Río Grande to contact Eyre, he put his men to work establishing a fortified supply depot at the station. While awaiting the arrival of General Carleton's main force, Sergeant Fountain, restless to be on to the Río Grande, led patrols along the Butterfield road eastward to the New Mexico border. The overland trek was nearly ended. This "somewhat remarkable march" of the Californians, over burning desert sands and through suffocating alkali dust,

[12] *Rio Grande Republican*, January 2, 1891.
[13] John C. Cremony, *Life Among the Apaches*, 164.
[14] *Rio Grande Republican*, January 2, 1891.

required, according to the Column surgeon, "men of stern stuff, else how could they have conquered the vast deserts and accomplished a march not equalled in modern times, traversing a distance of nearly a thousand miles . . . over a sterile waste."[15]

Sergeant Fountain's company was relieved at San Simon Station on July 28 with the arrival of Carleton's vanguard from Tucson. By evening of the same day, Roberts started his men for the Río Grande, and after a week of sustained marches, mostly at night to avoid the scorching desert heat, by way of Stein's Peak, Soldier's Farewell, Cow Springs, Mimbres River Station, and Cooke's Springs, the Column arrived at Picacho, a *placita* on the river.

The Californians were only six miles from Mesilla—jewel of the Union conquest—where, according to imaginative campfire tales (enriched by the enforced continence of a 1,000-mile march), seductive entertainment awaited them. Disappointingly, they found the river at high flood. After an extended drouth, the most severe in thirty years, heavy rains on the headwaters of the Río Grande had caused serious flooding, and the river was out of its banks, covering the lowlands in places for miles. Mesilla was an island, cut off from the west by a raging sea of muddy water. Above Picacho at the foot of the Jornada del Muerto was a ford used by travelers during high water—San Diego Crossing. Roberts camped there and awaited a fall on the river.

By August 7, the Río Grande had dropped to a level where men and animals could cross by swimming. On this day, General Carleton and headquarters company arrived at San Diego Crossing, and Sergeant Fountain and his men were directed to serve as a ferry detail, not only for Carleton's headquarters company, but for the cavalry, infantry, and artillery units expected momentarily.

Roberts' troopers turned to with a will. A guide rope was passed to the east bank and secured. Mules, horses, and commissary cattle swam across. Baggage, subsistence stores, and ammunition were transported in two leaky boats which had been recovered from a pile of drift. Then Sergeant Fountain and his men stripped

15 *War of Rebellion*, Series I, Vol. L, 136.

to the skin, swam into the current, and, aided by lines attached to straining mule teams on the east bank, pulled the wagons across. Men, animals, and supplies all crossed safely.

By August 11, the forward portion of the California Column had crossed, and, the river having dropped sufficiently to allow fording, Company E was relieved. Roberts was ordered to proceed to Fort Fillmore, near Mesilla, and garrison the post. All cavalry mounts and most of the quartermaster wagons and teams were kept at Fillmore because of the abundant grass and mesquite beans nearby.

The Californians were keenly disappointed that Sibley's Confederate brigade had retreated far into Texas. There was little likelihood of combat, and they were faced with the prospect of another hitch of prosaic home-guard duty. General Carleton expressed this regret during early August in a letter to General Edward R. S. Canby, commander of the Union forces at Santa Fe: "As the gallantry of the troops under your command has left us nothing to do on the Rio Grande, it would be a sad disappointment to those from California if they should be obliged to retrace their steps without feeling the enemy. . . . Could not a force . . . profitably be thrown into western Texas, where it is reported the Union men are only waiting for a little help to run up the old flag?"[16]

General Canby, his reassignment imminent, gave Carleton a free hand in southern New Mexico Territory and western Texas. Reports of fresh Confederate attempts to reconquer New Mexico and drive through Arizona into California caused Carleton to disperse his troops in companies throughout the larger towns and the military posts of southern New Mexico, extending his defensive perimeter as far down river as Franklin (El Paso) and nearby Fort Bliss.

Once billets had been assigned, the Californians swarmed in patrols along the river, searching for stragglers from the Sibley brigade, confiscating property of Confederate sympathizers, checking passports of travelers, and guarding the roads against spies

[16] *Ibid.*, Series I, Vol. IX, 559.

and small enemy forces which might attempt to infiltrate the New Mexican towns. Once each week the military routine was broken with a pass to Mesilla.

Before the war Mesilla had been a leading stop for the Butterfield Overland Mail and an important export center for trade into Chihuahua and Sonora. Low-running adobe buildings containing quaint shops, trading houses, and cantinas flanked Mesilla's cottonwood-studded plaza; the bell-towered church, set compactly on the plaza's west edge, was the only interruption in the town's architectural monotony.

Mesilla's predominantly Mexican population, thoroughly terrorized by the Texas Confederate occupation, responded to General Carleton's assurances that military rule by the California Column meant safety for life and property. *Acequias*, the gridiron of irrigation ditches crisscrossing around and through the town, were cleaned of military litter and flood debris, and again conducted life-giving water to the Mesilla valley. Buildings were repaired and whitewashed, streets cleaned, and in less than a month after Carleton's occupation, Mesilla sparkled in the desert sun. Proprietors removed shutters and barricades from the shops and cantinas, and free-spending California troopers brought a prosperity unknown before.

Of all that Mesilla had to offer, her *muchachas* appealed most to the lusty Californians. Women had been scarce in the West Coast mining camps; the few present were for the most part of the slattern, soiled-dove variety. Mesilla was a family community; the Mexican parents had many children and their daughters matured at an early age into voluptuous, dark-eyed beauties. Even Sergeant Fountain, generally stern and aloof toward the common soldier's preoccupation with the female, was smitten.

Since the Californians were unacquainted with the country, General Carleton authorized his company commanders to hire local Mexicans for guides and scouts. Captain Roberts employed Tomás Pérez, a youth from Mesilla, to work with Fountain on company patrol, and they struck up a warm friendship. On one occasion when the company received a two-day pass following a gruelling scout to Los Pinos, Pérez invited Fountain to visit in his home. The Pérez household celebrated Tomás' safe return, and during the festivities, Fountain was introduced to Tomás' sixteen-year-old sister, Mariana. In a few short hours this raven-haired beauty had charmed Fountain out of his dream of returning to Sacramento and establishing the law practice for which Judge Curtis had so well prepared him.

For the remainder of his assignment at Fillmore, Fountain spent his weekly passes in the Pérez home, wooing the vivacious Mariana as ardently as Hispanic courtship etiquette would permit. But, disappointingly, these happy times suddenly were cut short on August 27, when Company E was ordered to Franklin (El Paso). The day before his company departed, Fountain managed a special pass and rushed to Mesilla. An air of expectancy gripped the Pérez household throughout the evening. Finally, after rounds of prodigious toasts, Fountain, surprisingly facile in Mariana's native tongue, bowed and asked for her hand. Señor Pérez assented and it was decided to have the wedding during Christmas.[17]

The men of Company E were busy at Franklin establishing a forward defensive station for the California Column, and although Sergeant Fountain had little time off to travel the forty miles up river to Mesilla, Mariana was constantly in his thoughts. Soon after the California Column entered Texas and occupied Franklin and nearby Fort Bliss, cavalry patrols operating across the river at El Paso (Juárez) captured a large supply of hospital stores and quartermaster supplies cached in public buildings by fleeing Confederates. Roberts sent Sergeant Fountain and a detail of infantrymen across the river for the supplies. Twelve wagonloads of goods were gathered up and delivered to the headquarters depot at Mesilla. Also at Franklin, Fountain's squad captured a Confederate surgeon and twenty-five sick and disabled enemy soldiers. Believing there were additional Confederates hiding in the area, Fountain and his men combed the houses, public buildings, shops, and stores at Franklin and El Paso, and succeeded in rounding up

[17] Interview with Albert Fountain and Henry Fountain, August 12, 1961.

ninety-three additional Rebel soldiers. By General Carleton's order, the prisoners of war were paroled, issued rations and clothing, and sent to San Antonio, escorted by Captain Nathaniel J. Pishon's company of cavalry. Carleton authorized two wagons for the convoy to carry the prisoners unable to walk.

After a month of occupation duty at Franklin, another special assignment came to Company E. Along the valley of the Río Grande eastward into the Guadalupe Mountains of western Texas ranged the Mescalero Apaches. Before the war, the United States, with vigilant military patrols operating from Forts Bliss and Stanton and with rations issued by Indian agents, had made some progress in taming these fierce mountain people. In 1861, these posts were abandoned to the Confederates. The conquering Texans irritated the Mescaleros, incidents mounted, and before their retreat from New Mexico in 1862, the Confederates had provoked the Indians to all out war. The Texans showed poorly in their Apache campaigns; the Indians cut off and destroyed entire companies and captured substantial stores of provisions and weapons. Well-armed and more deadly than ever, the Mescalero Apaches were at the peak of their martial power when the California Column arrived in New Mexico.[18]

In a single month, August, 1862, Mescalero war parties killed forty-six settlers, carried scores of children into captivity, and ran off great herds of cattle, horses, mules, donkeys, and sheep.[19] These swooping Apache raids caused the Mexicans to abandon their *placitas* and flee to the garrisoned towns for protection.

On October 11, 1862, General Carleton sent his army after the Mescaleros. Colonel Kit Carson, with five companies of New Mexico Volunteers, was ordered to reoccupy Fort Stanton. Using this post as a base, Carson was to campaign to the south. A second arm of the Apache expedition, headed by Captain William Mc-Cleave with two companies of California troops, was to drive through Dog Canyon, moving east and south into the Mescalero Apache haunts.

[18] *Report of the Commissioner of Indian Affairs for 1861*, 122.
[19] *Report of the Commissioner of Indian Affairs for 1862*, 247–48.

The third arm, commanded by Captain Roberts, was to proceed from Franklin to the Hueco Tanks, and then northwest into the Apache range. Roberts' column included Gregorio García of San Elizario, a veteran Apache fighter, and twenty Mexican scouts. Captain Pishon's cavalry was to join Roberts' column, and since the expedition would travel through rough country, pack mules were to be used to carry ammunition and supplies. An ambulance and surgeon also were assigned to Roberts' column.

In handling the Apaches, Carleton advised Roberts that "there will be no council held with the Indians. . . . The men are to be slain whenever and wherever they can be found. Their women and children may be taken prisoner, but of course they are not to be killed." Roberts was to remind his troopers that "much is expected of the California troops. I trust that these . . . demonstrations will give these Indians a wholesome lesson. They have robbed and murdered the people with impunity too long already." Carleton cautioned Roberts to screen his preparations and troop movements so that Mexican spies and traders at Franklin could not warn the Mescaleros of the Indian campaign.[20]

When Fountain learned of his assignment to the Mescalero campaign, he wrote Señor Pérez that a change in orders made it impossible for him to be present at the Christmas wedding. An exchange of letters set October 27 for Mariana's marriage. Fountain was allowed a five-day leave, and on October 26 he hurried to Mesilla for the wedding. Through the succeeding months of tiring marches, Indian ambuscades, and lonely nights about the campfire, Fountain's spirit was nourished by the memory of this happy event—the houseful of Pérez relatives and guests, the marriage processional, candles and tapers, the pageantry of Roman Catholic church nuptials, Mariana strikingly beautiful in white lace and satin, and finally the bliss of her charms.[21]

Roberts' column departed Franklin on November 16 and marched 154 miles to Ojo del Martin, Texas. Using this watering point as a base, the Californians scoured the rough Guadalupe

[20] *War of Rebellion*, Series I, Vol. XV, 580.
[21] *History of New Mexico*, I, 349.

Mountain country for Apache *rancherías*. Apparently spies at Franklin had learned the purpose of the expedition despite Roberts' precautions, for, although García and his scouts located nine *rancherías* where they always before had found Indians, sign showed the camps had been abandoned several days ahead of the Californians' approach. In each case the Indian evacuation pointed westward to the Sacramento Mountains in New Mexico. After six weeks of futile searching, Roberts' footsore and disappointed column abandoned the base camp at Ojo del Martin on December 26, bound for Franklin.[22]

Sergeant Fountain and Company E arrived at Franklin on December 31, and on New Year's Day, 1863, the column marched to Mesilla where the men were allowed a two-day pass while Roberts awaited reassignment orders from Carleton. Although the Mescalero campaign had been a disappointment to Fountain insofar as no Apaches were found, he was pleased that his company had been routed to Mesilla since it meant a blissful reunion with his young bride.[23]

Refreshed by the delights of Mesilla, the men of Company E reported for muster on the morning of January 4. Sergeant Fountain learned from Roberts' briefing that Carleton had decided on a policy of containment for the Indian tribes within his jurisdiction. The primary function of the California Column, as Carleton had pointed out to his officers, was defending the Far West from a rumored Confederate offensive. New Mexico, in a state of military occupation by the California troops, was the most forward base in checking this expected assault. There had to be peace and order in New Mexico, for it to serve most effectively as a base for the California Column to carry out its primary function.

Apache and Navaho depredations had become so extensive that most of the effective companies of the California Column as well as the New Mexico Volunteers had to spend most of their time in the field chasing the predatory bands. Because the Indian

22 *War of Rebellion*, Series I, Vol. L, 267.

23 Albert J. Fountain to Fannie Fountain, Fort Craig, New Mexico Territory, January 12, 1863. Fountain Papers, University of Oklahoma Library.

campaigns diverted the Union forces in New Mexico from their primary purpose, General Carleton planned to eliminate the Indian problem once and for all by rounding up all hostile bands and forcing them to settle on a single military reserve. The reservation Carleton had selected for the Indian concentration was situated on the lower Pecos River at a place called Bosque Redondo. A military post, Fort Sumner, was to be constructed on the reserve to enforce residence once the hostiles were brought in. Carleton was optimistic about the future success of the Bosque Redondo reserve not only because of its isolation from the settlements, but because the open plains country for miles in every direction would make it easier for the troops at Fort Sumner to watch over the captives.[24]

Company E and most of the other effective units of the California Column, as well as the New Mexico Volunteer forces, were ordered to the field in an intensive Apache-Navaho roundup. Roberts' men, rated as the Column's veteran Indian fighters because of their victory at Apache Pass and their part in the recent Mescalero campaign, were assigned an operational base at Fort Craig, situated 120 miles above Mesilla on the Río Grande.[25]

Carleton's concentration policy was first applied to the Mescalero Apaches, whose customary range was east of the Río Grande. Vigorous campaigning by Company E and other units participating in the Indian roundup had brought good results by the late spring of 1863. California and New Mexico troops maintained a relentless pursuit against these hapless tribesmen. Springs and wells were guarded, closing every known watering point to the Indians; patrols watched the river, attempting to keep the Mescaleros from slipping through the defensive net and joining the Gila Apaches; and *rancherías* were scouted out and dwellings and stored foodstuffs were burned. The result was that during March and April well over four hundred Mescaleros voluntarily surrendered at Bosque Redondo. With eastern New Mexico safe, Carleton's

[24] 38 Cong., 1 sess., *House Exec. Doc. No. 1*, 230.
[25] Albert J. Fountain to Fannie Fountain, Fort Craig, New Mexico Territory, January 26, 1863. Fountain Papers, University of Oklahoma Library.

troopers concentrated on the Apaches and Navahoes located west of the Río Grande.

Sergeant Fountain's service in the Mescalero roundup won for him a special commendation from General Carleton and a promotion. In early May, 1863, Fountain exchanged his first sergeant's stripes for lieutenant's bars. Elation over the advance in rank, however, was tempered with regret, for, after a brief commissioning ceremony at Fort Craig, the young officer was separated from Company E and ordered to await reassignment. During the nearly two years' service with this group, Fountain had formed close friendships not only with the men in the ranks but the officers as well, especially the affable Captain Roberts.[26]

Lieutenant Fountain spent a restless two weeks at Fort Craig, watching his old comrades depart on Apache campaigns, writing ardent letters to Mariana, and speculating on his new assignment. After an eternity of frustrating inactivity, the reassignment orders arrived from Carleton's headquarters at Santa Fe—Lieutenant Albert J. Fountain was directed to report to Company G, commanded by Captain Henry A. Greene and presently billeted at Franklin, Texas.[27]

The Franklin road from Fort Craig passed through Mesilla. The happy possibilities of the journey to his new post caused Fountain to rush his packing to be ready to ride south with a Franklin-bound supply train early next morning. Three days later, resplendent in blue dress uniform, boots, and officer's equippage, he walked into the Pérez dooryard. The warm welcome, Señora Pérez' sumptuous hospitality, and stolen moments with Mariana made the day seem as an hour. Just before he left for Franklin, Mariana announced in her shy way that he would be a father by Christmas.

Fountain had hardly reported to Captain Greene when Company G was transferred to the Jornada del Muerto. The Jornada, a furnace-heat wasteland situated in the southern crescent of the Río Grande and extending ninety miles from San Antonio to just above Doña Ana, had become a scalp alley for travelers. Swift raids

26 Service Record of Albert J. Fountain (1861–66), National Archives.
27 Richard H. Orton, *Records of California Men in the War of Rebellion*, 332.

by renegade Apache and Navaho bands had strewn the Jornada's trackless sands with bones of famished animals, smashed wagons, and crude gravestones.[28] '

The shortest and most direct route between Santa Fe, military headquarters for the Department of New Mexico, and Mesilla and Franklin, lay through the Jornada, and General Carleton was determined to keep this vital communication link open. Indian raiders had become more brazen in their Jornada depredations during 1863. Besides countless miners, traders, and settlers suffering loss of life and property in attempting to make this dreaded crossing, several members of Carleton's army had been cut down too; one of them was Ed Fitzgerald, the General's express rider. Company G's mission was to establish a post on the Jornada for the purpose of protecting travelers and keeping north-south communications open.[29]

By mid-June, Fountain and other officers of Company G were combing the Jornada with survey details, searching for a location for the new post. Captain Greene decided to station his company at one of the few watering points on the Jornada, Ojo del Muerto (Spring of Death). The spring, forty miles north of Fort Craig, and adjacent to the north-south highway, was situated in a deep canyon surrounded by lofty mountains, enormous rocks, and, according to the troopers of Greene's command, "shut off from the world." Greene named the new station Fort McRae.

After raising tents about the spring and enclosing the camp with a crude stone breastwork, Greene's men went to the field in small patrols, guarding the Santa Fe–Mesilla road, intercepting escaping bands from the Bosque Redondo Reservation, and every now and then joining other units of Carleton's California Column–New Mexico Volunteer Army for a Gila Apache or Navaho expedition. Because of the strategic necessity of keeping north-south communications open, at least one-half of the Fort McRae garrison was reserved at all times for patrolling the Santa Fe–Mesilla road. Carleton regarded this mission so important that he sent a

[28] *Ibid.*, 332.
[29] Mesilla *Independent*, December 8, 1877.

consignment of mules and saddles from Santa Fe to mount the officers and men at Fort McRae. Great was the joy of these foot-sore troopers to be "mounted infantry."[30]

Greene's men, now mobile and thereby more effective, kept up relentless pressure on the Indians. Every raid on an Apache or Navaho *ranchería* netted a harvest of Indian prisoners for Bosque Redondo, rich plunder, and fresh samples of inventive barbarity. Liberating white captives spread-eagled over an ant hill or pitifully scorched from slow-burning soapweed fires, with their tongues cut out and privates mutilated caused Fountain to develop a strong stomach.

On one expedition during August, 1863, Fountain and twenty men pursued an Apache war party heading west of the Río Grande with several Mexican captives. On the tenth day, Fountain lost their trail and was about to abandon the search. That night a Mexican captive crawled into his camp. The poor devil was near death from thirst and pain. Attempting to prevent his escape, his Apache captors had torn the toe nails from his left foot and burned a hole through the mutilated limb. The captive gave directions to the Indian hideaway, and Fountain led his men to the *ranchería*. Hitting the sleeping Apaches with a dawn attack, the column forced the surprised Indians to flee on the first volley. After gather-ing up the surviving captives and booty and burning the village, Fountain returned to the Río Grande.[31]

Soon after the establishment of Fort McRae, mail contractors stocked the Santa Fe–Mesilla road and resumed mail service. In late August, 1863, the first coach reached McRae loaded with several months' accumulation of mail. Captain Greene offered an escort but the driver, Dave Knox, declined. Just before dark, Knox returned to McRae and reported that a large Apache war party had ambushed his stage at Point of Rocks, thirty miles south, and that the stock and mail had been captured. Captain Greene with

[30] Albert J. Fountain to Edward Fountain, Fort McRae, New Mexico Terri-tory, August 15, 1863. Fountain Papers, University of Oklahoma Library.
[31] *Ibid.*, and *War of Rebellion*, Series I, Vol. XXVI, 26.

Lieutenant Fountain and fifteen men left at once to search for the marauders.

Arriving at the ambush point at midnight, they found the ground strewn with wreckage of the coach and fragments of mail. At daybreak Greene's column took up the trail which led through a pass in the Sierra Caballo toward the Río Grande. Fountain estimated from the tracks that the hostile force numbered at least thirty warriors. About noon, as the column entered a narrow, high-walled canyon, Greene sent Fountain and four troopers forward to reconnoiter. The scouts had hardly ridden a mile down the canyon when they stopped short. Just beyond a sharp bend the sandy floor flared toward the river, a hundred yards ahead, and lined along the east bank dismounted Indians were watering their horses.

Just as Fountain turned up the canyon to alert Greene, he noticed sentinels along the heights on either side of the canyon racing for a position to cut him off. Quickly he ordered his men forward, and charging across the flat toward the river, and waving their weapons, and yelling, the scouts forced the Indians to scatter and run for cover.

A solitary warrior turned on a sand bar and stood his ground. Coolly stringing his bow, the Apache fitted an arrow that zipped close to Fountain's ear. On the troopers charged. At ten yards, and before the warrior could slip another arrow, Fountain flattened him into the soft sand with a blast from his Sharps.

The noisy troopers hit the water, splashed across the ford, and raced for a protective knoll. Looking back, they saw that while their swift thrust had startled and scattered the Indians, they were regrouping for an attack. Just as the warriors formed, Captain Greene's main force charged down the canyon and struck their rear. The confused Indians fell back to the river, and the water boiled with naked warriors and blue-uniformed troopers slashing and clubbing in close combat. Then suddenly the Apache line faded into the dense chaparral thickets that lined the west bank.

Making contact with Fountain, Greene ordered him to take

ten men and beat the thick brush for hiding Indians. For two sweating hours the searchers bellied through dense underbrush without finding even the sign of an Apache. Finally, on Fountain's right, Private Fred Dickey flushed a warrior from the chaparral. Both fired at close range and Dickey fell back with a gaping stomach wound. As the Indian rushed for the river bank, the dying Dickey fired again. The wounded warrior pitched into the water, came up, and limped across a sand bar. Fountain fired at fifty yards and hit the Indian between the shoulders. He landed face down, rose to his knees, and stumbled several steps when Greene's riflemen cut him down. Further search was futile. The Indians had vanished, abandoning their horse herd, the stage company mules, and camp booty to Greene's column. Sadly the men carried Private Dickey's body to Fort McRae for a soldier's burial.[32]

Four months of furious campaigning by Company G had tamed the Jornada; for the first time in years travelers could pass from Santa Fe to Mesilla without fear of an Indian ambush. By October, life at Fort McRae had settled down to a routine of garrison duty, periodic patrols along the Jornada road, and an occasional expedition west of the Río Grande.

Confederate defeats in the East during early 1864 erased all possibilities for the long expected Rebel offensive west of Texas into New Mexico, Arizona, and California. Happily, life and property in the Department of New Mexico seemed safe at last from murderous raids as General Carleton's Apache-Navaho roundup had brought together nine thousand hostile Indians on the heavily guarded Bosque Redondo Reservation. Thus, the men of the California Column, feeling their mission had been accomplished, eagerly looked forward to the end of their three-year enlistments which would occur during the summer.[33]

In the barracks and about the campfires the Californians dis-

---

[32] Mesilla *Independent*, December 8, 1877, and *War of Rebellion*. Series I. Vol. XXVI, 26.

[33] General James H. Carleton to General Lorenzo Thomas, Santa Fe, New Mexico Territory, May 31, 1864. Fountain Papers, University of Oklahoma Library.

cussed little else except their approaching return to civilian life. Many of the volunteers had decided to remain in New Mexico and Arizona. Several planned to seek their fortunes in the new gold and silver fields in the Pinos Altos and Upper Gila country, and a good number of the younger men, including Lieutenant Fountain, who had married Mexican girls and several with families already started, had been persuaded to remain in New Mexico.[34]

[34] Service Record of Albert J. Fountain (1861–66). National Archives.

CHAPTER III

Carleton's Scout

DURING THE LATE SUMMER of 1864, an era passed when the troopers of the fabulous California Column were discharged from military service. Lieutenant Albert J. Fountain, on temporary duty at Fort Craig, returned to civilian life on August 31. Believing the separation ceremony ended his military service for all time, he hurried by stage to his young wife and son at Mesilla, eager to begin a new life with his family in a land he had known up to this time only as a soldier.

The Fountains set up housekeeping in a four-room adobe situated just off the plaza in Mesilla. Albert, twenty-six and eager to begin his professional career, found civilian life (so promising in the plans Mariana and he had made) an endless chain of frustrations. Best prepared as an attorney, he studied the possibilities of establishing a law practice at Mesilla. He discovered, however, that four other attorneys were having a difficult time supporting their families from the lean practice available at the time, due largely to the continuation of military government which left but little business for the civil courts.

From his California newspaper experience Fountain carried the secret hope of editing a newspaper. Only one paper, the Mesilla *News*, was published in the entire lower Río Grande Valley, and this journal issued only sporadically. Here again, military censorship imposed by the occupation high command restricted news reporting and editorial comment. Censorship, added to lack of financial backing for a printing plant, ruled out the newspaper project for the time being.

Other business opportunities beckoned, but everything seemed to hinge on the war's end, which presumably would terminate military occupation and allow a full resumption of civilian pursuits. For the time being, the only local opportunity with honor or recognition seemed to be military service, and General Carleton and his staff regularly appealed to Fountain and other veterans of the California Column to re-enlist.

Carleton was distressed that "a mere handful" of his West Coast volunteers had signed for additional duty, for, while the threat of a Confederate invasion had passed, the Indian menace continued. Former Lieutenant Fountain was especially solicited by the military authorities. His reputation as a first-rate Indian fighter was an asset few veterans on the Río Grande frontier could match. Fountain's special value to Carleton's command, however, was his intimate acquaintance with southern New Mexico. He had campaigned over most of the country south of Albuquerque and knew the region like the back of his hand—the mountain passes, river crossings, every watering place, and the likely spots for secret Indian *rancherías*.[1]

By late autumn, 1864, Carleton's army was so decimated by expiration of enlistments that he could manage only skeleton garrisons for Sumner, Craig, McRae and other strategic southern posts. Faced with mounting Apache-Navaho depredations, he appealed to Fountain to serve the posts of southern New Mexico as a civilian scout and guide. Mariana protested, pointing out that since her husband had come through the Indian wars during his regular enlistment without a scratch, there was no need to expose himself further, and, besides, he was needed at home since she was in a family way again. Fountain was bored with two months of civilian inactivity and longed for the old excitement and action of an Indian campaign. Badly needing the five dollars a day Carleton's appointment carried, he accepted over his young wife's tearful pleas.

For nearly three months Fountain served as a scout and guide for the garrisons at McRae and Craig, his primary duty that of tracking Bosque Redondo runaways. On several occasions Fountain scoured the snow-covered Sacramento Mountains for Apache

[1] *War of Rebellion*, Series I, Vol. XLI, 743.

renegades ensconced in warm winter hideaways, and twice he guided parties of immigrant miners to the new gold camps in western New Mexico. During his service as civilian scout, Fountain was home only three days to comfort his lonely, *enceinte* Mariana.

Military forces in New Mexico Territory were supplied from Fort Leavenworth and other posts in Kansas. Until 1865, the wild Plains tribes, preoccupied with other sources of plunder, had not bothered Carleton's life line. Then in January of that year, well-armed Kiowa and Comanche raiders extended their forays into eastern New Mexico and threatened to cut all communications with the Kansas depots. To meet this fresh crisis, Carleton drew on his scanty forces at the southern Río Grande posts and from as far away as Franklin, Texas, and concentrated most of his effectives along the Cimarron in northeastern New Mexico. This shifting of military forces eased the pressure on the tribes in southern New Mexico. Apache and Navaho bands, forcibly settled at the Bosque Redondo Reservation and ever restive and watchful for an opportunity to escape, began slipping away in small bands, murdering settlers for horses and weapons, and then flying for the Río Grande and freedom in western mountain fastnesses.

Fearing a stampede of hostiles from Bosque Redondo, Carleton issued another appeal to the men of New Mexico Territory to enlist and protect their settlements against this peril. The New Mexico commander offered Fountain a commission as captain, New Mexico Volunteers, with authority to raise a special company of scouts and guides for service at the Río Grande posts. Men of effective military age and physical condition were scarce in southern New Mexico, most of them having been lured to the new gold camps. Carleton, desperate for fighting men, authorized Fountain to promise a bounty to each recruit.[2]

With the inducement of a one hundred dollar enlistment payment, Captain Fountain went after recruits. By the first of February he had signed forty men from Mesilla and Las Cruces. Colonel Edwin Rigg, commanding at undermanned Fort Craig, appro-

2 Service Record of Albert J. Fountain (1861–66), National Archives.

priated these recruits for his depleted companies, and Fountain had to start over again. During February and March, 1865, Captain Fountain visited Paraje, Chilili, Torreon, Doña Ana, and San Diego in New Mexico and Franklin and adjacent Texas towns for recruits. His top men came from the old squadron of Mexican scouts at San Elizario.[3]

By early April, when Captain Fountain had raised a force of seventy-five men, he informed General Carleton that his new company was in training and soon would be ready for assignment. He added that his was truly a bastard company, containing Anglos and Mexicans from New Mexico and western Texas, French deserters fom Maximilian's army in Mexico and Mexican deserters from Juárez' patriot army, and Indian mixed-bloods, the "rakings and scrapings of the frontier," men with no respect for "shoulder straps," sadly deficient in military order and discipline, who if threatened with punishment for insubordination, gave the stock reply "the army can go to hell."

Captain Fountain later recalled that "it was not the Indian alone who learned to dread these fellows, for whenever I was compelled to inflict a town with their presence, the good people would barricade their doors, hide their daughters, and declare they would rather see the Navajoes amongst them." Undisciplined though they were, Fountain praised the men of his company, claiming that they rendered valuable service to Carleton's regular army. Fountain boasted that his motley force was unexcelled on the frontier for ability to follow the dim trails, crawl into the enemy camp, count his numbers, stampede his horses, and outmaneuver the savage in all the wiles of Indian warfare. Besides being "wicked fighters," Fountain claimed his men had no equals for enduring heat, cold, hunger, thirst, and fatigue without complaint.[4]

After the briefest training in tracking and general tactics by Captain Fountain, this renegade force, the so-called lost company was scattered in squads along the river, watching the crossings, reporting daily to the garrison commanders, and leading

---

[3] *Ibid.*

[4] *Mesilla Valley Independent,* August 11, 1877.

regular troops on campaigns against runaway tribesmen. Fountain established his headquarters at Paraje, a Mexican town of five hundred population situated on the northern perimeter of the Jornada del Muerto. There he rented a house, and Mariana joined him at his new station to await the arrival of their second child.

Although the Civil War came to an end in April, 1865, with the surrender of Confederate forces at Appomattox, the most brutal kind of war continued in New Mexico. With General Lee's capitulation, troops from units in the eastern United States were being mustered out of the service and returned to civilian life. But on the Río Grande, Carleton's army remained on active duty. Rich strikes in the mountains of western New Mexico and Arizona set off a stampede of gold seekers to the new mines. Since many of the choice strikes had been made in the old homeland of the Bosque Redondo captives, Carleton feared trouble for the miners should the Indians be allowed to return and, therefore, decided to extend their confinement.

Disease and discontent were rampant among the Bosque Redondo captives during the spring of 1865, and every week a band or so would attempt to slip through Captain Fountain's line of scouts on the river. Generally the fugitives were intercepted and escorted back to their Pecos reserve.

On June 16, Ganado Blanco, Barboncito Blanco, and several lesser Navaho chiefs with about five hundred followers slipped away from the reservation stockade at Bosque Redondo under cover of night. Late the following morning, when the escape was discovered, Major Emil Fritz with a cavalry detail searched for signs but found the task an impossible one since the wily chiefs had sent decoy squads in several directions.

When the Fort Sumner dispatch concerning Ganado Blanco's escape reached General Carleton at Santa Fe, he wrote Colonel Edwin Rigg at Fort Craig that "Captain Fountain at Paraje would be one good man to employ on this business." Rigg was to tell Fountain that "these Indians must be recaptured or destroyed before they cross the Rio Grande," and that he would promise his men they could keep "all stock captured as booty."[5]

When Colonel Rigg's order reached Paraje, Fountain, anticipating that Ganado Blanco's band would strike directly for a crossing on the river, relayed an all-points alert to his squads which were scattered along the river from Paraje to San Diego. Nearly two weeks passed, and Fountain and Rigg were puzzled by the daily reports from all stations—"no crossings attempted." Since the Indians were still east of the river, among the likely places where they could hide and yet find grass and water would be any one of several spring-studded canyons in the San Andres Mountains, a low-running range on the eastern edge of the Jornada.

After two weeks on the river with no results, Fountain decided to ride into the San Andres and attempt to locate the Indian hideaway for Colonel Rigg's cavalry. Planning only a quick reconnaissance and reluctant to draw a detail from the thinly manned river stations, he decided to take only his orderly, Corporal Val Sánchez. Armed with revolvers and the new Henry repeating rifles, and each carrying a field glass, light rations, a blanket, and canteen, Fountain and Sánchez set out on the afternoon of July 2, carefully pacing their horses to cross the dreaded Jornada in the cool of evening.

A steady night ride brought them to Hermosilla Springs on the western slopes of the San Andres. Finding no sign of Indians, they watered their tired mounts, filled the canteens, and, after obliterating all signs of their stop, climbed to a small canyon on the heights above the spring and slept until early afternoon. Before departing Fountain walked to the low-lying Andres' divide and searched the plains on either side with his field glass. Northward on the east flank of the mountains his eye picked up a swirling dust cloud. He watched the low-hanging haze thicken as it drifted southward.[6]

Returning to the canyon, Fountain related his discovery to Sán-

[5] *War of Rebellion*, Series I, Vol. XLVIII, 942.
[6] *Rio Grande Republican*, January 16, 1891.

chez and surmised that since Hermosilla Springs was the only water in the region, if this was the runaway band, it would cross to the San Andres' west side by a low pass a mile or so above the springs and make camp at the water. Sánchez hid the horses far up the canyon, and Fountain selected a covered vantage point to observe the expected arrival of the fugitives.

Just before dark the cavalcade passed within one thousand yards of their hiding place and made camp near the springs. Certain that this was Ganado Blanco's runaway band, Fountain and Sánchez were about to slip away to advise Colonel Rigg of the discovery when Indian herders began driving the livestock to the uplands around the springs in search of grass. A movement now would alert the Indians and destroy the chances for a surprise attack by Rigg's cavalry. For the time being, Fountain and Sánchez were trapped.[7]

The scouts watched the camp all night and at daylight they calculated the party to contain about five hundred Indians. Since Hermosilla Springs was the westernmost water in the San Andres, it was evident the Indians were at long last moving toward the river. Fountain and Sánchez remained concealed above the camp all day. They narrowly escaped discovery during the afternoon by children hunting rabbits on the mountainside when several of the young hunters walked within a few yards of their hiding place.[8]

Just before dark, twenty warriors rode out of camp in a southwesterly direction toward the Point of Rocks. Sánchez offered that this was a scouting party sent out to spy on the passes through the Fra Cristobal and Caballo ranges which led directly to the river. The herders and livestock having returned to camp during the evening, Fountain decided the time had come for them to slip away. Moving quietly across the heights above the camp, they descended to the Jornada and padded through the sand in the direction taken by the scouting party. By daybreak they had reached the approaches to a small spring situated east of the Point of Rocks. Sign revealed that the Indians had passed but a short

[7] *Mesilla Valley Independent*, August 11, 1877.
[8] *Ibid*.

time ahead of them. While Sánchez held the horses, Fountain crawled to a summit and scanned the country all around. A mile north he could see the warriors lolling on a grassy flat near the spring, their horses grazing nearby.[9]

Suddenly Fountain saw the Indians jump to their feet and run toward the horses. Then, hearing a crackling noise behind him, he turned and saw the cause of the Indians' alarm. Sánchez had lighted his pipe, the wind had blown a spark into the grass, and already the fast-spreading fire was sending up smoke. Hastily throwing their coats over soapweed to decoy the onrushing warriors, Fountain and Sánchez mounted up, and, covering their flight with the low-lying hills, raced northwest toward Fort Mc-Rae, thirty-five miles to the west. Fountain's hope was that at least one of them could reach McRae and from there send messengers to headquarters at Fort Craig with intelligence of Ganado Blanco's location.

Before they had ridden twelve miles, however, it was apparent the Indians had anticipated their direction. Finding the Fort McRae route closed by the warriors' flanking movement, Fountain and Sánchez changed to a due north course for Paraje, sixty miles away. The rolling foothills, spurs from the San Andres jutting onto the Jornada, screened their direction and a steady ride brought them by evening to a malpais-fringed basin, a landmark from which Fountain identified their position as about thirty miles from Paraje.

Hopeful that they had eluded their pursuers, Fountain and Sánchez walked their travel-worn horses across the basin floor, and at sundown they reached a basalt wall rising abruptly to a height of twenty feet and extending for miles on either side in a crescent, its center cut by a narrow gap which led to the mesa above. Considering the prospects of an ambush, the scouts rode several hundred yards on either side of the pass opening and out from the wall some distance examining the ground carefully for Indian sign.

Finding nothing, but still apprehensive, Fountain directed Sánchez to take up position two hundred yards from the wall to cover

[9] *Rio Grande Republican,* January 16, 1891.

his ascent, and, should he be ambushed, Sánchez was to ride to McRae with the message of Ganado Blanco's whereabouts. Then Fountain urged his weary horse into the slender pass, the Henry rifle ready on the pommel. Halfway up, two huge rocks pinched the trail so tightly that a mounted man could barely squeeze through.

Fountain had just passed the gap when suddenly the horse arched his neck in fright, and at the same instant Fountain saw an Indian not twelve feet away bearing down on him with a rifle. At the same instant a dozen weapons cracked, bullets whined and glanced off the rocks all about, and the narrow cut seemed full of whizzing arrows. Instinctively Fountain lowered himself onto his horse's neck and the animal lurched back against the rocks, his head riddled with bullets. Fountain, his left side most exposed, was nearly wrenched from the saddle by a close-range blast striking his left hip. An arrow twanged into his left shoulder, and another sliced the underside of his right forearm.

The falling horse jammed his rider into a pocket among the huge boulders, and the attackers rushed down the trail for the kill. Fountain twisted his pain-racked body low behind the horse's carcass, rested the Henry across the saddle, and poured a withering point-blank fire into the rushing foe. In a matter of seconds the pass was glutted with writhing bodies. The last assailant to make the charge, "a villainous-looking fellow whose only garment was a red shirt" rushed Fountain with lance upraised for a thrust. Holding his fire until the warrior was but three feet from the Henry's muzzle, Fountain's point-blank fire drove the limp remains of the attacker backward into the rocks.[10]

A deadening silence gripped the bloody pass. The surviving Indians could not attack without exposing themselves, and the pass was so narrow they could rush Fountain's position but one or two at a time. Approaching darkness brought a chilling night breeze which smarted Fountain's open wounds. His left shoulder, jammed into a corner of the rocks, throbbed with each heartbeat, and each breath caused the deeply imbedded arrow shaft to rise

[10] *Mesilla Valley Independent*, August 11, 1877.

and fall. The thigh wound was painful, but the wound requiring immediate attention was in his right forearm. An arrowhead, probably fashioned from a sheet steel skillet, had sliced the flesh and cut into an artery, and the blood was pumping out in jets. With his skinning knife, Fountain cut the sleeve from his wound. Taking the steel wiping rod from the rifle butt, he twisted the tourniquet until the flow of blood stopped. Then he scribbled a note to Mariana on a leaf torn from his memorandum book, placed a small rock over the message, drained one of the canteens, and resting his head against the rocky wall, he waited for the end.[11]

Long after midnight, Fountain's senses, made highly acute from the pain of his wounds, heard a sound like that of a shod horse striking a stone far away. The noise increased, and a rushing about in the rocks above indicated that the waiting warriors had also discovered the approaching party and were preparing to flee. Then Fountain heard a voice he recognized as that of Lieutenant Pat Healy from Fort McRae calling his name. In a matter of minutes the rescuers had dismounted, moved up the gap, and Healy was holding Fountain's head in his arms and proffering a drink from his whisky flask.[12]

Healy explained that when Sánchez saw his captain fall in the ambuscade, he put the spurs to his horse, and, after a desperate ride which killed the already wearied animal, he reached Fort McRae at ten o'clock that night. Post commandant Colonel Ned Willis, after dispatching Healy's column to the rescue, informed cavalry units up and down the river of the discovery of the Indian hideaway. Fountain learned later that Sánchez guided the force to Ganado Blanco's camp at Hermosilla Springs, and the Navahoes were driven back to Bosque Redondo.[13]

Healey's men fashioned a litter and carried the battered Fountain to his old post, Fort McRae, and then by easy stages he was moved by army ambulance to Fort Bliss, near El Paso, where an army surgeon cut the arrow from his left shoulder. The intense

---

[11] George Griggs, *History of Mesilla Valley or the Gadsden Purchase,* 106.

[12] *Rio Grande Republican,* January 30, 1891.

[13] *Mesilla Valley Independent,* August 11, 1877.

summer heat, combined with high fever and delirium, further weakened Fountain and reduced him to a shadow of his former vigorous self. While the hip and forearm wounds healed quickly, the shoulder festered for weeks, and on several occasions the hospital orderlies were convinced that their patient was close to drawing his last breath. But the will to live sustained him, and the crisis passed, although the ordeal had so sapped his vitality that he was months on the mend. The grieving Mariana closed the house at Paraje and returned with little Albert to her people at Mesilla to await the arrival of their second child.[14]

14 Service Record of Albert J. Fountain (1861–66), National Archives.

Major Fountain and his staff

Standing, left to right, Lieutenant Pedragon, Lieutenant Fountain, Lieutenant Botello; seated, Captain Van Patton, Major Fountain, Captain Salazar.

Mariana Pérez Fountain
"Her life was her home, children, and religion."

*

CHAPTER IV

The Carpetbagger

CAPTAIN FOUNTAIN'S SHOULDER WOUND finally began to heal, his strength gradually returned, and he became a familiar sight on the El Paso streets acquainting himself with the citizens and considering his future prospects there. He noted that El Paso had changed little from 1862 when he patrolled its streets with Roberts' company searching for Confederate stragglers. Businesses and residences were squat adobe structures shaded by cottonwoods and peach trees. The town's three Roman Catholic churches and associated school contrasted with an equal number of saloons, a gambling parlor, and whore house. Down river on the edge of town were the jacals of the *pobrecitos*, crude huts constructed from upright sticks, plastered with mud, and covered with thatched roofs.

The harshness of the desert in all directions from the valley was softened by the productive river bottom. *Acequias* conducted life-giving water from the Río Grande to the ribbon of farms and orchards nestled on either side of the river. Cotton, clover, alfalfa, corn, wheat, a variety of vegetables, chili, and onions, staggered here and there with vineyards and orchards, flourished on the little plots. Herds of cattle, horses, mules, sheep, and goats grazed on the sparsely grassed uplands.

A string of towns extended down river from the Pass for twenty-five miles. Ten miles southeast of El Paso was Ysleta, with a Mexican population of sixteen hundred. Socorro, four miles beyond, contained seven hundred Mexicans, and six miles farther down river was the largest town in the county, San Elizario, with two thousand Mexicans. While the county seat shifted between Ysleta and San Elizario, El Paso (still called Franklin), with a population

45

of eight hundred, and all but eighty of these Mexicans, was by far the most important town in the district.

Fountain soon learned why that El Paso, while not as populous as some of the other district towns, was the most important. First of all, before the war, El Paso had been a division point on the Butterfield Overland Mail. The heavy volume of passengers and mail on this line had been responsible for the company establishing at the Pass its largest station east of Los Angeles. A wagon shop employed workmen to repair the coaches and blacksmiths to look after the draft animals. The vast corrals at El Paso station never contained less than three hundred head of horses and mules. Hay and grain needs at the station provided added markets for farmers on the river. An adjunct to the passenger and mail traffic was freighting, which also improved local markets.

Westbound immigrant trains using the southern route made El Paso a regular stop, and the merchants did a lively business supplying food and grain, repairing wagons, and replacing worndown ox teams. Mining in the Franklin Mountains of Texas and the nearby Organ Mountains of southern New Mexico increased business at El Paso, too. In 1854, Hugh Stephenson opened the rich Organ silver mines. The war brought a halt to operations, but with the collapse of the Confederate threat and the reduction of the Indian menace, old mines were reopened and new locations sought.

Military posts in the area, very likely required on a long-range basis because of the Indian problem, added to the prosperity of El Paso since procurement officers provisioned the garrisons from local markets and troopers on passes swarmed to the town every week for the ribald entertainment it furnished. But the oldest and most reliable basis for El Paso's existence came from the great concourse of commerce, an ancient road that passed by way of Santa Fe through the pass to Chihuahua. Trade goods came from as far away as Kansas City by way of Santa Fe. A new route had recently developed; merchandise from New York and St. Louis was shipped to Lavaca Bay, and thence overland to El Paso for export to the Mexican provinces south of the river.

Because of its strategic location, El Paso had been designated by the Treasury Department as a port of entry, its revenue district extending over a vast territory including New Mexico and Arizona. The location of the customs house at El Paso gave the town prestige and added significance from the staff of customs officers assigned there. The principal businesses of the Pass District and most of the eighty Anglos in El Paso County were there too.

Fountain discovered that the social center for the town's leading men was Ben Dowell's saloon. The post office being situated in the saloon added to its importance. Dowell, one of El Paso's early settlers, discreetly avoided the factions and cliques inevitable among the power-hungry Anglos resident at the Pass. Through the years he profited remarkably from his studied neutrality; by 1875 besides being the wealthiest man in the county, he was also the town mayor.

Dowell's was a peculiar saloon, for while drinking and gambling were in evidence, these universal western pastimes were patronized with a sophistication, an urbanity that made his place seem more like a private club. El Paso's leading citizens spent several hours there each day, less in their cups and cards and more in discussing politics and making business deals.

For most of his young life, Fountain had lived in frontier communities, and he observed from the individuals he met at Dowell's that El Paso had attracted more than its share of strong-willed, independent, ambitious men. A common maxim Fountain heard at El Paso was that "every man was a king as long as he lived and a corpse of no importance when he died." This and the convenience of the town graveyard, where, it was said, there were more people who had died of violence than all other causes, came to have a special meaning for Fountain before he had been in El Paso a year.[1]

At Dowell's, Fountain met the most powerful figure at the Pass, W. W. Mills, collector of customs. From New York and an old settler like Dowell, this runty, quick-tempered man with a "razor-sharp tongue" had been appointed to the collectorship in 1862 by

[1] Robert J. Casey, *The Texas Border and Some Borderliners*, 73. Quoted by permission of the publisher, The Bobbs-Merrill Co., Inc.

President Lincoln.[2] The Democrats had run Texas and El Paso before the war, and for nearly two years the town had been a Confederate base for operations into New Mexico and Arizona. Mills had suffered at the hands of the Democrats and Confederates, and he was determined to have his vengeance. Besides encouraging the confiscation of Rebel property, he believed the best way to continue the Democratic humiliation was to organize a strong Republican party in the El Paso District. Mills was well into this project when Fountain met him.

Also at Dowell's, Fountain became acquainted with the mysterious Luis Cardis, an Italian revolutionist recently arrived in the United States and at El Paso; Gaylord Clarke, a lawyer from New York, a schoolmate of Mills, and, like Cardis, a recent arrival at El Paso. Too, he met Frank Williams, former Confederate lawyer and converted Republican; A. H. French, a Bostonian from California and an acquaintance of Fountain from the California Column days; Henry Cunliffe; and J. P. Hague.

Fountain's law practice began as a result of contacts made at Dowell's place. During December, 1865, when he had completely recovered from the Ganado Blanco campaign wounds, the United States government was perfecting title of confiscated Rebel property and arranging for its sale at public auction. Fountain met the property commissioners over a drink, made known his qualifications, and was assigned to the staff to investigate titles for ranches, mills, businesses, private residences, and other properties of former Confederates in the El Paso District. Fountain was proud of his fee for this work, not only because it represented the first earnings from the profession Greene Curtis had so well prepared him for, but more especially because his long recovery period had reduced his family to near destitution. Now he could support Mariana and the children in the style he considered appropriate for a rising attorney's family.

During the confiscation proceedings, the Overland Mail property at El Paso was repossessed and held in trust for the company. Fountain was named trustee and appointed local agent for the

2 C. L. Sonnichsen, *Tularosa, Last of the Frontier West*, 58.

property. This position was important less for the income and more for the privilege it carried of living on the property. The low rambling adobe Overland Station contained quarters for travelers. Fountain selected one of the apartments for his family and moved them from Mesilla to El Paso. He also arranged quarters for Gaylord Clarke and J. P. Hague and their families.[3]

Even before the confiscation proceedings and auction sales were concluded, Fountain was casting about for new assignments. No one could patronize Dowell's for long without becoming involved in politics. Fountain, though still a youngster when compared to the other saloon habitués, already was an experienced politician, his first exposure to politics occurring in the California mining camps. As an eighteen-year-old, he had campaigned for the Frémont ticket in 1856 and thus could claim to be an original Republican. The Lincoln campaign four years later not only added to his political experience, but also integrated his political philosophy—Fountain came to equate justice, honor, and all that was good with the Republican party. His enlistment and service in the Union Army during the Civil War had been for him but a natural application of the tenets of militant Republicanism. Thus, it was natural that he should become associated with the Republican party cell that Mills was organizing at El Paso.

Fountain was admirably fitted for a career in the rough-and-tumble politics of the Southwest, for, besides his zeal, striking personal appearance, and great physical strength, he was a talented orator. His sparkling command of the English language very soon made him much in demand as the keynote speaker for Republican conventions, Fourth of July celebrations, and other occasions where a ringing public address was required. And he had local advantages too. Mariana had coached him in Spanish, not only flawless Castilian, but Pass patois as well. Skill in the use of the Spanish language was essential for local law practice (court proceedings and arguments to juries were in Spanish), and since the Mexican vote decided all elections, an aspiring politician had to be

[3] Roscoe P. and Margaret B. Conkling, *The Butterfield Overland Mail, 1857–1869*, II, 62.

able to make political speeches in the language of the natives, too.

Postwar politics got underway at El Paso in January, 1866, when Captain David H. Brotherton, commandant at Fort Bliss, issued special orders terminating military rule. In the subsequent election which restored civil officers to power, Mills's Republican machine presented a slate of candidates for all county offices: A. H. French for police or county judge; J. J. Lujan, county clerk; Maximo Aranda, district clerk; and Albert J. Fountain, county surveyor. Vigorous campaigning by the surveyor candidate and other party workers won a smashing victory for the Republicans. Fountain had some surveying experience from military service, primarily laying out roads and military posts, but this, his first elective political office, was more of a sinecure since he hired a deputy to perform the field work associated with the County Surveyor's office, thus making himself available for another political position which was tendered to him shortly after the election.[4]

W. W. Mills was so pleased with Fountain's work for the local Republican party organization that he offered him the appointment of customs inspector and chief assistant to the collector at an annual salary of $1,800. An assured income compared to the uncertainty of a struggling law practice led Fountain to accept Mills's offer. At the Customs House he joined Mills's staff consisting of H. B. Amity, clerk, and D. K. Wardwell, John F. Stone, and Charles Eaton, deputy inspectors.[5]

The duties of customs inspector included enforcing United States revenue laws over the vast El Paso District, watching for smuggling, and assisting in collecting duty on goods entered at the Pass. Grain, fruit, and certain other foodstuffs imported in small amounts were no particular problem, the daily cash collected from this traffic amounting to less than fifty dollars. Chihuahua whisky, Tampico tobacco products—especially cigars—and Juárez wine were popular import items. Tobacco products were weighed and taxed by the pound while whisky was levied a flat $40 a barrel. Fountain had not been on the job very long before

[4] 45 Cong., 2 sess., *House Exec. Doc. No. 93*, 127.
[5] Austin *Republican*, September 29, 1869.

he discovered that wine was the most difficult commodity to tax, because importers regularly attempted to enter barrels of wine as vinegar. The tax on vinegar was ten cents a gallon, that on wine, $1.25 a gallon.

Aside from the customs inspector job providing Fountain with the means to support his family, it also brought him into contact with the leading men of the Southwest, men he dealt with later in his political career. The biggest importer was Miguel Ortiz, a Santa Fe merchant, who entered cigars by the hundred pounds, whisky in forty-barrel lots, and wine ten barrels at a time. Others he became well acquainted with were Peter Dues, distiller at Juárez, El Paso merchant Ernest Angerstine, Henry Lesinsky, a trader from Las Cruces, and representatives of Tully and Ochoa of Tucson.[6]

Even though Fountain held the county office of surveyor and federal appointment of customs inspector, these posts were not so demanding that he could not spend some time pursuing his first love—politics. For two years a surprising harmony prevailed in the Republican party at El Paso, the members helping one another in public as well as private activities. Then, in 1868, trouble developed in the ranks and, curiously, over salt. One hundred miles east of El Paso at the base of Guadalupe Peak was a scattering of salinas or salt beds. These pure salt deposits were on public land, and natives came from all over the El Paso district and from as far away as Chihuahua and Sonora to Guadalupe to gather their annual supply of salt.

In 1866, Samuel A. Maverick of San Antonio, who held some Texas land scrip, applied to Fountain as El Paso County Surveyor for a survey in the Guadalupe salt beds. Jarvis Hubble, Fountain's assistant, made the survey and Maverick located on 640 acres. Since Maverick's section embraced only about one-half of the beds, the Mexicans continued to have free access to the salt.[7]

Shortly after the Maverick patent was issued, Mills proposed to his El Paso cronies that they form a company, obtain title to the

[6] *Ibid.*
[7] 45 Cong., 2 sess., *House Exec. Doc. No. 93*, 127.

remaining salt beds, and collect a fee for each *fanega* (about one and one-half bushels) of salt taken out. In 1867, such a company was formed, its membership made up of Mills, Fountain, Lujan, Clarke, and Williams. While negotiations were underway to obtain a land patent to the remaining salt beds, news of the formation of Mills's company leaked out.[8]

Strong resentment against the Anglo plan to take in the remaining salt beds and convert them to private use built up among the Mexicans at the Pass, and Fountain, concerned with his political future and shrewd enough to realize the danger of alienating the all-important Mexican vote, proposed to Mills that the salt company abandon the Guadalupe enterprise. Mills with the other members insisted on carrying through. Besides political expediency, there was an element of humanity in Fountain's stand on abandoning the salt project. Mariana's point of view had more and more become his; he sympathized with these gentle people who had been bullied, harassed, and abused for years by the aggressive Anglos.

From Mariana he learned that when the Gringos began arriving at the Pass around 1850, hundreds of native families fled westward into the Mesilla valley and established new settlements. Mariana's people, originally at San Elizario, had joined this exodus. Fountain observed that while the Anglos had become less overt in their rapacity, they "considered themselves representatives of a superior race," consistently disregarded Mexican rights, and generally held the so-called Greasers in contempt. He regarded the Mills-inspired project to appropriate the salt beds as the climax to nearly two decades of Anglo greed.

For the time being, Fountain kept his views to himself, and the salt company members did not seem to bear a grudge against him for withdrawing from their enterprise. This was probably because at the time they did not understand or appreciate the political consequences of the salt question and because there would be one less associate to share in the anticipated profits.

Meanwhile, the Pass Republicans became involved in state

8 *Ibid.* Also see C. L. Sonnichsen, *The El Paso Salt War.*

politics. With the close of the Civil War, Texas as a former Confederate state was organized into the Fifth Military District, occupied by United States troops, and subjected to martial law. After several attempts to restore civil government by President Johnson's mild reconstruction plan, Texas and the other Confederate states were subjected to the severe Congressional Reconstruction Plan. The so-called Radical wing dominated both the Republican party and the Congress. The Radicals opposed a soft treatment for the late Confederate states; many of its leaders advanced the view that by the act of secession these states had committed "state suicide" and therefore had to be completely reconstructed before they could return to the Union. The Radical Reconstruction formula for each former Confederate state included a tutelage period of military rule, a more or less permanent disqualification of Confederates by the ironclad oath, drastic state constitutional revision, adoption of the thirteenth, fourteenth, and fifteenth amendments, extension of civil and political rights to former slaves, and general abeyance of the secession-tainted Democratic party to provide an opportunity for the Republican party to develop.

The Radical Reconstruction Plan was set in motion in Texas during early 1868 when General J. J. Reynolds, Fifth District military governor, authorized calling a constitutional convention. Military-supervised balloting and rigid enforcement of the ironclad oath assured a Republican assembly with the Radicals holding a majority of the seats. The El Paso District Republicans named their political chief, W. W. Mills, as delegate.[9]

The Reconstruction Convention, in session at Austin from June, 1868, until February, 1869, selected Edmund J. Davis, a Radical, as president. Leader of the Conservative Republicans, who favored a soft reconstruction for Texas, was A. J. Hamilton. Over the protests of Hamilton's faction, the Davis Radicals followed the national Republican Reconstruction formula to the letter including the extension of suffrage to former slaves.[10]

An important convention footnote for El Paso Republicans was

[9] Austin *Republican*, December 1, 1869.
[10] W. W. Mills, *Forty Years at El Paso, 1858–1898* (El Paso, 1901).

the marriage of their delegate to the daughter of the Conservative Republican leader, A. J. Hamilton. Up to this time, Mills had been neutral concerning a Radical or Conservative commitment. Thereafter, his political thinking and action crystallized, and he became an echo of his father-in-law.

During Mills's year-long stay in Austin, the El Paso Republican party leadership fell upon Fountain, and, aside from him, little heed was paid to the proceedings at Austin for the local politicos were preoccupied with the salt project. Fountain regarded the Radical Reconstruction program as a natural and desirable application of his militant Republicanism—Texas Democrats must be punished for their treasonous affiliation with the Confederacy, and any person or group was suspect who opposed disfranchisement of former Rebels and elevation of freedmen to full citizen status including the right to vote and hold office. Fountain was alarmed by the rise of the Hamilton-Mills faction in the Republican-dominated convention. On several occasions he wrote sharp letters to Mills, criticizing his advocacy of soft reconstruction, and challenging his political apostasy by reminding him that the Hamilton faction's stand on Reconstruction for Texas was contrary to the national Republican reconstruction program. When the sensitive Mills reacted to this needling by suspending Fountain as customs inspector for the El Paso District, he set off a vendetta which filled several new graves at the Pass, wrecked numerous political careers including his own, and assured the early demise of the Texas Republican party.[11]

The first act in this tense political drama was staged in 1869 when, the Austin convention having completed its work on the Texas constitution, the Fifth District Military Governor authorized state elections for November. The convention battle over "soft versus tough reconstruction" had split the Texas Republican party, and each faction called a nominating convention. Among those candidates selected by the "pure white" Conservative Republicans at their Austin convention were Hamilton for governor

[11] See W. W. Mills, *El Paso—A Glance at Its Men and Contests . . . Fountain the Infamous* (Austin, 1871).

and Mills for legislative representative from the El Paso District.[12]

Radical leader Edmund J. Davis, claiming his following to be the only legitimate Republicans in Texas since they had the backing of the national party, convened his partisans at Corpus Christi. Fountain encouraged the Pass Republicans to accompany him to the Radical convention. Only Williams agreed to go; French, Clarke, and the others stuck with Mills. At Corpus Christi, Fountain made several ringing speeches to the convention, composed of black and white delegates, and became acquainted with Radical leaders from both groups, including the Negro delegates G. T. Ruby of Galveston and Matt Gaines from Brenham, who were expected to deliver the heavy Texas freedmen vote for the Radicals in November.[13]

Fountain was elected vice-chairman of the convention and played a key role in selecting candidates and developing the Radical platform. During his conferences with Edmund J. Davis, he reminded the Radical leader that W. W. Mills, a "soft reconstructionist," held one of the most lucrative federal posts in Texas. Davis' influence with the national Republican party leaders was quickly shown, for even before Fountain and Williams returned to El Paso, Mills had been removed from the collectorship and a carpetbagger from Michigan, Dr. D. C. Marsh, had been appointed in his place. Before the Radical convention closed, Davis was nominated for governor, and Fountain for state senator from the Thirtieth District which included El Paso.[14]

Fountain and Williams immediately began their compaign to promote a Radical Republican victory in west Texas at the November elections. Since "soft versus tough reconstruction" meant little to the Mexican voters at the Pass, a local issue had to be found, and, conveniently for Fountain, there was the Guadalupe salt project. The Mexicans were anxious over rumors that an Anglo company had nearly completed arrangements to obtain private title to the salinas after which the historic free use would be ended and they would have to buy salt from the company.

[12] Mills, *Forty Years at El Paso.*
[13] Austin *Republican*, December 5, 1869.   [14] *Ibid.*, June 16, 1869.

Fountain learned from local informants that the El Paso associates had obtained a land certificate authorizing the company to locate on the remaining salt beds, but before the survey had been completed it was discovered that the document was defective, and the company had to make a fresh start for a title. This meant that the Guadalupe salinas were still public land and open for entry, and Fountain decided to develop his platform around the pledge that if elected to the Texas senate he would obtain the salt beds for the citizens of El Paso County under a community trust arrangement, open and free for the use of all.

He shrewdly injected local prejudice into the campaign by attacking the Mills crowd for attempting to appropriate from the Mexicans what he claimed was rightly theirs. Even though Mills had been in Austin for over a year, he was still powerful at the Pass, and Fountain's friends called his campaign reckless and daring and warned him to desist or dire consequences would result.[15]

Fountain refused to relent and, with Williams' help, carried on a vigorous campaign throughout the Thirtieth District. The election began on November 30, 1869, and extended for four days. Voters could cast their ballots only at the county seats, and each polling place was guarded by a detail of United States soldiers. El Paso County's election center was at San Elizario where Lieutenant J. P. Verney and a squad of soldiers examined the registration credentials of voters and counted the ballots. By December 5, it was evident that the Davis Radical Republicans had swept all state offices from the "soft reconstructionists" led by Hamilton and Mills. Albert Fountain, thereby, had won his first major political victory.[16]

[15] 45 Cong., 2 sess., *House Exec. Doc. No. 93*, 128.
[16] Austin *State Journal*, February 11, 1870.

CHAPTER V

The Senator from El Paso

POSTELECTION EL PASO was like a town about to explode. The Anglos studiously shunned Fountain and Williams, assassination rumors circulated, and both carried weapons while on the streets. Only the Mexicans were friendly. From Austin, Mills screamed charges of election frauds, threatened Fountain with lawsuits, and published nasty letters about Fountain in the Texas newspapers friendly to his father-in-law, A. J. Hamilton, the defeated Conservative leader.[1]

A few days before Senator-elect Fountain departed for Austin for the opening session of the Twelfth Legislature, he had a caller—Antonio Borajo, priest of the San Elizario–Socorro parish. Fountain knew him as an old tyrant who unhesitatingly mixed religion and politics. It was said of Padre Borajo that before each election he visited the homes in his parish, warning that those who did not vote according to directions would "not be buried in consecrated ground, but on dung hills, like dogs." On election day he gathered his flock like a herd of sheep, and marched them to the polls.[2]

Borajo got right down to cases. First, he claimed that he had won the election for Fountain by directing the Mexican vote, and second, he implied that, since Fountain had won, he was indebted to him. Borajo asked the Senator what he intended to do about the Guadalupe salt beds. Fountain repeated his election pledge to introduce legislation assigning title to the salinas to the people of El Paso County. Borajo answered that in his view it would be better if the lakes were in private hands and that Fountain should

---

[1] Austin *State Journal*, February 11, 1870.
[2] Sonnichsen, *The El Paso Salt War*, 16.

put them in his (Fountain's) name, collect a fee for use, and split the proceeds (which, according to the Padre, would amount to a "snug revenue") with Borajo. The Padre assured Fountain that the people would submit to such an arrangement. Fountain rejected the proposition, and when Borajo became enraged and began making threats, Fountain ordered him from the house.[3]

On New Year's Day, 1870, Fountain bade Mariana and the children good-by and boarded the Austin stage. He stopped at San Elizario, county seat of El Paso County, long enough to read his salt proposal to the Mexican leaders. When he explained that his bill would vest title to the salinas in the citizens of El Paso County, the use to be administered by a board of trustees selected by the people, he received an enthusiastic ovation and expressions of civic gratitude.

Senator Fountain's coach was slowed by storms and high water, and he did not reach Austin until January 11. This was his first visit to the Texas capital, and he was impressed above all else by the beauty of the countryside. Austin, hemmed by low-lying mountains and nestled in a well-watered valley, was a friendly contrast for a traveler accustomed to the bald mountains and desert flats of the El Paso District. Austin's center of gravity was the statehouse, looming over the city on a high hill; all streets radiated from the shrubbery-banked capitol grounds.

Compared to El Paso, Austin was lively too. Already the town was being readied for Governor Davis' inauguration which would take place on January 17. Well-groomed couples promenaded Congress Avenue, Austin's busiest thoroughfare, and stages arrived daily from all directions bringing additional citizens to swell the throng assembling to view the installation of Texas' first Republican governor.

At the stage station Fountain learned that Austin's most popular and reasonably priced inn was Raven's on Bois d'Arc Street. He engaged rooms there and found the food exquisite—even oysters on the half-shell. For several days, while waiting for his appointment with Governor Davis, Fountain explored the town.

[3] 45 Cong., 2 sess., *House Exec. Doc. No.* 93, 128.

The best patronized place, he noted, was a beer garden on Pecan Street.

Senator Fountain found that entertainment at the state capital ran the gamut of human taste—from the bawdy Wren Company burlesque to Mitchell and Pardey's Galveston Dramatic and Musical Combination. Those with more intellectual tastes could attend Professor Leslie Fowler's lecture on phrenology, which was offered each night in the senate chamber because no other hall in town was available.

The men of Austin preferred the Austin City Jockey Club. The spring racing season was soon to begin, and crowds gathered each afternoon to watch the animals being conditioned and timed for opening day. Several favorites from last season were back, including the top money winners Stonewall, Choctaw, Rebel Chief, Rabbit, Sandy Walton, and Tamerlane.

But of all that Austin had to offer, her churches appealed most to Senator Fountain. The wide range of denominations, most of them housed in elegant sanctuaries and served by eloquent divines, reminded him of his youth on Staten Island when his interest in the Episcopal faith had been strong. He had found it next to impossible to maintain an abiding religious faith in the rough West Coast mining camps, and the vulgar tone of military life during the Civil War had further abated his convictions. Marriage to Mariana further reduced his religious interest, for as a condition of the marriage, her family and Father Donato had exacted from him the promise that any children issuing from their union would be reared in Mariana's faith. Fountain had kept this pledge, and as his children came of age they were instructed in the dogma of the Roman Catholic church. While agreeable to this as far as the children were concerned, he could not bring himself to accept it, and because the only churches in the El Paso District were Roman Catholic, his spiritual apathy continued. Now, for the first time in years, living in a community which supported other churches, he found his old interest quickened, and he began to develop a plan to establish an Episcopal church at El Paso.[4]

[4] Esther D. MacCallum, *The History of St. Clement's Church*, 35–36.

Senator Fountain met with Edmund Davis on January 14 and spent two days with the Governor-elect planning the Radical legislative program and discussing patronage and means of strengthening the Republican party in Texas. Florida-born Davis, trained in the law, had arrived in Texas in 1848 and during the Civil War had led a regiment of Texas Unionists on the lower Río Grande. The fact that he was favored by President Grant, the Radical leaders in Congress, and the military governor of Texas, General J. J. Reynolds, made him the most powerful man in the state. Davis, recalling the vigorous leadership qualities Fountain had shown at the Corpus Christi convention, proved his esteem for the senator from El Paso by designating him as his choice for senate majority leader, and by selecting him to appear on the upcoming inauguration program as one of the featured speakers.[5]

The Radical formula for Reconstruction in each former Confederate state included, besides a drastic revision of the state constitution, political disqualification of former Confederates, and military supervised elections which included Negro voting (thereby guaranteeing a Republican regime in each state), the approval of the thirteenth, fourteenth, and fifteenth amendments to the Federal Constitution, and election of "ironclad oath" United States senators and congressmen. Then, after the military governor had certified that satisfactory reconstruction progress had been made and that the state was qualified to return to civil government, and when the revised state constitution had been approved by Congress, a special act was passed readmitting the state to the Union. Only then was the state completely reconstructed. Until the readmission act had been passed, the governor and legislature were designated "provisional." Davis was inaugurated on January 17 as the "Provisional Governor of Texas," and the Twelfth Legislature, which convened on February 8, was likewise designated as the "Provisional Legislature."[6]

Most of opening day was spent in calling the roll and taking the oath. With Lieutenant Governor J. W. Flanagan presiding,

[5] Galveston *Tri-Weekly News*, January 20, 1870.
[6] Twelfth Legislature, Provisional Session, *Senate Journal*, 4–46.

Justice Morrill of the state supreme court administered the oath. The text had been devised by Texas Military Governor Reynolds and was based on the ironclad oath which was designed primarily to purge the state government of former Confederates and thereby most of the leading Democrats. Since the senators were taken by order of district, Senator Fountain, from the Thirtieth District, was the last to make his affirmation which read: "I do solemnly swear (or affirm, as the case may be) that I have never held the office, or exercised the duties of a senator or representative in Congress, or been a member of the legislature of any state of the United States, or held any office created by law for the administration of any general law of a state, or for the administration of justice in any state or under the laws of the United States, or held any office in the military or naval service of the United States, and thereafter engaged in insurrection or rebellion against the United States, or held any office under, or given any support to, any government of any kind organized or acting in hostility to the United States so help me God."[7]

Looking to the future when he would have responsibility for ramming Governor Davis' program through the senate, Fountain appraised the party structure of the Twelfth Legislature. Compared to the house which contained fifty-three Republicans (eight of them Negroes) and thirty-seven Democrats, the senate could muster eighteen Republicans to oppose those twelve Democratic members who had managed to pass the ordeal of the ironclad oath. Probably the most colorful members of the Republican majority in the senate were the two Negro senators—G. T. Ruby from Galveston and Brazoria counties and Matt Gaines from Washington County.[8]

Ruby, born in New York City and educated in the schools of Maine, had worked as a newspaper correspondent in Haiti for the *Pim and Palm*, published in Boston. In 1864, he arrived in New Orleans as an adviser to assist the United States military authorities with the slave problem. His duties included supervising freed-

[7] Galveston *Tri-Weekly News*, February 8, 1870.
[8] Austin *State Journal*, February 11, 1870.

man education with the title of traveling school agent for the Louisiana Military District. In 1866, Ruby was transferred to the military governor's staff in Texas where he organized the Loyal Union League, a Republican party adjunct among the freedmen, and he stood high in favor with the Texas Radicals because of his skill in lining up the Negro vote for the Davis regime. Of medium height and olive skin, Ruby soon proved himself to be one of the most skilled debaters in the Texas Senate.

Senator Gaines was from another world. Born a slave in Louisiana, he was sold to a trader while a child and taken to the New Orleans slave market, where he was purchased by a planter from Arkansas. Gaines arrived in Texas just before the outbreak of the Civil War when C. C. Hearne of Robertson County purchased him. In 1863, Gaines fled for Mexico, but was captured at the river by Texas Rangers. He labored near Fredericksburg until the war closed when he settled in Washington County. The Austin *State Journal* characterized the Washington County Senator as "a pure African, small in stature . . . compactly build . . . with a vein of rich humor. . . . He is a natural stump orator, but his education being very limited, his ideas are often crude. He is, however, improving rapidly, and nobody will be surprised to see him a member of Congress some fine day."[9]

At ten o'clock each morning the senate convened. Many of the members wore their greatcoats into the bleak chamber since the open fireplace in each of the four walls heated only those fortunate ones with seats nearest each hearth. On February 11, Lieutenant Governor Flanagan named Fountain, Ruby, and Joseph P. Douglas (senator from the Sixth District) as a special committee to wait upon Governor Davis with the information that the senate had completed its organization and was ready for business.[10]

On the same day, Governor Davis submitted the Reconstruction Amendments. Between February 11 and February 22 the senate and house approved the amendments and in joint session elected M. C. Hamilton and J. W. Flanagan to the United States

9 *Ibid.*, February 25, 1870.
10 Twelfth Legislature, Provisional Session, *Senate Journal*, 8.

Senate. After listening to speeches from the senators-elect as to the vigor with which they would, once in Washington, work for an early return of civil government to Texas, Majority Leader Fountain moved that the Chair appoint a committee to inform the Commanding General and Governor that the senate had dispensed with the business assigned it and was ready to adjourn. The Chair named Fountain with M. H. Bowers (senator from the Twenty-eighth District) and W. A. Saylor (senator from the Seventeenth District) for this purpose. They returned with a message from General Reynolds in which he congratulated the senate on the "harmony of its session and the expedition with which it . . . transacted the business laid before it" and authorized the session to close. The "Provisional Legislature" adjourned on February 24, 1870.[11]

Fountain was lonely for Mariana and the children, but as senate majority leader, he was obliged to remain in Austin to work out the Radical program which would be placed before the legislature at its regular session, expected to be called in April. Finally, Mariana agreed to leave the children with her family at Mesilla and arranged passage on the Austin stage. With her husband until the legislature reconvened, Mariana was captivated by the strange new world Albert led her through at Austin. The plays, music, and new fashions were all delights beyond her provincial imagination, but her proudest moments were those Congress Avenue promenades on the arm of her husband, thrilling at the deference all passing paid them.

On the afternoon of April 26, 1870, the Twelfth Legislature assembled, this time in regular session. The previous session had been designated as provisional, so each member had to take the oath again, this time administered by Judge M. B. Walker of the state supreme court. Since J. W. Flanagan had been elected to the United States Senate, the Texas senate was without a presiding officer. Fountain and Governor Davis had discussed this beforehand, and it was decided that the best man for the position would be Don Campbell (senator from the Eighth District),

[11] *Ibid.*, 43–44.

who, as a moderate Republican, might well attract some of the opposition to support the Davis Radical program. Therefore, as the first order of business, with Secretary of State James P. Newcomb presiding, Fountain nominated Campbell for the presidency of the senate, and he was elected with only two dissenting votes.[12]

Just as the members of the legislature had to take another oath changing their status from provisional to regular officers, so did Governor Davis. All legislative business stopped for his second inauguration. With throngs (both white and black), brass bands, flags, and speakers, Edmund Davis was properly installed at noon on April 28. In the afternoon the First Texas Cavalry gave a barbecue with three long tables loaded with meat, bread, pickles, and cake. Symbolic of the superficial character of Texas Reconstruction was the comment by the Galveston *News* reporter: "I was glad to see the colored people wait until their white brethren got through; this was as it should be."[13]

The following day, Governor Davis delivered his message to the legislature. Besides announcing that on March 30 the United States Congress had readmitted Texas to the Union, he reminded the assembled representatives and senators that "so long time has elapsed since the session, within this state, of a body competent to legislate, that your duties must be many, and their performance tedious and laborious. In addition to ordinary matters of legislation, you will find it incumbent upon you to remodel, to a great extent, the General Statutes, and to accommodate them to the new order of things, and to the radical changes engrafted on our institutions by the constitution lately adopted." Davis called for legislation providing for a railroad development program for Texas, a state militia, an expanded public school system, a state police, improved frontier defense, and a special code protecting the rights of Texas' new citizens, the Negroes.[14]

April 30 was one of the busiest days of the entire session. First

12 *Ibid.*, 5.
13 Galveston *News*, April 29, 1870.
14 Twelfth Legislature, *Senate Journal*, 13.

order of business was to elect a senate chaplain. Several senators placed their respective pastors' names in nomination. Through the Episcopal bishop at Austin, Fountain had become acquainted with Rev. J. W. Tays of Bryan and, esteeming his clerical qualifications, nominated him for the chaplaincy. Tays won handily over Baptist, Methodist, Roman Catholic, and other nominees.[15]

Next came the drawing for seats. The sergeant at arms produced thirty marbles, each numbered two, four, or six, placed them in a box, and shook it vigorously before a numbered marble was drawn for each senator by a page. Fountain drew a four-year term; Senators Ruby and Gaines were among those who drew six-year terms.[16]

The final order of business was the assignment to committees. The Republican caucus, headed by Fountain and attended by Davis, had the night before placed Radicals on key committees to assure success for their legislative program. Fountain's committee assignments included Nominations by the Governor (Patronage), Public Buildings, Printing (of which he was chairman), and Public Lands (an important committee in view of the anticipated subsidies to railroads). Because of the alarming increase in Indian depredations, the most important committee to the citizens living in the western half of Texas was the one on Indian Affairs and Frontier Protection. Since he was the only experienced Indian fighter in the Texas senate, Fountain was also named chairman of this committee.[17]

Once the routines of senate organization had been taken care of, legislative supporters of the Davis program began paving the way for reception and passage of the Radical measures. The Governor rented a suite for his legislative high command at the Avenue Hotel, and Fountain and other leading Radicals met there each night to draft bills, confer with the house leadership, and plan strategy for moving the legislation once introduced. Before the first two weeks of May had passed, the calendars of both

[15] *Ibid.*, 31.
[16] Galveston *Tri-Weekly News*, May 6, 1870.
[17] Twelfth Legislature, *Senate Journal*, 36–38.

houses contained the "Big Four" measures of the Davis program—the state police bill, the expanded education bill, the militia bill, and the frontier protection bill.

Then came a spate of private member bills and local legislation for bridges, ferries, roads, and other improvements, which each day so involved the rank and file on the senate floor that the major bills were by-passed. One of the few Texas newspapers favorable to Davis, Fountain, and the other Radicals, the Austin *State Journal*, noted this neglect of the Davis program, and in each issue demanded, in view of the urgent situations all four bills would meet, an early passage of all major legislation. Concerning the state police bill, the *Journal* pointed out that "To suppress crime and lawlessness is essential, if we desire to obtain emigration from the North and West, for the people from those sections, accustomed to security of life and property, hesitate to cast their lot with us when crime stalks unpunished in our midst. They reflect that over eighteen hundred murders have been committed in the State of Texas since the war, while less than half a score of legal executions of the murderers have followed as a result. An efficient force of mounted police, armed with State warrants for the apprehension of criminals, and acting under the orders of an efficient chief, would soon clear the State of criminals. . . . All orders should emanate from the chief, who should himself be under the orders of the Governor."[18]

Regarding Fountain's pet project, so important for his constituents in the El Paso District and all of western Texas, the frontier protection bill, which would reactivate the Texas Ranger system, the *Journal* encouraged early approval, "for every day of needless delay is paid for by a human life. The settlers on our border are as much entitled to the protection of the States, as the members who sit in our legislative hall." According to the *Journal*, settlers were met everywhere "by the war-whoop and the tomahawk of the savage. . . . Too long have the calamities and sorrows of the border been listened to with complacent unconcern. Our harassed and outraged settlers must have the guaranty of peace

[18] Austin *State Journal*, May 19, 1870.

and protection, if the savage tribes have to be swept from the face of the earth with the besom [broom] of extermination."[19]

Fountain noted this senate inertia toward the Davis legislative program, too, and he suspected that it was calculated and planned. But it was still early in the session, and he allowed the senators to dally with their private member bills and local pork barrel measures while he, for the most part, remained in the background and watched, planning for the showdown.

The only local bill Senator Fountain introduced during this early phase of the session was his measure proposing transfer of the Guadalupe salt beds to the citizens of El Paso County. It appeared that the bill would pass without a murmur when, suddenly, Senator M. H. Bowers advised Fountain that he had in his possession a "protest petition" which opposed the passage of the salt bill. The senator from El Paso examined the document and noted that it carried the same date of his appearance on the courthouse steps at San Elizario when he had read his proposal; that among the four hundred signatures were many of those present at the mass meeting; and that "the protest was to the effect that the people of El Paso County objected to the passage of any bill affecting the salt lake question." Fountain then declared to the senate that "if the citizens of El Paso County were determined not to accept the bounty of the state I should not try to force it upon them," and withdrew his proposal. While he was puzzled by this curious turn of events, it was not until his return to El Paso at the close of the legislative session that he learned the astonishing particulars.[20]

By the end of May, Majority Leader Fountain was able to identify a coalition of Conservative Republicans and Democrats formed, he suspected, for the purpose of scuttling the Davis Radical program. Irritated by their private member and local bill delaying tactics, Fountain moved in for the kill. The first, and least objectionable, of the "Big Four" measures, the frontier protection bill, he maneuvered onto the senate floor on May 28.

[19] *Ibid.*, May 27, 1870.
[20] 45 Cong., 2 sess., *House Exec. Doc. No. 93*, 128.

Fountain had drafted most of this proposal which would, if adopted, raise and equip twenty companies of Rangers for frontier service against the ferocious Kiowas, Comanches, and Kickapoos who were making a scalp alley out of western Texas. For two days Senator E. L. Alford, Conservative Republican leader of the coalition, and Fountain were pitted in furious debate on the issue of state versus federal action against the renegade tribes. When it appeared the youthful senator from El Paso had bested the Conservative leader, the latter turned to bill-killing amendments and aggravating points of order in an attempt to check the Radical steam roller Fountain had set in motion.[21]

On June 12, Fountain demanded and got a final vote of twenty-four to three in favor of his measure. The correspondent for the Galveston *Tri-Weekly News* warned the Conservative coalition that Senator Fountain had taken over and was moving the Davis program: "Things hereabouts are settling down amazingly fast. Those connected with the movement to clog the machinery of the administration . . . I think have arrived at the conclusion that their efforts in that direction would prove futile, and have therefore stayed their operations for the present. . . . This is apparently the programme of the administration: such measures as they deem necessary to put in motion to carry out the doctrines of the Republican leaders will be forced through regardless of any obstacles that may be put in their path."[22]

While many newspapers in eastern Texas strongly criticized the frontier protection bill and Senator Fountain for his so-called highhanded methods in achieving its adoption, the press of western Texas, serving the area exposed to the savage raiders, was favorable. Compliments for Fountain came from as far away as Santa Fe where the *New Mexican* declared: "El Paso County can congratulate herself on her good luck in being so ably represented in the person of Mr. Fountain."[23]

The Galveston *News* reporter's prediction that the Radical

---

[21] Austin *State Journal*, June 1, 1870.
[22] Galveston *Tri-Weekly News*, June 13, 1870.
[23] Santa Fe *New Mexican*, July 12, 1870.

leaders would force Governor Davis' program through the legislature "regardless of any obstacles that may be put in their path" was borne out in less than a week. Encouraged by his victory on the frontier protection bill, Fountain moved down the senate calendar, calling for the militia bill on June 15. Once it was on the floor, he pushed it relentlessly, and by limiting debate, restricting amendments, and calling those wavering Republicans into daily caucus and threatening to strip them of patronage and other senatorial privileges unless they got into line, he was ready for a vote on the measure by June 21.

This was the showdown, and Fountain had already been alerted to the reaction he would get by forcing a vote on either this bill or the state police bill. Private detectives employed by Governor Davis to watch the movement and learn the thinking and plans of the coalition senators had reported that insurgent Republicans E. L. Alford and W. Flanagan were meeting each night in Alford's rooms with ten Democratic senators. The operatives' reports revealed that leading officials of the ante bellum and Confederate Texas government, now proscribed by the ironclad oath, regularly met with and advised this clique on how the Davis militia and state police bills might be defeated.[24]

The private detective reports explained that the coalition opposed these measures because they feared that both, if enacted, would be used by the Radicals to perpetuate their "carpetbag tyranny" and "Negro Rule" in Texas. It was revealed that the reason Conservative Republicans and Democrats had remained fairly quiet during Federal occupation, many even working for the adoption of the new Radical constitution and the other Reconstruction requirements, was for the purpose of hastening the end of military rule, and the early return of civil government, when, with Federal troops no longer around to protect the Radicals and Negroes, it was expected that they could twist and turn the new order to suit themselves. Now, the military and state police bills would create what they regarded as a private army for Governor Davis which he could use to guard the polls, protect Negro voters, and assure a

[24] Twelfth Legislature, *Senate Journal*, 335–59.

continuation of the Radical regime, thus thwarting their plans to produce an early return of white supremacy in Texas.[25]

The intelligence brought to Governor Davis by his private detectives, which he passed on to Fountain, included a word on the plan to be followed by the insurgents. When Majority Floor Leader Fountain called for a vote on the militia bill, the twelve were to walk out, thus breaking the quorum and paralyzing senate action. Fountain prepared for this exigency by instructing the sergeant at arms to stand by, ready to intercept any senators departing the chamber when he called for the vote. Just before noon on June 21, as he demanded a roll call vote on the militia bill, he watched Senator Alford.

The insurgent leader suddenly stood erect as if seeking recognition by the Chair, and his eleven partisans rose as one, filed behind Alford, and stalked from the chamber. The sergeant at arms attempted to turn them back into the room, but was shoved aside as the determined group walked in a body toward the outer entrance. When the insurgents saw that three assistants to the sergeant at arms guarded this door, they turned suddenly into a committee room and slammed and bolted the door behind them. The sergeant at arms, having recovered from his rough handling, attempted several times to crash the heavy door. Fountain rushed into the hall and, speaking on behalf of the senate president, Don Campbell, ordered the bolters to return to their seats. When they refused, he directed the sergeant at arms to place the twelve under arrest and to return them to their seats to face charges of being in contempt of the Texas senate. After a whispered conference, the rebellious senators opened the door and, escorted by the sergeant at arms and his aides, returned to their seats in the chamber.

Senate President Campbell reminded the twelve of the serious nature of their action and advised them that they were under arrest pending an investigation of their conduct. Until such time as they were restored to full voting status, he instructed them to remain in their seats at all times when the Senate was in session. Campbell then named Fountain as chairman of a special committee to in-

25 *Ibid.*, 252–71.

vestigate charges that Alford and his followers had "conspired to break the Senate quorum for the purpose of arresting the machinery of government and thereby defeating reconstruction and the organization of the state government."

On June 29, Senator Fountain reported for his special committee. Except for Senator Alford, the committee report recommended a reprimand and release from arrest for each suspended senator. But, continued the report, since "Senator Alford did, in contempt of the Senate, violently resist . . . arrest, and did forcibly close the shutters and did refuse to submit to said arrest by sergeant-at-arms, your committee, therefore, submit the following resolution and recommend its adoption . . . . That in view of the flagrant and persistent contempt of the Senate by Senator E. L. Alford, in refusing to submit to arrest by the sergeant-at-arms, he, Senator E. L. Alford be expelled from the Senate." Fountain's committee report was adopted by a vote of fifteen to five.[26]

Fountain had tamed the insurgents. The last obstacle to passage of the Davis Radical program was removed, and both the militia and state police proposals became law before the Twelfth Legislature closed its first session. Fountain's handling of the Alford rebellion brought him praise, new honors, and demands for public appearances, including the Austin Fourth of July celebration. The program for this gala affair included a giant barbecue, after which a crowd of three thousand clustered about the speaker's stand on the capitol grounds and listened in rapt silence as Senator Fountain read in booming tones the Declaration of Independence.[27]

As the first session of the Twelfth Legislature approached adjournment, Fountain gave more and more thoughts to home, Mariana, and the children. He reflected on the tense political situation at El Paso, too, and gave some consideration to the possibility of mending his split with the Mills faction and uniting the Pass Republicans under his leadership. While he regarded Mills as irreconcilable, Fountain calculated that many of his followers could be won over—notably Clarke and French; and with

[26] *Ibid.*, 272–83.
[27] Dallas *Herald*, July 16, 1870.

71

this pair in his camp, the remaining Conservatives would very likely abandon Mills and follow him. Thus, the key to capturing control of the Republican party at the Pass was in winning Clarke and French. To achieve this, Fountain estimated their price.

As a senate leader, Fountain controlled substantial state patronage, the two most important local positions being the El Paso District judgeship and a captaincy in the newly established state police. Frank Williams, his Radical colleague and only loyal supporter among the Anglos at El Paso before and after the fateful December election, really merited one of these top posts. But regarding party unity at the Pass and his own political future of greater importance than satisfying his political debt to Williams, Senator Fountain directed the appointment of Gaylord Clarke to the district judgeship and A. H. French as captain, state police for the El Paso District.[28]

28 Austin *State Journal*, July 15, 1870.

*

CHAPTER VI

The Most Abused Man in Texas

SENATOR FOUNTAIN'S RETURN to El Paso in August was far pleasanter than his departure had been the preceding January. Most important, Mariana and the children were in good health. The deadly tenseness of election time had passed, and El Paso was its old happy, carefree self again. The Anglos were friendly, even deferential to Senator Fountain, and he felt safe walking unarmed on the streets. Williams was aloof, but Fountain had expected this, figuring that after a momentary pout he could be managed. As he had hoped, his managing the appointment of Clarke and French had healed the political breach, and he was the acknowledged leader of the Pass Republicans. His antagonist, W. W. Mills, had apparently taken up permanent residence in Austin, and Fountain and El Paso seemed to be rid of him at last.

Fountain's homecoming was important in another respect. He had brought the Episcopal clergyman, Joseph W. Tays, from Austin. While at Austin, he had spent several evenings with Bishop Alexander Gregg discussing the possibilities of establishing an Episcopal mission at the Pass, and Gregg had promised to establish a mission when a qualified clergyman became available.

A clergyman became available in the most curious way. After his election as chaplain of the Texas senate, Mr. Tays continued to serve both his flock at Bryan and the senate, his position with the latter carrying prestige but demanding little service. In May, the Reverend Mr. Tays officiated at a wedding in which a white man married a Negro woman. East Texas newspapers were indignant over this mixed-marriage and condemned Tays in scorching editorials, most of which pointed out that he was chaplain of the Radical senate and that this "loathsome union" was typical of the

73

type of society Texas could expect if Governor Davis and the Radical Republicans remained in power much longer. The Houston *Times* reported that "for this offense against decency many of his flock at Bryan refused to hear him preach." Tays's solitary defender, the Austin *State Journal*, raised the question "is not marriage more honorable than concubinage? The *Times* is continually fighting shadows about the legal mingling of the races, but it never says a word about that illicit and promiscuous intercourse which has ever been the bane of Southern society. Of course that is all right with the *Times* people."[1]

Bishop Gregg decided that Mr. Tays was just the man to establish a mission at El Paso; so at the end of the legislative session, Tays resigned his senate chaplaincy and accompanied Fountain to the Pass. Fountain introduced Tays to the townspeople and invited all Protestants to worship on Sunday. For several weeks, services were held in private homes attended by only a score of worshipers, but the Reverend Mr. Tays, a King's College graduate from Nova Scotia, was a vigorous worker and a compelling preacher, and in a few months he had established a congregation of seventy-five members.[2]

Now on the best of terms, Fountain and Clarke, fellow New Yorkers and Episcopalians, rented a vacant adobe building, and El Paso's St. Clement's Episcopal Church was born. This busy pair of laymen constructed an altar, a pulpit, and crude benches, and Fountain, "artistic to his fingertips," painted a large shaded cross on a canvas placed over the back window.[3]

Once St. Clement's Mission was ready for worship, Senator Fountain spent most of his time meeting with constituents to learn how he could best serve them in the next legislative session. Delegations from all over his district came in to discuss such problems as Indian depredations, railroad construction, public schools, and local tax assessments. Ben Dowell, the saloonkeeper and

[1] Houston *Times*, May 12, 1870, and Austin *State Journal*, May 15, 1870.

[2] Esther D. MacCallum to Albert J. Fountain, Jr., El Paso, October 26, 1925. Fountain Papers, University of Oklahoma Library.

[3] MacCallum, *The History of St. Clement's Church*, 35.

mayor of El Paso, headed a group of citizens promoting legislation to incorporate their town and designate it the county seat.

Of all the Senator's conferences with constituents, his most memorable one occurred in mid-October when Luis Cardis, a subcontractor for the Overland Mail, called. Fountain recollected that this dapper little Italian had arrived at the Pass in 1865, a refugee from Garibaldi's ill-fated Freedom Legion. By marrying a Mexican woman and adopting the language and mores of her people, Cardis gained much influence on the Río Grande, and he prospered as a trader and freighter.

It had come to Fountain on good authority that Cardis, in league with Padre Borajo, had inspired the "protest" against his Guadalupe salina proposal in the Texas legislature, so, after an exchange of pleasantries, he bluntly asked his visitor if he was in any way connected with the "protest" petition. When Cardis acknowledged that Father Borajo and he had prepared the document, Fountain inquired how the Mexicans had been persuaded to sign a "protest" which was so opposed to their interests. Cardis "laughed and replied that they had represented to the people that if the salt lakes became the property of the county of El Paso their friends and relatives residing in the towns on the Mexican bank of the river would be deprived of the privilege they then enjoyed of taking salt from the lakes," and that Borajo had also told them that the whole affair was a trick by Senator Fountain to "deprive them of the salt lakes."[4]

Fountain then inquired what Father Borajo and he expected to gain by these machinations to which Cardis replied that he would answer after they had discussed his proposition. Cardis reminded Fountain that his political future was dependent upon the continued peaceful relations between the Pass Republicans' two factions and that such relations could be assured if the Senator would submit to certain demands. In view of Fountain's controlling influence in the distribution of patronage, Cardis revealed that the price of continued party harmony would be the "removal of Marsh as collector of customs, the appointment of French in his place,

[4] 45 Cong., 2 sess., *House Exec. Doc. No.* 93, 129.

the appointment of Cardis as mounted inspector, and the distribution of patronage equally between the two wings of the party."[5]

Cardis continued that Father Borajo, the most influential man in the country since "he could turn the Mexican vote in any direction he desired, for his part . . . insisted upon having entire control of the public schools; the selection of teachers . . . and an arrangement . . . in regard to the salt lakes." Cardis said that "Borajo had salt lake on the brain; he thought there was a great fortune in the matter." Fountain's role in this arrangement would be "to enter the salt lakes in his name and to charge for all salt taken and divide the proceeds with Borajo." When Fountain asked Cardis why "he or Borajo did not locate the lakes in their own name, as they had a right to do, Cardis replied that such action on their part would completely destroy their influence with the people," but if Fountain would do it, "the people would not be surprised, as they had already prepared their minds to receive notice of such action. . . . Borajo would advise them to submit, and they would follow his advice."

Fountain then asked Cardis "what security he would have that . . . Fountain might refuse to divide the proceeds of the salt tax with Borajo" when he obtained legal title to the beds, and the Italian replied "We know that you would not do anything of the kind, because it would cost you your life, and you know it." Cardis added that "Borajo was determined to have the lakes, and that no other person should enjoy their possession adversely to him."

Senator Fountain flatly refused to go along on the salt project, the school proposition, and the Marsh ouster. Cardis, accepting the rejection somewhat expectantly, left Fountain's office with the sinister warning that "war will be commenced on Marsh. Let us alone and keep out of the fight if you won't help us."[6]

Preoccupied with his family, the new church, audiences with

[5] Dr. D. C. Marsh had been appointed collector of customs at El Paso to replace W. W. Mills in 1869. A carpetbagger from Michigan, Dr. Marsh arrived in Texas with the Union Army of Occupation as an army surgeon. Just before his appointment to the El Paso collectorship, he had been stationed with Federal troops at Seguin, Texas, where he also was postmaster for Seguin.

[6] 45 Cong., 2 sess., *House Exec. Doc. No.* 93, 129.

constituents, and preparations for the next legislative session, Fountain gave little thought to the Cardis meeting. For the present he had a bigger problem than trying to conciliate Cardis and Borajo. Frank Williams, his old Radical crony, had not come around as Fountain had expected he would. As a matter of fact, he became more surly and morose by the day, spending most of his time at Dowell's saloon, grumbling thick-tongued curses on Fountain, Clarke, and French. Fountain had attempted on several occasions to reason Williams out of his hostility with assurances of patronage preference as soon as the legislature reconvened. But Williams became increasingly belligerent, and, to avoid a showdown, Fountain shunned him.[7]

Then came that fateful December 7. The night before, Williams, influenced by Pass brandy, crowed his determination to avenge the shame and the loss of reputation he had suffered. Dowell's patrons had heard these fulminations so many times they hardly looked up from their cards until Williams capped his tirade by calling Fountain a "son of a bitch" and Clarke and French "spineless carpetbaggers."[8]

Bright and early the next morning Fountain went looking for Williams. Entering Dowell's, he found him standing at the bar. Fountain took a cigar, held it to his mouth with one hand, and, lighting it with the other, his cane hanging on his left arm, quietly addressed his old political colleague: "Williams, you have been talking a great deal lately about Judge Clarke, myself, and other gentlemen here, and you ought to stop it. You ought to put a curb on your tongue."

Williams replied, "Maybe you had better curb it," and at the same time making a sweeping motion with his right hand to his belt, he palmed a revolving derringer. Unarmed and anxious about the wild look in Williams' eyes, Fountain warned him, "Don't shoot me, for if you do, you will get more holes through you than you ever dreampt of."[9]

[7] MacCallum, *The History of St. Clement's Church,* 42.
[8] Austin *State Journal,* December 22, 1870.
[9] *Ibid.*

When he saw that Williams was not bluffing, Fountain rushed him with his cane and rained blows on his shoulder and right arm to deflect the pistol. Williams sent three quick shots into the Senator, then retreated out the back door, and ran down the street. His first shot had struck Fountain in the left arm, and the second hit his breast, penetrating his coat, five letters in his pocket, and striking his watch. The watch saved his life, for the shot was fired at point-blank range. Williams' third shot struck Fountain in the head, inflicting an ugly scalp wound from which blood flowed down over his face.[10]

Fountain staggered into the street and, meeting Clarke, explained that Williams had gone berserk and asked that he call a posse. Mariana screamed with fright when her husband stumbled onto the porch. She pleaded with him to remain in the house and let her clean and bandage his wounds, but, wiping the blood from his face with a wet towel, the Senator grabbed his rifle and joined the search for Williams.

As he approached the building where Williams roomed, he saw that Clarke had collected a posse and that three Mexicans, armed with axes, were chopping at the heavy front door. Captain French had just posted three armed men in the rear of the building to prevent escape and was deploying the remaining possemen along the street when suddenly the three Mexicans dropped their axes and fled, and Clarke, French, and the other searchers scurried for cover behind the adobe pillars which supported the portal extending from the building.[11]

Then Fountain saw the cause for this haste. Williams had opened the door and was stepping onto the sidewalk holding a double-barreled shotgun at hip level. Williams looked up and down the street, searched out Clarke's position, and fired one barrel, chipping adobe but missing the target. Then he rushed Clarke's pillar, dodging around it twice to decoy his quarry. On the second turn, Williams whirled abruptly and came face to face with Clarke. Williams snapped a point-blank charge into the

10 Galveston *Tri-Weekly News*, January 13, 1871.
11 MacCallum, *The History of St. Clement's Church*, 44.

Judge's chest. Clarke staggered off a few paces and fell mortally wounded into the arms of two possemen.[12]

Fountain approached the scene as fast as his tormented body would allow. Seeing Clarke fall, he pulled up at fifty yards, aimed, and fired. The shot spun Williams around and smashed him to the cobblestone walk. As Williams rolled over and felt for his pistol, French rushed in and finished him off with a shot to the head.[13]

Frank Williams was buried with a simple service on December 8. Judge Clarke's funeral occurred the following day and was the most elaborate burial ever conducted at El Paso. Mr. Tays officiated, and nearly all the prominent citizens from over the county and "the few ladies of El Paso" attended the rites. The procession, led by the brass band from Juárez included a company of rangers with the county unit of state police as honor guard.[14]

After Clarke's funeral, Senator Fountain submitted to Mariana's nursing, and her tender, loving care helped him conquer his weakness from the heavy loss of blood caused by the Frank Williams duel. The bullet intended for his heart, but deflected by the watch, had glanced downward, furrowing a gash in his side and breaking a rib. This wound and that in his left forearm healed quickly. The head wound, near the left temple, came along nicely, but the bullet had grazed a nerve and a paralysis developed in his right leg.

Despite his difficulty in walking and Mariana's protests, Senator Fountain decided on the second day after Christmas to leave for Austin to be present when the legislature convened on January 10. The racking 800-mile stage ride set him back, and after answering roll call, he was excused by Senate President Don Campbell to convalesce in his rooms at Raven's.[15]

Senator Fountain handled such legislative business as he could manage at his bedside and caught up on his newspaper reading. His vigorous constitution and strong determination enabled him

[12] Austin *State Journal*, December 22, 1870.
[13] MacCallum, *The History of St. Clement's Church*, 44.
[14] Austin *State Journal*, December 28, 1870.
[15] Galveston *Tri-Weekly News*, January 13, 1871.

to overcome the weakness of his wounds and paralysis, and by February 1 he was back on the senate floor managing the legislative fortunes of Radical Governor Davis. His first official act took place on February 24 when the legislature asked that he serve as marshal of the day for the funeral of Senator Amos Clark (Second District Democrat). Even the bitterly anti-Radical Galveston *Tri-Weekly News* praised the senator from El Paso for his efforts: "So well did he discharge the trust confided to him, as to draw encomiums from all. He had an eye to the large as well as the minutest details."[16]

The last of the "Big Four" measures of the Davis Radical program on the Twelfth Legislature's calendar, the education bill, had yet to be brought onto the floor and managed through to passage. The proposal was unpopular in many state circles and with certain members of the legislature because of, first, the cost and, second, the educational opportunities it provided for Negro children as well as white children. Senator Fountain had made an exhaustive study of the educational situation and discovered that of the 160,000 children of school age in Texas, only about 60,000 were able to attend classes, owing largely to lack of teachers and facilities.[17]

The education bill he proposed was described as a "practical and equable school law" by the Austin *State Journal*. It provided for compulsory attendance of all children in Texas between the ages of six and eighteen, on penalty of a \$25 fine, for at least four months each year. The public school system was to be administered by a state board of education, composed of the state superintendent of public instruction, the attorney general, and the governor. The state board was vested with the power to adopt rules for the operation of the schools, examine, appoint, and fix salaries of teachers, define the courses to be taught in these schools, and adopt all books used.[18]

The education bill evoked a lively debate in the legislature, largely on the grounds that it centralized education and made it

16 *Ibid.*, February 24, 1871.
17 Austin *State Journal*, April 11, 1871.
18 *Ibid.*, March 29, 1871.

the pawn of the governor and his aides. During late March, just as the school bill was moving through its final stages of consideration, Senate President Campbell was stricken with a serious illness which finally was diagnosed as typhoid fever with the bloody flux and other complications. Although Campbell lingered until November, Governor Davis, remembering the senate cabal of the previous session and wanting a strong hand to manage the upper house, pushed for an immediate replacement, and Senator Fountain, as ranking Republican senator, was elected to the presidency of the Texas senate on March 30.[19]

While pleased with this new post, won at the age of thirty-two, Senate President Fountain was anxious about the future of the Radical Republicans in Texas. Most of the state newspapers had been anti-Radical from the earliest days of the Davis regime, and they spared no effort to belittle the New Order. But of late the editorial critics had become more intemperate in their criticism, and, joined by many papers heretofore moderate or neutral, seemed to be carrying on a vigorous, calculated, hate-mongering campaign aimed at destroying public confidence in the Davis government, encouraging the end of Radical Reconstruction and a return to the Old Order.

It disturbed Senator Fountain that the emerging image of the Radical Republicans was that of a public enemy intent on bringing ruin to Texas. While his party still held a comfortable majority in the legislature and Governor Davis seemed invulnerable in his hold on Texas with his militia and state police, reports came in daily from over the state of open public defiance to the Davis system. Fountain suspected that this growing attitude was symptomatic of the eventual and inevitable collapse of Radical Republicanism in Texas.

One method used by the critics in their campaign to discredit and destroy public faith in the Davis regime was to expose Radical Republicans to ridicule and public censure. None escaped their editorial venom. The early sniping at Mr. Tays, carefully identi-

[19] Twelfth Legislature, *Senate Journal*, 583, and Galveston *Tri-Weekly News*, March 31, 1871.

fied by the papers as the chaplain of the "Radical Republican" senate, for marrying the white man and Negro woman was a case in point. Many citizens resented Negroes holding public office, and newspaper correspondents at Austin kept their readers informed of the antics of the Negroes in state government, eternally poking fun at them. For example, wide coverage was given the resolution presented by the playful senator from Washington County, Matt Gaines, to procure "at public expense for each member of the Legislature a Horace Greeley Hat." This needling of the Negro members of the legislature became so regular by the Houston *Times* that Senator Ruby on several occasions offered resolutions to expel that paper's correspondent from the senate. Every Radical officeholder was watched, and every possible unfavorable item concerning public as well as private behavior was published. When Senator Gaines was convicted of bigamy and sentenced to one year in the state penitentiary, his so-called lechery was described as typical of Radical conduct.

From the earliest days of their first session, the Radicals had been the object of editorial blasts from papers like *Flake's Bulletin*, whose Austin correspondent kept writing "what a blessing it will be when they adjourn, especially if they don't do more than an average amount of mischief." But this criticism was mild compared to the Galveston *Tri-Weekly News* charge that the Radical legislature was "more wicked than the Romans that stood guard at the foot of the cross. Our legislators have fought and quarreled over the spoils—the soldiers made a peaceable division, and cast lots for that which remained. Personal interest . . . and personal aggrandizement have occupied the chief attention of our legislature."[20]

As the Twelfth Legislature approached adjournment, the *Tri-Weekly News* gave a parting shot which was more prophetic than the correspondent realized: "Poor fellows! I pity them. Ere the first of January, 1872, the requiem of the Republicans as a party will be chanted from every house-top in the state of Texas. A happy day that will be for our glorious state; speed it along say I."[21]

[20] Galveston *Tri-Weekly News*, March 10, 1871.   [21] *Ibid.*, June 2, 1871.

Davis, Fountain, and other Radical leaders, raw from this incessant editorial whipping, watched with grave concern a gathering which took place at Austin in September, 1871. Called the "Non-Partisan Tax Payers Convention" and held ostensibly to protest "abuses of government" under the Davis regime, its membership contained most of the prominent Texas Democrats plus A. J. Hamilton and W. W. Mills and their Conservative Republican followers. Besides declaring the acts of the Davis administration unconstitutional, the convention mapped strategy for the upcoming fall elections.[22]

Senator Fountain's fears concerning the uncertain future of Radical Republicanism in Texas were confirmed by the results of the Congressional elections held during October, when the Radical candidates took a dreadful beating. The solitary spokesman for the Radicals, the Austin *State Journal*, charged that Democrats had won over their Republican opponents because the Ku Klux had ridden the countryside intimidating Negro voters; Negro tenants and sharecroppers were threatened with loss of jobs and credit and were faced with "poverty and starvation for their families" if they registered and voted.[23]

The legislative elections were even more disappointing, for when the returns were all in, it was clear that the Democrats would have a majority of eighteen to twelve in the senate and overwhelming strength in the house when the Thirteenth Legislature convened in January, 1873. While Fountain did not have to stand re-election since he had drawn a four-year term, it was disconcerting for him to witness the defeat of his Radical colleagues district by district by Democratic candidates.[24]

Senator Fountain had planned to help his party by campaigning in certain critical districts, but his involvement in federal grand jury indictments absorbed his time and talents until the very eve of the fall elections. Part of the strategy of the Democratic opposition had been to embarrass, discredit, and ruin Radical office-

[22] See Charles W. Ramsdell, *Reconstruction in Texas.*
[23] Austin *State Journal*, October 11, 1871.
[24] Dallas *Herald*, November 23, 1871.

holders by whatever means available. Unable to nail top Radicals by the methods found successful in harassing the lesser fry, Democrats and Conservative Republicans turned to the grand jury. During January, 1873, the three leading Texas Radicals—Governor Edmund Davis, Secretary of State J. P. Newcomb, and Senate President Albert J. Fountain—were indicted by federal grand juries. The charge against Davis was declaring martial law in Limestone County without the concurrence of the legislature. Newcomb was accused of conspiracy in showing a United States commissioner (allegedly drunk) disrespect. Fountain faced seventeen felony indictments, the charges ranging from conspiracy and forgery to defrauding the federal revenues.[25]

Right after the indictments were published, Davis and Newcomb traveled to Washington for conferences with President Grant and other high government officials. Soon after their return the indictments against each were quashed. Senator Fountain did not fare as well. The charges against him stemmed from his service as a customs inspector at El Paso under W. W. Mills. Interestingly, the chief witnesses for the prosecution, besides one Ynocente Ochoa, were W. W. Mills and Luis Cardis, and the prosecution was led by A. J. Hamilton, Mills's father-in-law, and Buck Walton, both leading Conservative Republicans.

It took the prosecution from January to July to move through the seventeen charges, against which Fountain was defended by Colonel Allen Trigg. Both Mills and Cardis perjured themselves early in the proceedings. The other star witness for the prosecution, Señor Ynocente Ochoa, a Mexican citizen and prominent businessman in the Southwest, had been arrested and forcibly brought to Austin by the prosecution to testify against Fountain. Furious at the treatment he had received at the hands of federal officials, Ochoa gave testimony which refuted charges of fraud against Fountain, after which he lodged a heavy bill for damages against the United States for his "arbitrary arrest, conveyance to Austin, and long detention there."[26]

[25] Galveston *News*, January 27, 1872.
[26] Austin *State Journal*, March 5, 1872.

Fountain held his temper and stood up well under the harassment by the prosecution which according to the *Journal* became so vicious that "Hamilton . . . in his harangue to the jury, poured out the rankling grief of his bosom to such an extent that he was stopped and admonished by the court." Hamilton stoutly "declared his fixed resolve to annihilate the whole Republican Administration of Texas from Governor Davis down to the town constable. They were all rascals and thieves and he was bent on their annihilation."[27]

Finally, after months of castigation by the prosecution, even the anti-Radical *Flake's Bulletin* came to Fountain's defense, pointing out that "the entire amount of money claimed to have been lost was less than five hundred dollars. The trial of these cases shows that every cent was paid over by Fountain—not one mill was lost by the Government—and that Senator Fountain did not forge any one's name, did not personate any other person, did not illegally collect a dime, and did not neglect his business either criminally or carelessly. I believe the court and jury to be fair, conscientious, and impartial—at least no man will accuse them of bias in favor of Fountain.

"These trials have conclusively proved the entire innocence of Fountain. Any other conclusions would prove the corruption of the judiciary, the perjury of jurors, and the incapacity and stupidity of the prosecutors. Senator Fountain has been the most abused man in Texas for the past six months. . . . He vindicates himself and is honorably acquitted. Yet the prosecution continues a case which inflicts upon Fountain another trial, the expenses of which are ruinous to him. In view of this I say prosecution has become persecution."[28]

By midsummer, Senator Fountain had been acquitted of all seventeen charges and was released from custody. Even though each offense had been considered at jury trial proceedings, the Democrats and Conservative Republicans, piqued at their failure to win a conviction on at least one of the nearly a score of indict-

[27] *Ibid.*, February 27, 1872.
[28] *Flake's Bulletin*, March 16, 1872.

ments, charged that the Fountain case had been tampered from Washington. The dissidents turned the acquittals to political advantage by incorporating into their Democratic platform for the November elections the statement: "Resolved that the administration of President Grant merits condemnation of all law-abiding men for interfering with the course of justice in the Federal Courts of Texas."[29]

Physically, Senator Fountain had stood up under his ordeal magnificently. Financially, he was ruined. All the money Mariana had saved over the years had been drained to help pay for his defense, and even this was not enough, for he had to borrow heavily from Newcomb and other friends in Austin before he could settle with his attorney. When Fountain returned home, free and penniless, he was invited to join Allen Blacker and Charles Coldwell in a law firm they had only recently established. Being newcomers, they found Fountain's legal acumen and knowledge of the language and ways of the region splendid assets for increasing their business, and the firm of Coldwell, Blacker, and Fountain prospered.[30]

Fountain looked with dread to returning to Austin for the convening of the Thirteenth Legislature, not only because he would be of the minority party, but also because of his recent ordeal, Austin held only heartache and disappointment for him. Mariana hated Texas and Texans for so ill-using her beloved, and when Fountain returned from the recent trials, she urged him to resign his senate seat and take her and the children back to New Mexico. But feeling a duty to his party, which faced its darkest hour, he determined to return to Austin and serve as the leader of an effective minority.

The Democratic-dominated Thirteenth Legislature convened on January 14, 1873, with the election of E. R. Pickett, Democrat from the First District, as president of the senate. Fountain and the Radicals found it awkward and frustrating to be the minority after running the senate for two years, and they maintained a

[29] Dallas *Herald*, June 12, 1872.
[30] Mesilla *News*, March 14, 1874.

tightly knit, articulate opposition to the majority's efforts to undo the Reconstruction program. But despite their efforts, the basic measures of the Radical regime fell one by one, Fountain's pride—the education bill—receiving the axe just before the session closed.

One of the most hotly contested proposals offered by the Democratic majority was an election law providing for general state elections in November, 1873. Fountain saw the threat of this for it would shorten the terms of Davis, himself, and other surviving Radicals and force them to run for re-election one year early. Fountain pointed out that abridging the terms of senators and representatives might well bring two legislatures to the capital. The election law restored the old method of voting by precincts (rather than county seats) and shortened the election period from four days to one day, thereby making it easier for local groups to intimidate the Negro voters, control the electoral machinery, and hasten the return of white supremacy.[31]

Probably the sharpest protest Senator Fountain raised as senate minority leader concerned a resolution to invite Jefferson Davis, former President of the Confederate States of America, to include a visit to Austin and an appearance before the legislature on his projected journey through Texas. Despite Fountain's objections, the resolution carried, but as it turned out, Davis was detained at Memphis and had to decline.[32]

One of the most interesting proposals brought forth during the first session of the Thirteenth Legislature was Senator Fountain's resolution advocating the adoption of woman's suffrage in Texas. The Democratic-dominated legislature was much more concerned with restricting suffrage (especially as it concerned the Negro) than extending it, and with all his emphasis on "justice" and "natural right" Senator Fountain's appeal on behalf of Texas womanhood was half a century premature. Despite his minority role, he was able to drive through several important local bills, the most significant one being a law providing for the incorporation of El Paso.[33]

[31] Thirteenth Legislature, *Senate Journal*, 753.
[32] *Ibid.*, 592.   [33] *Ibid.*, 865–68.

Senator Fountain's proudest hour of the entire session occurred on June 5 when he was honored with a banquet at the elegant Raymond House. Sponsored by a delegation of grateful constituents, the senator from El Paso sparkled amidst the toasts and compliments. The Galveston *Daily News* reported that Fountain received "a very fine gold watch" and "many good things were said by the members present. . . . It was an occasion that Senator Fountain will long remember with pleasure and pride. We all know how extreme he has been in his partisanship, but his Democratic constituents, who were present last night, acknowledged that he had never let an opportunity pass when he could benefit the great West."[34]

[34] Galveston *News*, June 6, 1873.

CHAPTER VII

Frontier Editor

RETURNING TO EL PASO after the close of the Thirteenth Legislature, Senator Fountain busied himself with catching up on his share of the Coldwell-Blacker-Fountain law firm work and contemplating his future. Several important decisions had to be made, and each night Mariana and he discussed the course best for them and the children.

The recently adopted Texas election law nullified his four-year senate term and required that should he continue in the affairs of state government he must stand for re-election. Mariana favored returning to Mesilla where her husband could make a fresh start. There was merit in her urging, for his lengthy Mills-inspired federal court trial, even though he had been exonerated on all charges, had embarrassed him socially and politically and ruined him financially.

If his political prospects were generally uncertain, of greater moment was his dismal future at El Paso. This was disappointing since Fountain, planning to live out his years at the Pass, had put in much time and effort at improving the town and promoting the district's economic development. Even if he remained at El Paso and eschewed politics, which would be most difficult to do, he still had to live with his neighbors, and he was despised by many. The Williams-Clarke killing had left scars. The greedy salt ring crowd, busy again conniving to gain control of the Guadalupe salinas, hated Fountain for thwarting their earlier efforts. And Mills continued to stir up trouble whenever and wherever possible.

Emotionally, Fountain was ready for a change, and each day Mariana's proposal that they return to Mesilla and make a fresh start appealed to him more. Above all else he was devoted to his wife and children, and, his duties as senator and party leader requiring that he be away from home much of the time, he felt a sense of guilt at neglecting them. Albert already was ten, Thomas would soon be eight, Edward was six, Maggie was five, and Marianita, the raven-haired image of her mother and the pride of the Fountain household, was four.[1]

Another appeal the move to Mesilla held for him, should he decide to continue in political affairs, was the unlimited opportunity New Mexico Territory offered experienced Republicans. As a territory, New Mexico was completely at the mercy of the federal government—its laws and other official acts were subject to the scrutiny of Congress, and its leading officials from the governor on down were appointed by the President. The President and Congress had been Republican since 1861, and the prospects were good that the Republican party would continue to dominate national affairs. The parent party in Washington had nourished New Mexican Republicans, and the party was all-powerful in the territory. Unlike Texas, where the political die had been cast in the Democratic image and where Republicanism was but a passing fancy, New Mexico was a political frontier where unlimited opportunity awaited all Republicans.

With all these persuasive reasons for leaving El Paso, and unable to find a single justification for staying, Fountain began winding up his affairs at the Pass and preparing for the move. Mariana, anxious to be in her old town for Christmas, happily went about the packing chores. Fountain rented a wagon and team, hired local Mexican helpers, and had completed the move to their rented house at Mesilla on December 15, just in time for his family to participate in the Virgin of Guadalupe Festival which opened the Yule Season.

Fountain was as happy as Mariana to be back in New Mexico, and life at Mesilla, compared to the heartache and hardship of El Paso, was more pleasant than they ever dreamed it could be. This quiet, peaceful, law-abiding town of two thousand popula-

1 Interview with Albert Fountain, August 12, 1961.

tion, 90 per cent Mexican, compared favorably to its noisy neighbor two miles north, Las Cruces. An Anglo center of fifteen hundred people, it was an ugly town like El Paso, where on the average one murder and from four to six shootings and cutting scrapes occurred each week.[2]

As the leading town in the valley, Mesilla was the judicial center for federal, territorial, and county courts, and thus a strategic town for an attorney. Besides being the county seat for Doña Ana County, Mesilla had the United States Land Office and other public offices. Furthermore, Mesilla was a pretty town; pleasantly laid out, it was arranged in regular squares on streets running from the plaza, the streets with shade trees, and orchards and vineyards all about.

From his doorstep Fountain could see to the northeast the Organ Mountains, nearly twenty miles away, and many times he wondered at their rugged beauty and ever-changing panorama of beautiful scenes—at sunset when the peaks were "lavishly tinted by nature's hand" or in early spring when the desert browns changed to hues of green. To the south he could study the spacious homes of Mesilla's leading citizens; some of the most elegant residences in the Territory were there, including the homes of Thomas J. Bull, the wine-maker; Mariana Barela, land baron; Warren Bristol, federal judge; and J. E. Griggs, Joseph Reynolds, and Thomas Casad, merchants and traders. On the main plaza were the leading mercantile establishments, which included nine general and grocery stores, one hotel, a saloon and billiard hall, three carpenter shops, two printing offices, a bakery, two meat markets, and the offices of three doctors, a dentist, and five lawyers. On the west edge of town were two mills—one a steam gristmill and the other a water mill.

After Fountain became established in his law practice, he began looking about for a better residence for his family. The rented house and yard were too small for the children, Mariana was in a family way again, and he sought a place on the edge of town convenient to his office, yet so situated as to provide space for play

[2] *Rio Grande Republican*, November 26, 1881.

and a garden and chores for the children. After some search, he located five acres of undeveloped land south of town. He negotiated with native workmen for the building of his new house, and he found it interesting to watch them construct in the mode of the Southwest. First, the laborers made the brick, or adobe, by shaping a mixture of thick mud and straw into bricks twenty-two inches long, eleven inches wide, and three inches thick. Pine frame moulds were used, and the adobes were left on the ground to dry in the sun. Next, the workmen, using common mud for mortar, laid the adobes into a wall twenty-two inches thick. When the six-room structure was completed, the walls were plastered inside and out and covered with a calcimine finish. The dull white walls and protruding *vigas* made a handsome, though modest, dwelling, warm in winter and cool in summer.

Fountain could not help noticing that, unlike strife-ridden El Paso, where a man had to stay tense, his hand near his gun ready to defend his life at all times, in peaceful Mesilla a man could relax and thoroughly enjoy life. He appreciated this, put his pistol and belt in his desk drawer, and threw himself into the stream of civic affairs, casting his creative talents here and there.

Among the many things he had had in mind for some time was the formation of an association of California Column veterans. Many of his comrades had settled in New Mexico, and he had hopes of organizing an annual encampment. He began locating and corresponding with the scattered members and soon had sufficient interest stirred up to arrange for a reunion which was held at Mesilla in the autumn of 1874. While only a handful attended the first meeting, it was a start, and the California Column reunion, a predecessor of the New Mexico G. A. R., became an annual affair. By 1876, the association had grown to two hundred members, and in that year the Californians convened at Mesilla for what was described as "the best reunion ever." The program included a memorial service for deceased members of the Column, capped by the firing of salutes, and a huge banquet and ball at Reunion Hall, the premises "handsomely and tastefully arranged and decorated with flags, evergreens, and pictures." A Mexican band furnished music for dancing which continued until daylight.[3]

The Masonic Order was another civic activity which absorbed a good deal of Fountain's time and interest. He had joined the Order at Austin during his senate days and had attempted to organize a lodge at El Paso, but that hate-filled town was poor ground for transplanting the Masonic tenets of brotherly love, charity, and service. Mesilla being a thoroughly Mexican-Catholic town was without a Masonic cell, but the nearby Anglo town, Las Cruces, sponsored a Lodge, and a few weeks after his return to Mesilla, Brother Albert J. Fountain was accepted into the Las Cruces fraternity.[4]

Aztec Lodge No. 3 of Las Cruces, organized in 1866 under a dispensation from the Grand Lodge of Missouri, was the third unit established in the Territory, only the Santa Fe and Las Vegas lodges antedating it. Thus, when the Grand Lodge of New Mexico was organized in 1877, Las Cruces' Aztec Lodge took the number "3" for its identity, and its members included besides Fountain such notables as James J. Dolan, Thomas B. Catron, John Blazer, S. B. Newcomb, and G. W. Maxwell. In his Masonic work, besides serving several times as worshipful master, Fountain traveled over the territory to Grand Lodge meetings held at such places as Santa Fe, Albuquerque, and Las Vegas and became well-acquainted with brother Masons who were also leading territorial politicians, Henry L. Waldo, W. G. Ritch, and Max Frost.

At the same time that he was advancing socially, Fountain was putting his creative talents to work. His dream was to transform Mesilla and to produce there a cultural oasis in the generally barbaric Southwest. Already he was talking up the idea of a public library—using his personal library as a nucleus, extending the public school system, organizing drawing and painting classes, and presenting dramatic productions.

During the summer of 1874 the indefatigable Fountain organized the Mesilla Dramatic Association, rented a vacant build-

[3] *Mesilla News,* June 24, 1876.
[4] Interview with Henry Fountain, August 10, 1961.

ing on the northwest corner of the plaza, hired workmen to clean, paint, and renovate it inside and out, and emblazoned on its front "Mesilla Opera House." While he designed and painted the stage sets, Mariana and the girls produced the costumes. All the while he was coaching the members, rewriting several plays for local presentation, and finally selected *Bombastes Furioso*, a burlesque, for the association's first public effort. The cast included: Albert Fountain as Bombastes Furioso, the redoubtable general of the Bosque Guard; Ira Bond, king of the Río Grande; L. H. Baldy, Fusbus, the prime minister; Page Otero, Distaffina, a gushing damsel; and Alex Bull, the grand chamberlain.

By November 9, Fountain thought that his troupe was ready for their first public appearance, and he sent out printed invitations announcing the production and cast to the leading citizens of the region. To the editor of the Mesilla *News* he included a note: "Extenuate naught, and set nothing down in malice . . . but bestow praise and blame where it is deserved."

The editor not only reported his amazement that a refined effort could be produced from such crude material, but, in addition, he extended a tribute to Fountain as a playwright, producer, and actor. First of all he noted that "the pretty little theater was filled to overflowing with the elite of the Mesilla Valley, the 225 seats sold out and 'standing room only' crowded over 300 into the hall." Furthermore, the editor observed that the "stage, curtain scenery, and other appointments were in excellent taste," all the work of Fountain, which "reflects great credit upon that gentleman's good taste."

Since this was an amateur production, the editor pointed out that the crowd did not expect too much; for "like most amateur performances, there would be a drag, lack of finish, and forgetfulness of parts. . . . To say that they were agreeably disappointed but feebly expresses the truth. . . . At 7:30 precisely the curtain went up on a parlor scene. Mr. Fountain stepped forward in evening costume and delivered a short, humorous opening address in verse. A few minutes after, the curtain went up on the burlesque of

Bombastes Furioso, rewritten by him for this occasion and interspersed with local allusions and hits.

"We have witnessed the performance of this piece by professional actors on the boards of metropolitan theaters and we assert that the performance on Monday night was not inferior, taken as a whole, to any performance of the same piece, that we have ever before witnessed. All the gentlemen were not only perfect in their parts, but performed them with so much spirit and abandon that the audience was kept in a state of enthusiastic delight until the fall of the curtain."[5]

Mesilla's first dramatic production was talked about for months, and there was a popular demand that Fountain's troupe not only repeat *Bombastes Furioso*, but also present a regular schedule of plays each year. As word spread of Mesilla's stage talent, the dramatic club received invitations, with full-house guarantees, from Albuquerque, Las Cruces, El Paso, and other towns in the region. With this unexpected response, the members met soon after the first *Bombastes Furioso* presentation and created the Mesilla Amateur Club, complete with permanent organization, constitution and bylaws, and officers: Fountain was elected president; J. E. Griggs, vice-president; Ira Bond, secretary; and L. H. Baldy, treasurer.[6]

Even though Fountain's law practice, dramatic productions, and his many civic interests absorbed most of his time and energy, every now and then he felt that old urge to edit a newspaper. With southern New Mexico Territory on the verge of a boom inspired by imminent railroad connections, Fountain believed as never before that a very special type of newspaper was needed to interpret the Mesilla valley to the world. The big problem in this regard was money for equipment, for while his earnings were substantial, he was strapped most of the time because of the demands of his ever-growing family. Fountain expected and received obedience, respect, and love from all his children, but he was notorious for indulging their every want, with the result that he could never

[5] Mesilla *News*, November 14, 1874.   [6] *Ibid.*, November 21, 1874.

accumulate enough reserve for investing in this or any other promising enterprise.[7]

On several occasions he had attempted without success to persuade his friends of means to join in a publishing venture, and it appeared that his talents, including far better intellectual background than most frontier editors, plus crusading zeal with ideas and creative energy to burn would be wasted. Then, one summer afternoon in 1876, two local merchants, John S. Crouch and Thomas Casad, agreed to back him in producing a paper, and the Mesilla Valley Publishing Company was born.

The publishers looked about for equipment, and finally Crouch located a rusty old press stored at Las Cruces. The "Carleton Press" as they dubbed it, had a remarkable history. Freighted out from the East just after Mesilla became an important stop on the Butterfield Stage Line, the press first published the Mesilla *Times*, original paper in the valley. Confiscated by the Texan Confederate Army during the invasion of 1861, it was used to print Confederate money, occupation general orders, and Rebel propaganda. The Confederates abandoned the press during the disastrous retreat by Sibley's brigade, and the California Column took it over in August, 1862, and used the equipment to print army blanks and "rag money," the only medium of exchange then in circulation. Following the war, various persons used the orphan press, one of them an itinerant printer who published a Spanish syllabary. Subsequently, the press became the property of W. L. Rynerson of Las Cruces who gained title to it during the Rebel property liquidation sale and he used it as a job press, shortly renting it to H.W. Sherry who published the *Rio Grande Gazette*, the first paper at Las Cruces. N. V. Bennett succeeded Sherry in the use of the press and used it briefly to publish *The Borderer*. From Sherry's plant it went into storage, and from there Crouch moved it to Mesilla.[8]

After months of collecting supplies and putting the equipment in working order, the firm went to press with its first issue on June

[7] Interview with Albert Fountain, August 12, 1961.
[8] *Rio Grande Republican*, April 8, 1882.

23, 1877, with a masthead announcing weekly publication under the name *Mesilla Valley Independent* and its editors, Albert Fountain, John Crouch, and Thomas Casad. Feeling an obligation to the Mexican population which comprised nearly 90 per cent of the valley's population, the company published a separate weekly Spanish edition, *El Independiente del valle de la Mesilla*. For the Spanish edition, Fountain did the translating, helped at times by his son, Albert, who by now was a precocious fourteen. Crouch was business manager in charge of advertising and circulation; Casad edited the agricultural material; and Fountain was chief editor, responsible for the columns and editorials.[9]

Fountain's lead article in the first issue of the *Independent* informed subscribers and the world of its purpose: "The object of this journal is to advocate what will best advance the interests of Southern New Mexico. We shall endeavor to stimulate new industries . . . . We shall seek to aid so far as our ability extends, in eradicating whatever shall operate to obstruct a healthful public sentiment. We shall hold it to be our highest duty to oppose and defeat dishonest schemes. We shall at all times oppose maladministration in public affairs, and uphold good government . . . . We shall contribute our share towards elevating the morals, purifying the politics, and improving the business of the Mesilla Valley. We distinctly deny that this paper is published for the purpose of either advancing or retarding the political aspirations of any man or set of men. Whatever views it shall give utterance to will be in the interest of no political party, faction, or clique. We wear no party shackles, seek no selfish rewards. We intend to be independent in the true higher sense of that word."[10]

With this statement as a guideline, Editor Fountain loaded each issue with instructive, interesting articles on national and local affairs. Regarding his newspaper office as a sort of classroom, he lectured editorially on the issues of the day, presented interpretative comment, muckraked social problems, and at every opportunity boomed the Mesilla valley.

[9] Interview with Henry Fountain, August 10, 1961.
[10] *Mesilla Valley Independent*, June 23, 1877.

The territorial legislature was one of his targets for sharp, barbed editorials. Fountain carefully watched their deliberations each session and showed no mercy when the solons neglected legislation which he regarded as essential for the greater good of the territory. One of his chief concerns was an extended and improved public school system for New Mexico. When, during the 1878 session, the legislature showed signs of dallying with this issue, the *Independent* editor hit them with a nasty editorial which included a tongue-in-cheek admonition: "Now gentlemen of the legislature, give us a decent public school law, and don't forget to insert a clause prohibiting the employment as teachers of persons who sign their pay vouchers 'his "X" mark.' "[11]

The telegraph line was generally the vanguard for railroad construction and Fountain promoted the extension of the communication link which had reached Mesilla from Santa Fe, on to El Paso. Construction was held up because the federal appropriation had been exhausted. The *Independent* solicited donations from local citizens with the result that the line reached El Paso on November 6, 1878. Fountain showed his delight at the response to his fund-raising campaign and the completion of the line by writing: "It indicates the dawn of a new era, and awakens slumbering hopes that the railroad will soon follow the telegraph and furnish us a means of transporting to the markets of the country the products of our farms, our pastures, and our mines."[12]

In view of all that he had done locally to attract railroad connections for the Mesilla valley, Fountain was irritated and impatient with the slowness of construction. It appeared that the first line to reach the valley would be the Texas Pacific, and his railroad editorials explained to the public that the delay was due to harassment of Texas Pacific by New York interests and the Union Pacific. Fountain pointed out that the Texas Pacific could build from Fort Worth westward through the Mesilla valley only if the company received aid from Congress, and the New York interests had joined with Union Pacific to defeat the Texas Pacific Bill in the Congress.

[11] *Ibid.*, January 19, 1878. [12] *Ibid.*, November 6, 1877.

The *Independent* editor called the Texas Pacific opponents a "giant monopoly" and charged them with "conspiracy." He wrote "New York opposes the granting of aid because she fears that the construction of a southern route to the Pacific will divert a portion of her commerce to southern ports."[13]

Among other civic improvement projects, Editor Fountain did a good deal of work with his *Independent* on human relations. To many of the immigrants entering New Mexico, and especially those from Texas, the Mexicans were greasers and held in low regard. Fountain, having lived among the natives for nearly twenty years and with a Mexican wife and a family of mixed-blood children, found these people kind and gentle almost to a fault, hospitable, sensitive, and generally much more law-abiding than their Anglo critics. He defended them in court and out against their fair-skinned oppressors, and as their champion and protector, Fountain shared the Mexicans' resentment of the gringos' superior attitude, and when he became editor of the *Independent*, he published articles aimed at destroying the greaser image which certain Anglos attempted to perpetuate.

While as a general rule, Fountain was affable and gentle, he was never known to go out of his way to avoid a fight; he was at his best in conflict. In his long years on the southwestern frontier, he had faced knives, fists, and bullets without flinching, but in taking on the Jesuit Order of New Mexico in an editorial war, he not only met his match, but also precipitated the demise of the *Independent*.

In 1878, the Jesuits began promoting bills in the New Mexico legislature to exempt their property from taxation and to permit the members of the Order certain teaching privileges in the public schools. When information of the Jesuit proposals reached Mesilla, an indignant Editor Fountain began the publication of a three-month series of anti-Jesuit articles. He charged the Jesuit Order with influencing legislation which would enable the Order to capture control of the schools of the territory, adding that they were attempting to unite all Mexicans against the Anglos.

[13] *Ibid.*, November 17, 1877.

The *Independent*'s vitriolic pieces described the Society of Jesus as "the most powerful and insidious secret order in existence. . . . The General of the order has more real power than the Pope. From his headquarters in Europe he commands and receives the implicit obedience of his inferiors in this Territory. These in turn have obtained control of the Legislative Assembly of New Mexico. Therefore, the General of the Society of Jesus dictates what laws shall be made or unmade by the Legislature of this Territory. . . . The people of the United States will never consent that the General of the Society of Jesus shall dictate laws for the government; and although a majority of our Legislative Assembly may be as puppets in the hands of their Jesuit masters, there fortunately is a body that is not controlled by Jesuit influence and which will protect our liberties. We appeal to Congress."[14]

When the Jesuit *Revista* replied to Fountain's charges with a five page counterattack on the *Independent*, calling it a "reptile, infidel journal," he responded, "The infamous society which has stolen the livery of heaven to serve the devil with is seeking to justify the recent Jesuitical attempt to control political affairs in this territory."

Fountain added for good measure: "The wind which has been so effectually sown by these pious frauds has been, is, and will continue to return like a whirlwind. These are marplots who have been spewed from bourbon, bandits, and Jesuit-ridden Naples upon these fair lands. . . . People of New Mexico, how much longer will you contribute your subsistence to the building up and support of the schools of treason established by these people? How much longer will you permit your children to be subject to the liberty-destroying precepts of the Italian outcasts?"[15]

Fountain's anti-Jesuit campaign had little effect except to alienate many Catholics who had been his friends and supporters before the Society of Jesus conflict and to assure the early demise of his paper. But Fountain was able to make one last crusade before his paper folded. The famous Lincoln County war eventually over-

14 *Ibid.*, January 26, 1878.
15 *Ibid.*, March 2, 1878.

flowed into Doña Ana County as gunmen, horse thieves, and cattle rustlers, most of them imported from Texas as hired partisans of one faction or the other, extended their depredations as far south as Mesilla. As reports of local murders, stock thefts, and robberies mounted, Fountain was distressed that Mesilla's longstanding utopian peace should be cut so abruptly, but he met the threat with characteristic directness. Besides organizing a *posse comitatus* now and then to drive the marauders from the valley, he also waged a newspaper war against outlawry. His lead articles in the *Independent* admonished the people to rid their homeland of this plague from the north: "Citizens of Doña Ana County; how long will you permit the band of thieves and murderers that infests this county to commit crimes with impunity? You know that these men have committed murders; you know that they live by stealing; you know that they walk your streets and defy and spit upon and spurn your laws."

He reminded his readers that "laws are made by the people, for the protection of life and property of the people. When the laws protect neither life nor property what are they worth? Of what value are the laws when a band of lawless ruffians can at any time murder a citizen, or steal his property, with the utmost impunity?"[16]

A few days after the *Independent*'s appeal for action against the Lincoln County marauders was published, Fountain received several anonymous notes warning him that he "would be shot down like a dog" and that he could expect to be "killed on sight" if he continued to encourage the people to act. To these he replied in the *Independent*: "The character of the persons who make these threats leaves us no room for doubt regarding their being carried into execution if an opportunity occurs. If the persons making these threats intended to give us a fair notice of what we have to expect at their hands, we thank them for the warning and shall act upon it, and sell our life as dearly as we can. If on the other hand they are mere words of braggadocio intended to frighten and intimidate us from making further comment on thieves and murderers, then we say that the persons making such threats are en-

[16] *Ibid.,* July 21, 1877.

tirely ignorant of the character of the writer of these lines. We are not to be frightened by the threats of any man or band of men, and this paper is not to be muzzled by any band of thieves and assassins."[17]

Fountain's challenge did not receive an immediate and open response as he had hoped. It was his habit on certain nights to stay at the *Independent* office to catch up on neglected law practice work, and several times on his way home lurking assassins took pot shots at him. Luckily he escaped these ambuscades without a scratch, but rather than intimidate him, the attempts on his life only increased the vigor of his editorial war on crime in southern New Mexico.

Mariana knew what was going on, and she begged her husband to either abandon the law and order crusade or get out of the newspaper business altogether. But Fountain would not be dissuaded. Then came the night of March 1. Fountain was at Hillsboro attending court. Around midnight his two oldest sons, Albert and Thomas, were at work in the *Independent*'s composing room. Gunmen hiding in the shrubs on either side of the building, riddled windows, lights, walls, and furniture with a crossfire fusillade. The boys ducked to safety under a table and escaped injury. But when Fountain returned home next day and learned of the incident, it caused him to stop short. Attacks on his own life were one thing; on the lives of his children, another. So reluctantly he decided to liquidate his publishing interest. Other factors entered into his thinking on the matter—writing and editing duties had taken up much of his time; he had neglected his law practice; and his debts were mounting again. He had poured most of his earnings into the paper, and it had done exceptionally well until he began his war on the Jesuit Order. The society had placed the *Independent* on the local Index; most of his readers were Catholics, and circulation had plunged. Casad and Crouch were grumbling, too, and even though it saddened him that there yet were great causes to promote, Fountain decided the time had come to terminate the *Independent*.[18]

17 *Ibid.*, July 28, 1877.   18 *Ibid.*, March 2, 1878.

CHAPTER VIII

Mesilla's Avenging Angel

As MATTERS WORKED OUT, Fountain's obsession for law and order found an outlet many times more effective for eradicating crime and violence in southern New Mexico than his newspaper had ever been. And equally as important for Fountain's ego, this outlet brought him prestige, honors, and public praise and acclaim in excess of anything he could have expected to receive as a frontier newspaper editor.

Shortly after the *Mesilla Valley Independent* folded, a brutalizing Indian war struck the American Southwest. General Carleton's long-standing peace among the Indian tribes was ruptured in 1879 when a band of Mimbreño Apaches (also known as Ojo Caliente or Warm Springs Apaches), led by Victorio, a protégé of the mighty Mangas Coloradas, went on the warpath.

Under Carleton's direction, Victorio's people had been assigned a reservation at Ojo Caliente, a pleasant, happy place in the Cañada Alamosa country of central New Mexico. Before long, miners and cattlemen encroached on this Apache domain, incidents mounted, and, in 1877, under the curious charge that they had aided the intractable Chiricahuas, Victorio's people were forcibly removed to the San Carlos Reservation on the Gila River in Arizona—a settlement of dirt-roofed adobe buildings, sand, cactus, and miserable desert waste. At San Carlos the Ojo Caliente Apaches joined White Mountain, Coyotero, Chiricahua, and other groups in a combined Indian community of 4,500.

Victorio's people were unhappy at San Carlos from the start, and the determined chieftain led his band away on two different occasions with the result that the government finally gave up and allowed him to return to Ojo Caliente. Fountain interviewed Vic-

torio on his return to New Mexico in 1878 with the idea of publishing feature stories in the *Independent* depicting life among
the Apaches. Victorio told him, "the government had forced him
to go to San Carlos Agency twice, and he had broken away; that
if they did it a third time, he would go out on the warpath and
leave a trail of blood and fire behind him, and die fighting."[1]

Demands by miners and ranchmen that all Indians be evacuated
from the Cañada Alamosa country caused the government once
again to drive the Ojo Caliente Apaches back to San Carlos, and,
true to his promise, Victorio cut a trail of blood, fire, and death.
The so-called Victorio War broke out on May 7, 1879, when the
Apache chieftain began a series of local depredations. His most
substantial stroke was an assault on a Coyotero band on Eagle
Creek. Killing eleven, he plundered their sheep, cattle, and horses.
From there Victorio cut a swath of terror along the New Mexico–
Arizona border, killing two white men on Ash Creek, stealing
horses from local ranches, and hitting the Bunker Hill mining
camp near Tres Alamos. Army patrols searched for nearly two
weeks after the Tres Alamos affair for some sign of the marauders;
then out of nowhere Victorio appeared east of the Río Grande.[2]

Settling his people in the pine forests and brush-choked canyons
of the Mescalero Apache Reservation, Victorio spent the three
months of late winter and early spring, 1880, in council with
Mescalero warriors, urging them to join him in his campaign of
retaliation. According to the Mescalero Apache agent, Victorio's
"almost uninterrupted success in skirmishes with the military"
helped his recruitment, and by April 1 about 250 Mescaleros had
joined the raiders.[3]

Rested, well-mounted, better armed than ever, and strengthened by the Mescalero recruits, Victorio raised hell in the settlements, ranches, and mining camps of southern New Mexico and
Arizona during the spring and summer of 1880. His fantastic mo-

[1] Deposition of Colonel Albert J. Fountain for Court of Claims (*Giddings* vs.
United States and Kiowa, Comanche, and Apache Indians), National Archives.

[2] *Report of the Commissioner of Indian Affairs for 1879*, 114.

[3] *Ibid.*, 1880, 129.

bility and shrewd generalship were both at once the marvel and the curse of his stalkers. When pursued by United States forces too strong to challenge, Victorio would cross into Mexico, returning now here, now there, like a ghost, dividing his people into small bands and leaving scattered trails to baffle the pursuers. Each week Victorio was out, the toll of death and destruction mounted. On a single raid near Hillsboro, eighteen settlers were killed; "in the cemetery at Lake Valley there were thirty-three graves, twenty-eight of these killed by Indians"; and before the summer had passed, three hundred had been killed to satisfy Victorio's vengeance-hungry warriors.[4]

As Victorio's plunging raids came closer and closer to the Mesilla valley, Fountain called a public meeting for the purpose of organizing local defenses, and there followed the organization of the Mesilla Independent Cavalry, or Mesilla Scouts as they were called in the field. At first muster, held on November 9, 1879, after thirty troopers—practically all of them Mexicans—were enrolled, John Crouch was elected captain, Fountain, first lieutenant, and Charley Bull, second lieutenant. Crouch was an old California Column man, but he had passed his prime and was not up to hard campaigning, so he resigned his commission after the first muster, and Fountain was named captain.[5]

Fountain held weekly drills for his company, instructing the men in those basic maneuvers that he recalled had worked so well during his Apache hunting days, imparted to them all the tricks he had learned as an Indian fighter, and obtained Sharps carbines and ammunition for his command from the Territorial Arsenal at Santa Fe. Among other precautions, he established a command post on the town plaza and assigned scouts to watch all approaches to Mesilla.

Shortly after Victorio left the Mescalero Reservation, United States military authorities in New Mexico and Arizona began a campaign to trap the marauder band and thus end its reign of terror. Since many of the field officers knew little of the Apache haunts, Captain Fountain was again called upon to serve as a

[4] *Lone Star*, August 5, 1882.   [5] *Thirty-four*, November 12, 1879.

scout and guide. Dividing his company and leaving a core of defenders at Mesilla under Lieutenant Bull, he joined the command of Colonel Edward Hatch, the ranking United States commander who had brought one thousand troops from Texas and New Mexico posts for the offensive against the Apache raiders. When Mexican spies sent word via the El Paso telegraph that Victorio was moving back into New Mexico, Hatch divided his force. Calculating that very likely the wily Apache chieftain was bound for the Mescalero Reservation, Hatch sent one column to the agency with orders to disarm all resident warriors, confiscate their ponies, and hold the Indians as prisoners of war.[6]

The other column was directed to follow Captain Fountain and other scouts recruited from over New Mexico in a search for Victorio's immediate whereabouts. Wide-ranging patrols finally picked up sign on the edge of the San Andres, and Fountain, who knew the country well from his Ganado Blanco campaign days, led the column into the well-watered Hembrillo Canyon. As he suspected, Victorio's band was camped at the spring, and the United States forces, alerted to the location, moved in for the kill. The poorly managed, green troops were no match for Victorio's battle-scarred veterans, and the beleaguered Apaches fought their way out rather easily.[7]

After the Hembrillo Canyon fight, Victorio led his band westward across the Río Grande, raiding settlements along the way, hitting ranches and sheep camps for provisions, arms, and fresh horses, and scattering cattle and sheep to the four winds. By late summer, Hatch's army had increased to two thousand, including a hastily formed New Mexico militia and Texas Ranger units since Victorio's peregrinations carried his depredations east of El Paso. To ensure his ultimate investment, a Mexican army was moving north in Chihuahua.

Fountain and his Mesilla Scouts had a busy time of it leading weary cavalrymen through punishingly rough country, casting over Apache sign, now hot, now cold. During August his scouts

[6] Report of the Commissioner of Indian Affairs for 1880, 129.
[7] Report of the Secretary of War for 1880, I, 95.

traced the renegades into the Candelario Mountains of Chihuahua, sixty miles south of El Paso. All outlets were plugged with rifle squads; Gatling guns were positioned at the likely exits; and cavalry pushed through every canyon in a effort to flush the hiding Apaches. Just as the investing force was ready to spring the trap, orders came in to proceed north on the double—Victorio was already in New Mexico, reportedly moving east of the Black Range.[8]

In September, Captain Fountain and his Mesilla Scouts were assigned as guides for Colonel George Buell's column, the Fifteenth Infantry from Fort Stanton. Victorio had been positively located in the Tres Costillos Mountains of northern Chihuahua. Fountain knew the place and set a fast pace for Buell's foot soldiers as they moved in for what they hoped would be the kill. But before the Fifteenth could reach the hideaway, Mexican forces struck the Apaches, killing eight-six warriors including the vaunted Victorio.[9]

The old chief, Nana, with fifty warriors, escaped the Mexican trap, flew into the Río Grande country, and made contact with the Mescaleros. These people, smarting under the treatment they had received from Colonel Hatch, were vulnerable to Nana's overtures, and it appeared New Mexico faced another blood bath. But General Ranald Mackenzie, fresh from sparkling victories over the seemingly unconquerable Kickapoos and Comanches, had been brought in to direct military operations against the renegade Apaches. From his headquarters at Santa Fe, Mackenzie established a new order and stiffened morale in southwestern military affairs. While Nana ran wild for a few months, he was never able to operate with the freedom enjoyed by Victorio. The Mescaleros, chief source of fresh horses, arms, and warriors, were especially watched, and when Honesco, principal warrior of the Nana band, came in to recruit Mescaleros, he was promptly arrested,

[8] Report of Captain Albert J. Fountain, Mesilla Scouts, Independent Cavalry, March 1, 1882. New Mexico State Records Center, Santa Fe. (hereafter SRC).

[9] Martin L. Crimmons, "Colonel Buell's Expedition into Mexico in 1880," *New Mexico Historical Review*, Vol. X (April, 1935), 133-42.

disarmed, and turned over to General Mackenzie as a prisoner of war.[10]

New Mexico Territory rose to the occasion, too. Militia units, so active and effective during the days of General Carleton, had deteriorated to the point that the only local military activity was of an extralegal, grass-roots response such as Captain Fountain's organizing the Mesilla Scouts. In 1880, the territorial legislature authorized the formal organization of militia units to operate in conjunction with federal forces against the hostile Indian tribes. Militia companies were organized in most of the territory's counties. Fountain, as captain of an independent company already in the field, was directed to organize a unit for Doña Ana County, using his old Mesilla Independent Cavalry as a nucleus. With the territorial commission as captain, he recruited his quota of troops from San Miguel, Bosque Seco, and Mesilla. Fountain's cavalry participated in capturing Nana and shared New Mexico's relief at the eventual assignment of the Warm Springs recalcitrants to San Carlos Reservation. Since the militia was only recently organized, the Mesilla cavalrymen furnished their own horses, forage, and rations and received "no pay beyond the letter of thanks from Colonel Buell and the consciousness of having performed their duty."[11]

Nearly two years in the saddle leading infantry and cavalry columns into the Apache haunts had restored Fountain to his old trim, tough self. He had gloried in the excitement and adventure of the Victorio and Nana campaigns and was almost regretful to see his command end, for it meant that his hard-riding troopers would return to inactive service. Then, quite unexpectedly the Mesilla Scouts got a new life. In the general confusion and disorder accompanying the nearly three-year-long Indian war, a development had taken place in southern New Mexico which, because of the emergency situation facing the region, had not received prompt attention.

For years, West Texas had been cursed with daring highway-

10 *Report of the Commissioner of Indian Affairs for 1882*, 124.

11 Report of Captain Albert J. Fountain, Mesilla Scouts, Independent Cavalry, March 1, 1882. SRC.

men, rustlers, and professional gunmen. Travel between towns had been at great risk, and no ranch was safe from swooping raids. Texas Ranger companies finally moved in, and broke up the robber and rustler bands, so about the time the Apache wars ceased, the Texas underworld fugitives moved into southern New Mexico. Many of them settled in the boom mining camps of Lake Valley and Kingston—raw, rip-roaring towns generally free of law and order restraints. Peace officers and courts in neighboring communities who might protest their doings were bullied or bought, with the result that they had things their own way. The Texans, joining with local renegades, shortly had spun a web of crime which nearly choked out free and honest industry and threatened to make a wasteland of Doña Ana, Lincoln, and Grant counties.

During the Indian wars, Governor Lionel Sheldon had received petitions from the people of southern New Mexico praying for relief from the Apache menace. Now, Doña Ana, Lincoln, and Grant counties' citizens, claiming that local law enforcement and courts were helpless, again appealed to Santa Fe, this time for aid in ridding them of their new torment—the gunmen, rustlers, and highwaymen—and including in their petitions long descriptions of depredations against life and property. During the spring of 1882, reports from the troubled zone of livestock and personal property losses and homicides mounted; in Grant County alone seven Chinese were slain, and dozens more bullied and beaten.[12]

The incident which stirred Sheldon to action occurred on May 24, 1882. A telegraph message from Las Cruces reported a raid on the R. S. Mason ranch, located on the Silver City road, twenty-five miles west of Mesilla. Sheldon, recalling the charges of inertia on the part of local peace officers, responded with a wire to Captain Fountain at Mesilla, directing him to muster his company, ride to Mason's ranch, look into the reported raid, and take whatever steps his investigation might justify.

Finding only twenty-three troopers available on the sudden muster he called, Fountain had the column supplied with five-day rations and was pounding leather on the Silver City road by dawn

[12] Santa Fe *New Mexican*, February 13, 1883.

of May 26. At Mason's ranch he learned from the household that five men had entered the kitchen during breakfast and at gunpoint had hog-tied the Mason family and their riders and locked them in a small room, ransacked the house of all valuables and clothing, gathered up two hundred head of cattle, and had ridden off.

Taking up the raiders' trail, the Mesilla cavalry traced them south to Ura Springs, thence toward the Mexican border over a waterless plain to Palomas Lake, just across the international boundary. This watering point, ninety miles from Ura Springs, was reached in just under thirty-six hours. Stopping on the Llanos River deep in Chihuahua on May 29, Fountain's outriders discovered an old campsite which was identified as one used by the Mason raiders, for scattered all about was plunder including women's clothing and some ransacked letters bearing Mason's name. Two days later the searchers arrived at the town of Ascensión and received permission to continue the pursuit if organized in parties of no more than five men each. The *alcalde* co-operated further by sending couriers in all directions with descriptions of the fugitives. The Mesilla cavalry reprovisioned at Ascensión and divided into parties of five to continue the search. One squad moved west toward Sonora and on June 7 was met by one of the Ascensión couriers who brought news from General Lupe Reyes, Sonoran *jefe político*—his police had captured the fugitives.

Fountain's report of the expedition to Governor Sheldon continued: "When satisfied that they were beyond the reach of human punishment and that they had gone to a place where a writ of extradition would not be likely to reach them, the command rallied together and returned to Mesilla on June 11." The Mesilla cavalry commander continued: "The expedition cannot fail to have a salutary effect if no more has been accomplished than to teach organized bands of rustlers that they cannot carry on their nefarious occupation in Doña Ana County with impunity. The fate of the band that attacked Mason's Ranch should be published far and wide as a warning to all others of that ilk."[13]

[13] Report of Captain Albert J. Fountain to Adjutant General, New Mexico Territory, June, 1882. SRC.

When the Mesilla cavalry returned from the Chihuahua expedition, the happy townspeople celebrated with a parade, barbecue, and *baile*. For Captain Fountain, his greatest joy, next to being reunited with Mariana and the children, came from the letter awaiting him from Adjutant General E. L. Bartlett at Santa Fe: "The Governor desires me to express to you his personal and sincere thanks for your prompt action in this matter, and to assure you that your zeal and wisdom is fully appreciated by him to which I add my own views to the same effect. I have the pleasure to announce your promotion to be major of the first regiment."[14] Equally as important to Fountain as his promotion in rank was Bartlett's citation for the Mesilla cavalry which was published in all territorial newspapers. It read in part: "The militia's zeal and watchfulness in a great measure discouraged depredations by the Indians; and outlaws have been greatly discouraged in their nefarious operations. . . . Fountain's command has rendered great service in this direction."[15]

Major Fountain ordered his troops to inactive status and turned his attention to long-neglected personal affairs. He had hardly made a good start in this direction, however, when he was ordered to active duty again. Beginning in January, 1883, a wave of rustling hit Lincoln, Grant, and Doña Ana counties. Reports came in to the governor's office of substantial stock thefts from practically every ranch in the three-county area; the entire town herd of the little village of Doña Ana was run off in broad daylight.[16]

The primary goal for Sheldon, Fountain, and other leading citizens was statehood for New Mexico at an early date. Fountain for one had put much time and energy into promoting the territory and its resources in the East, and encouraging railroad development and immigration. Therefore, he shared Sheldon's concern over the effect these fresh disorders might have on New Mexico's reputation. The Lincoln County war and the Victorio-Nana

[14] Bartlett to Fountain, Santa Fe, May 28, 1882. Governor's Letter Books, SRC.

[15] Report of Adjutant General, New Mexico Territory for 1882. SRC.

[16] *Rio Grande Republican*, January 27, 1883.

rampage had embarrassed the statehood advocates, but both, it was hoped, were past history the better to be forgotten.

Many of the leading territorial newspapers, typified by the Santa Fe *New Mexican*, shared this official concern over the resurgent lawlessness: "Life and property must both be as safe in the mountains and on the plains of New Mexico as they are in New York and Massachusetts. This is the whole thing in a nutshell, and it is to secure this very condition that Governor Sheldon has decided that the law must be enforced and regularly constituted authority respected and feared. The Billy the Kids of the territory must get up and get out. They must move on. We care not where they may find a final resting place, we only know that they must leave New Mexico."[17]

Irritated at the apathy of local law enforcement officers toward the crime wave in southern New Mexico, Governor Sheldon decided to use Major Fountain's cavalry to purge lawlessness from the troubled zone once and for all. His first step in this direction consisted of a militia reorganization which strengthened Fountain's command. Units from the First Regiment, New Mexico Volunteer Militia, were fused into the Second Cavalry Battalion with headquarters at Mesilla, and commanded by Major Fountain. Its components were to include Company A, Captain Van Patten; Company B, Captain Salazar; Company F, Captain Black; and a new company to be organized at Tularosa. Sheldon's general order instructed Fountain that his companies were to be armed with the carbine, equipped as cavalry, and were to conform to United States cavalry drill as prescribed in army tactics. When on active duty the personnel were to be paid at the rate of regular United States troops plus allowance for horse.[18]

Fountain whipped the battalion into operational readiness by holding week-end drills, and in less than a month he enthusiastically described his company commanders "brave as lions," singling out Captain Francisco Salazar of Company B as espe-

---

[17] Santa Fe *New Mexican*, January 19, 1883.

[18] Bartlett to Fountain, Santa Fe, January 28, 1883. Governor's Letter Books, SRC.

cially impressive. The major was also proud of his son, Albert, a conscientious sergeant during the Chihuahua expedition, who had been promoted to second lieutenant in Company A.

As his law practice took him to Hillsboro, Lincoln, and other towns of southern New Mexico, Fountain made inquiries and observed firsthand the region's rampant lawlessness. His unofficial investigation began to explain the phenomenal increase in stock thefts. Great quantities of fresh beef were needed to feed the railroad crews building lines across Texas and New Mexico. The booming mining camps of southern New Mexico and Arizona were demanding markets too. The Indian agencies purchased thousands of head of cattle each year to supply beef rations for the resident tribes. In addition, there was the heavy demand for cattle to stock new ranges in the rapidly developing range cattle industry to the north.

Fountain discovered that the ranches of southern New Mexico were especially vulnerable to rustling, owing largely to the loose methods in vogue for handling stock. Bills of sale too frequently were not required to close a livestock transaction; brands were carelessly registered, if at all; there was no stock association to protect the industry, no brand inspectors, or other controls.

As Fountain's dossier on southern New Mexico lawlessness continued to build up, he began to identify individuals. As he was prominent throughout the region, he decided to use certain lesser known of his battalion officers for some of the more intimate sleuthing. Lieutenants Pedragon and Ransom, dressed as itinerant cowboys, filled in nicely. Their reports to Fountain disclosed that a band of from thirty to forty gunmen, many of them fugitives from Texas, was headquartered at Lake Valley. The more prominent members were John Joy, Frank Emmons, Marguerito Sierra, Bob Reese, William Galliard (alias Bill Rush), John Watts, Doroteo Sains, and Baldy Johnson. Sains was rated the most deadly of the rustler crowd except for the leader, whom Fountain's operatives identified as John Kinney. A bit of investigation revealed that Kinney had come to New Mexico with the Eighth Cavalry, and, following a brawling service hitch at various Río

Grande posts, had taken up with a dance-hall queen, participated in the Lincoln County war, and lately had settled at Lake Valley. Shrewd and bold, Kinney was regarded by those who knew him as one of the most dangerous and "desperate characters . . . since Billy the Kid."[19]

Fountain knew Kinney through his sprees in Las Cruces. On one frolic he pistol-whipped his crony, Frank Emmons, in broad daylight in front of the Thorn Hotel. The attack left deep cuts all over Emmons' skull, his face was bruised and blackened in every feature, his lips and ears were slashed open, his jaw broken, and several teeth and a piece of jawbone completely knocked out. Kinney had the town so thoroughly intimidated that the sheriff and other local officers did nothing. Besides being a bully, Kinney apparently was a shrewd businessman, for Fountain learned from one of his informants that he was banking large sums of money at the El Paso bank each month.[20]

Pedragon and Ransom reported that the Kinney gang, its nerve center at Lake Valley, was scattered in bands of four or five members each from Concordia, below El Paso, into Chihuahua and northward as far as Socorro County in New Mexico. A common pattern was for the squad in Socorro County to gather up a local herd, drive the animals to a rendezvous in Doña Ana County, turn them over to local representatives of the ring who in turn drove the stock to the next relay, the Socorro group returning with cattle taken from Texas and Mexico. While much of the local stock was driven on to a ready market on the expanding northern ranges, some of it was slaughtered for local sale to the railroad construction camps and mining towns. When Pedragon and Ransom discovered that large quantities of fresh beef were shipped regularly from an obscure railroad siding near Rincon, they traced it to a butcher shop at El Paso, from which railroad crews and local mining camps were supplied.[21]

Fountain kept in close touch with Sheldon, sharing with the

[19] Santa Fe New Mexican, February 21, 1883.
[20] Rio Grande Republican, February 17, 1883.
[21] Lone Star, February 10, 1883.

Governor the more significant evidence he or his operatives turned up, and, looking to the day when he would receive orders to move in, he worked out arrangements with Texas Ranger officials and Mexican authorities whereby he could pursue fugitives in all directions.[22] During early February, 1883, cattle stealing reached an all time high in southern New Mexico, and local newspapers reported there was "hardly any use engaging in the stock business there. The herds along the Rio Grande and from the Texas line to Paraje have been cleaned out. Lincoln and Grant counties have been plundered too."[23] The raiders were reported as "even running off oxen of farmers in the Mesilla Valley so they cannot plow, and the country is a wasteland."[24]

Petitions from afflicted cattlemen deluged the governor's office, and many leading citizens of Santa Fe with large interests in the southern part of the territory demanded action, claiming that since the first of the year, ten thousand head of stock had been swept from southern ranches and driven to old Mexico, Arizona, and the northern range pastures.[25]

Convinced that Major Fountain had sufficiently identified the ring members and was acquainted with their operations and whereabouts, Governor Sheldon sent him a coded message on February 10, placing his battalion on alert. Fountain had his companies mustered, provisioned, and ready to move in twenty-four hours.[26]

Two days later, he received operational orders and territorial warrants for each of the identified ring members. He was directed to "act in every way upon his own best judgment," including unlimited telegraphic use at territorial expense, authority to commandeer railroad boxcars for his men and cattle cars for the horses, and complete freedom to operate in all counties of New Mexico.[27]

[22] *Rio Grande Republican*, February 24, 1883.

[23] *Lone Star*, February 10, 1883.

[24] Santa Fe *New Mexican*, February 18, 1883 .

[25] *Ibid.*, February 17, 1883.

[26] Sheldon to Fountain, Santa Fe, February 10, 1883. Governor's Letter Books, SRC.

[27] Bartlett to Fountain, Santa Fe, February 13, 1883. Governor's Letter Books, SRC.

Major Fountain lost no time dispersing his companies in a pre-arranged attack pattern—Captain Black and Company F were sent into Lincoln County; Salazar's Company B rode south along the river toward the Texas line; and Fountain, hopeful of being in on the capture of the rustler chief, raced northwest with Van Patton's Company A toward Kinney's hideaway, Cottonwood Ranch. Before moving in, the column halted at Padilla, established a headquarters camp, and approached the ranch from four directions. Disappointingly, the searchers found the hideout abandoned, sign showing hasty flight, with trails scattering in all directions. Noting one trail which indicated a large party moving toward the railroad, Fountain first sent squads obliquely up and down the line, then led the balance of the column directly to a siding near Rincon.[28]

All during the night the soldiers stopped trains running between Randall and Rincon and searched each car, their efforts yielding only two Kinney partisans—Mariano Cubero and Leonardo Maese. Abandoning the train vigil at dawn, Company A searched all houses, barns, and jacals as far as San Diego on the river, picking up two additional members of the gang, Gaspar Montenegro and Juan Bernal. But there was no sign of Kinney, and the prisoners refused to give his whereabouts. Mystified how Kinney had escaped the carefully conceived net, Fountain refused to believe that he was out of the area and for over a week kept Company A on patrol scouring the country both east and west of the river for a distance of forty miles, finally abandoning the Padilla camp on February 29 and returning to Mesilla for supplies.[29]

The dispatches awaiting Fountain at Mesilla told that while Black's column was returning from Lincoln County empty-handed, Salazar's men were having good hunting to the south. The number two man in Kinney's ring, Doroteo Sains, rated as a cold-blooded killer with the fastest gun on the river, was reported to be using La Mesa, a village fifteen miles below Las Cruces, as

---

[28] Reports of the Adjutant General, New Mexico Territory, February 12 to March 14, 1883. SRC.
[29] *Ibid.*

his headquarters. Salazar's cavalry hit the town at evening on their first day out and found the entire local cadre of the Kinney gang *en casa*. Eugenio Pedraza, one of the men for whom Salazar held a warrant, was discovered in a house with a woman. He was overpowered and disarmed, placed under arrest and guarded by a sergeant and five troopers. Moving through the town, Company B surrounded the cantina and found five Kinney men, including the deadly Doroteo Sains, inside. Salazar's men rushed the place and took three prisoners. Doroteo and his brother Mario escaped through a window. Before Salazar's men returned to pick up Pedraza, the prisoner slipped his bonds, but as he ran into the street, his guards shot him to death.[30]

While much remained to be done in the way of bringing an enduring peace to southern New Mexico, especially since Kinney and Sains were still at large, Fountain's cavalry had made a start, and already he and his men were the toast of the territory. The *New Mexican*, in an editorial captioned "Law and Order," epitomized the good results of the campaign: "Under the wise policy of our present territorial administration, law and order is rapidly asserting itself. The lawless and reckless are being effectually repressed. Honest settlers are feeling a confidence never felt before, and the good effect of this is seen in every direction. There is already a greatly increased inquiry for agricultural lands, stock ranges, and the like.[31]

The prisoners gathered up by companies A and B were placed in the Las Cruces jail, the one at Mesilla being too small and not strong enough for holding the prisoners. Lacking confidence in Sheriff Guadalupe Ascarate and his deputies, Fountain selected a detail of eight men from Company B to guard the prisoners. All the while, Fountain kept patrols in the field continuing the rustler roundup; Van Patton's men bringing in seven fugitives captured near Rincon on March 3.[32]

On the same day of Van Patton's coup, Fountain received a

30 Santa Fe *New Mexican*, February 21, 1883.
31 *Ibid.*, February 23, 1883.
32 *Ibid.*, March 9, 1883.

telegram from Captain Baylor advising that his rangers had captured three New Mexico fugitives at Concordia, Texas—José
Caballero, Néstor Cubero, and Doroteo Sains—and that the prisoners could be picked up at El Paso. Black was near Lake Valley,
Van Patton at Rincon, and Salazar, operating closest to Mesilla,
was on a scout near Doña Ana. Leaving word for Salazar, when
he reported in, to ride south along the railroad and meet him on
the return trip, Fountain with his son Albert caught the south-
bound train for El Paso.[33]

At the depot, Baylor turned over the prisoners and papers taken
from Sains, and Fountain and he visited while waiting for the
return train. Just before Fountain boarded with the prisoners,
"Baylor chided Fountain for not wearing a cord to fasten his pistol
to his belt, as then did all the Rangers, to prevent its loss from the
scabbard in a running fight." Then Baylor detached his own cord,
looping one end to Fountain's belt and the other to his pistol.[34]

After the train got underway, Fountain left Albert to guard the
prisoners and walked back into the car to visit with friends. The
youth was sitting on the coal box at the forward end of the car,
facing the prisoners on the front seats. As the train slowed to make
its stop at Canutillo, Fountain noted a commotion in the front of
the car, and running forward to the platform saw Albert rolling on
the ground attempting to gain his feet; then ahead he saw Sains
already on his feet and racing for the mesquite thickets fringing
the river.[35]

Fountain jumped from the moving train, rolled twice to gain his
feet, and reached for his pistol; "finding it gone—lost evidently
in the tumble—and fearing to lose his prisoner entirely if he
stopped to hunt for it, Fountain hit the best pace he could in
pursuit. But almost at the first jump something gave him a thump
on the shin . . . and, looking down, there, dangling on Baylor's
pistol-cord, he saw his gun." Dropping to one knee, he "sky-lined
his man on the crest of a little hillock he had to cross" and poured

33 *Lone Star*, March 3, 1883.
34 Edgar B. Bronson, *The Red Blooded Heroes of the Frontier*, 100.
35 *Lone Star*, March 3, 1883.

four quick shots into the target. Sains dropped to the ground, mortally wounded.[36]

The engineer stopped his train and backed the string of cars to Fountain's position, and just as Sains's body was carried aboard, Salazar's column came into view. The two remaining prisoners were turned over to him with "instructions to kill them if they attempted to escape."[37]

With all his success thus far in the campaign, Fountain fretted that Kinney was still at large. True, the Las Cruces jail bulged with prisoners, but with the exception of Doroteo Sains, the cavalry dragnet had caught only the lesser fry. The Major was irritated by the boastful challenges Kinney sent to him from the safety of his secret hideout—that Fountain and his greaser militia were afraid to face him and his gunmen in an open fight, and that no man or set of men would ever capture him alive.[38]

Fountain was certain that Kinney would make his move soon. Pedragon and Ransom had reported that after the militia raid on Kinney's Cottonwood Ranch the rustler king's mistress and brother, Mike Kinney, had withdrawn large sums of money from Kinney's account at the El Paso bank. Fountain had men watching the railroad stations on the main line of the Santa Fe, and he had taken all other possible precautions to assure that Kinney would not escape once he left his secret hideout. Then on March 5, a message from Frank Cartwright, superintendent for the Sierra Mining Company, arrived at his Mesilla headquarters which told that Kinney had been seen in Silver City buying supplies and that he had left town traveling southwest. Fountain rushed a special messenger to find Captain Black and Company F, operating somewhere between Lake Valley and Silver City.[39]

Three days later, the telegraph lines hummed with messages from Lordsburg. Black reported that Fountain's courier had reached him in time to pick up fresh sign of Kinney; he was

---

[36] Bronson, *The Red Blooded Heroes of the Frontier*, 102.

[37] Santa Fe *New Mexican*, March 4, 1883.

[38] *Ibid.*, February 24, 1883.

[39] *Rio Grande Republican*, March 10, 1883.

traced to Ash Springs on the Gila, eight miles into Arizona Territory. Black's column surrounded Kinney's camp and caught the rustler chieftain, his mistress, and brother completely unaware. Besides a substantial amount of cash, Black recovered twenty-five head of horses and mules. The prisoners were brought to Lordsburg, locked in a boxcar, and placed under heavy guard by Black's cavalry. A local justice of the peace ordered the release of Kinney's mistress and his brother and nearly freed Kinney, but "stiffened by telegrams from Sheldon and Fountain," the local judge remanded the outlaw to Black's custody. Kinney was reported to have said that he would "as soon be sent at once to hell as to be taken to Las Cruces."[40]

Sheldon arranged for a special train to transport the prisoner and cavalry escort to Deming and Las Cruces and telegraphed Fountain to personally supervise the transfer. Fountain selected Salazar and six troopers to accompany him. The entire party returned with their prize to Las Cruces, arriving without incident.[41]

News of Kinney's capture electrified the territory. A fiesta-like atmosphere pervaded both Las Cruces and Mesilla; those cavalrymen not assigned guard duty over the prisoners were treated to a round of tribute they would not soon forget. Even as far away as Santa Fe the excitement was evident; according to the *New Mexican*: "Governor Sheldon and Major Fountain last night shook hands across the wires over the capture of John Kinney and gang by Captain Black. The news of the capture spread rapidly throughout the city and Governor Sheldon was generally congratulated. During the evening he visited the Palace and the crowd there shook hands with him till his Excellency begged for a rest."[42]

40 *Lone Star*, March 10, 1883.
41 Santa Fe *New Mexican*, March 10, 1883.
42 *Ibid.*

CHAPTER IX

The Lake Valley Raider

MAJOR FOUNTAIN and his cavalry were the toast of the territory; congratulatory messages poured in from officials and private citizens from as far away as Arizona, Colorado, and Washington, D.C.; and the battalion's rustler war exploits were described and praised in effusive detail by most of the region's newpapers, the *New Mexican* outdoing all others in ecstatic comments: "The wonderful energy displayed by Major Fountain in his present campaign against the lawless in the south is above all praise. His movements have all the certainty of fate and the rapidity of a lightning's stroke . . . . He is an avenging angel in the hands of outraged justice. He is as brave as he is determined and active, and as thorough and complete in his operations as some of the best Ranger captains Texas ever sent out against the robber bands which at one time made her frontier a perfect hell on earth. . . . The day has passed entirely when the lawless freebooters and thieves can run one of the states or territories of this union. They must turn honest or get out, or what is better still, get captured by Fountain and attempt to escape."[1]

People from miles around filled Las Cruces' cantinas and hotels and crowded the streets, generally celebrating Kinney's capture and hoping for a chance to see the rustler king in captivity. In this they were disappointed, for Fountain, having received word that the members of the Kinney gang still at large would try to liberate their chief, permitted, besides Kinney's mistress, only Governor Sheldon and Adjutant General Bartlett (who had taken the train to Las Cruces to personally congratulate Fountain and his cavalry) even to approach the adobe cell block. When the Governor

[1] Santa Fe *New Mexican*, March 25, 1883.

returned from his interview with Kinney, he observed that not a single ray of light could penetrate the thick-walled, windowless jail and that the Las Cruces calaboose was more like a dungeon.[2]

Well aware of the loyalty of Kinney's men to their chief, his alert sentries having already intercepted two notes, the Major increased the guard to twelve heavily armed troopers, dividing the detail by sending half the men to the rooftops of buildings overlooking the jail and stationing the others on the ground on all sides. All the while, squads from companies A and B continued to capture rustlers. Captain Van Patton caught Bob Reese and Tom Coyn butchering cattle near Rincon, and the indefatigable Salazar brought in Pauche Sains, cousin of the noted Doroteo.[3]

The number of prisoners was now seventeen and it appeared that, until the Doña Ana County grand jury convened on March 28, Fountain would have little to do except oversee the guarding of the bulging Las Cruces cell block. Then on March 19 he was ordered to Santa Fe for a conference with Governor Sheldon. Reports had come to the chief executive's office from mining companies operating in the Black Range country that members of the old Kinney gang had been seen near Kingston and Lake Valley; mine officials offered to guide Fountain's cavalry to their hide-outs. Fountain returned home, mustered companies A and B, and, leaving well over half the command for guard duty on the prisoners, he loaded forty-five troopers, their horses and ammunition in railroad cars, bound for Nutt Station, the prearranged rendezvous point. Frank Cartwright and Charley Forsythe, Sierra Mining Company superintendents, met the column at the siding. Before leaving Nutt Station, Fountain divided his command; Salazar's column led by Cartwright moved on Kingston, while Fountain, accompanied by Forsythe and Van Patton's company, left for Lake Valley.[4]

A whirlwind ride brought the column to the outskirts of Lake Valley about half-past two on the morning of March 22, to a place

[2] *Ibid.*, March 13, 1883.
[3] *Rio Grande Republican*, March 17, 1883.
[4] Santa Fe *New Mexican*, March 24, 1883.

the guides identified as Irwin's ranch, one of the hide-outs. The troopers surrounded the ranch house, fired shots into the windows, and gave orders to surrender or be burned out. One by one the surprised occupants filed out, arms upraised in surrender, shoeless, and in their underwear. While Van Patton called off the names in the territorial warrants, Major Fountain and Forsythe examined the corrals and butcher pens where cattle from Doña Ana and Lincoln counties reportedly were driven for slaughter. After Van Patton's prisoner muster, which identified the captives as Hurricane Bill Phillips, Jimmy Hughes, Matt Irwin, Bill Leland (alias Butch Hill), John Watts, and Jim Colville, they were tied to their mounts and the column moved toward Hillsboro.[5]

Shortly after daylight the party stopped for a hasty breakfast. The captives were roped together in a circle near one of the campfires. While the guards were drawing coffee, three of the prisoners—Hill, Watts, and Hughes—slipped their bonds and raced for the timber. The sergeant of the guard discovered the escape and yelled to his men. Coffee cups were flung aside, rifles snatched up, and a fast, deadly volley cut the fugitives down into the rocks on the timber's edge. The surviving prisoners were co-operative with their Mexican guards thereafter. The militia proceeded to Hillsboro where the townspeople gave Fountain's men "a royal reception at the schoolhouse and left nothing undone to prove their entire sympathy and support."[6]

Meanwhile, Salazar's flying column struck Kingston. John Shannon, one of the fugitives named in the warrants, was captured at the Royal Hotel. He broke from his captors and nearly escaped over the roof, but he was shot to death by cavalrymen stationed in the street. Hank Brophy and Baldy Johnson, wanted in Lincoln County for murder and stock theft, were reported to be hiding out at Kingston with Shannon, but after Company B squads had scoured the town and surrounding ranches without finding a trace of either man, Salazar learned that a small party, including two men who matched the descriptions of Brophy and Johnson, had

[5] *Ibid.*, March 23, 1883.
[6] *Ibid.*, March 27, 1883.

ridden hurriedly from town while the cavalry was chasing Shannon over the roof tops. Salazar called in his squads on the evening of March 23 and pushed for Nutt Station for his rendezvous with Fountain's column.[7]

The Lake Valley raid had immediate repercussions. Governor Sheldon received anonymous letters postmarked Lake Valley and Kingston, complaining of the use of military force to "intimidate and torment local citizens," and charging that the rustler killings by Fountain's "Greaser militia" were cold-blooded and needless. This was nothing new. From the earliest days of the rustler war the Governor and Fountain had been sternly criticized in certain quarters for using territorial cavalry for law enforcement. Several newspapers, notably the Albuquerque *Journal*, had been conspicuously bitter in their railings at Fountain and the Governor, but these law-and-order champions had their defenders, too, as indicated by a March 10 editorial published in the Santa Fe *New Mexican*: "Sheldon has been unmercifully severe upon Kinney and his compatriots. But it is quite observable that none but the rogues regret it. All honest men applaud the governor. It is a great sin . . . to use the militia for this purpose. . . . A state militia is maintained solely for ornament, only for the purpose of wearing fine uniforms and give proper eclat to Washington's birthday and the Fourth of July. Use them for any other purpose, say to capture, kill or break up a gang as Kinney's was, is a desecration, unwarranted tyranny—and a terrible assumption of power which stamps Sheldon a dangerous man. . . . In the eyes of such papers as the Albuquerque *Journal*, this is sinful energy on Sheldon's part, and it deserves repression. But his excellency has the satisfaction of knowing that the people of the whole territory, of all parties, and shades of political belief warmly applaud."[8]

Sheldon called the hand of Fountain's critics after the Lake Valley raid by forming a court of inquiry, consisting of Colonel Max Frost, Lieutenant Colonel Perfecto Armijo, and Captain Harold Eaton, all officers of the Second Regiment, to investigate

[7] *Ibid.*, March 24, 1883.
[8] *Ibid.*, March 10, 1883.

the anonymous charges.[9] The Governor invited those citizens of Lake Valley and Kingston "who thought Fountain's authority had been excessive . . . to present their facts before the Court of Inquiry."[10]

Sheldon had no takers on his offer, for not a single person appeared to offer evidence that Fountain had exceeded his authority. The Governor regarded this as vindicating his policy of using territorial cavalry to crush lawlessness. But Fountain was not satisfied, and he asked the Doña Ana grand jury, convening to investigate the twenty-five prisoners held on stock theft charges, to look into the Lake Valley raid complaints. After examining thirty witnesses and reams of depositions and other evidence, the grand jury declared that since Fountain's cavalry was acting on orders from the Governor in serving lawful writs issued by the territorial courts, and because no one was arrested except those for whom there was a legal warrant, it was unable to find that any crime had been committed.[11]

While the grand jury was investigating Fountain's military conduct, John Kinney was trying to gain his freedom. In casting about for an attorney, he "made a strenuous effort to retain Fountain" offering the Major a $3,000 retainer with "more to come." Fountain, amused at the rustler's brass, refused, and finally W. T. Thornton of Santa Fe, one of the most prominent attorneys in the Southwest, agreed to serve as defense counsel.[12]

Once the grand jury finished with Fountain, the members began to study the cases of the twenty-five accused rustlers he had brought in, and within two days the Doña Ana investigators handed down 132 indictments, binding all twenty-five over for trial. Fourteen charges were lodged against Kinney alone. Once specific charges had been filed, Thornton went to work applying all the wiles of the criminal lawyer. First, he tried for a continuance (an indefinite postponement of Kinney's trial) which Judge Warren

[9] *Rio Grande Republican*, April 7, 1883.

[10] Bartlett to Fountain, Santa Fe, March 31, 1883. Adjutant General's Files, SRC.

[11] *Rio Grande Republican*, April 7, 1883.

[12] Santa Fe *New Mexican*, March 31, 1883.

Bristol promptly rejected; next, he requested that old favorite of the southwestern underworld—the change of venue—and in this proposal, too, he was unsuccessful. Last he tried bail for his client. Bristol, well informed of Kinney's daring and aware of the risks involved in setting him free, refused this, even when Thornton offered $2,000. Money seemed unimportant for bail offers were jumped, one thousand dollars a time, until finally when counsel offered $6,000, the Judge, well versed on the rule of excessive bail, ordered, over the remonstrances of District Attorney S. B. Newcomb and Major Fountain, the prisoner released on bond. Kinney loose on the streets of Las Cruces caused considerable uneasiness; the citizens were shocked that one so notorious could obtain bail. The *New Mexican* in a furious editorial, pondered the question of since it "cost $10,000 to bring in Kinney and his gang [how could] Judge Bristol allow him freedom on $6,000 bail?"[13]

Fountain, taking every precaution to ensure that Kinney did not jump bail to Mexico, detailed Lieutenant Pedragon and five handpicked men to follow him day and night; so that whatever may have been Kinney's plans, he was so closely watched that the Major knew every move he made. Thus, when the vigilant spies reported that Kinney had approached a number of jurors impaneled for the upcoming district court session, Fountain notified Judge Bristol who held that Kinney was in contempt and ordered the prisoner returned to jail to await his trial, which was to commence at ten o'clock, April 12.[14]

As Kinney's trial neared, the rustler king's alleged case history of crime was recited by the *New Mexican*. Its readers were reminded that while "Billy the Kid was bad enough, so far as the business interests of the territory and its good name, as a desirable place in which to build homes, Kinney was a worse man and exercised a far more destructive and malign influence," and the editor recalled that since Fountain had turned down the $3,000 retainer offered him by Kinney, the Major deserved "some competent reward from the territory for his refusal of the fee, and in this way

13 *Ibid.*, April 8, 1883.
14 *Ibid.*, April 12, 1883.

and from all circumstances should be allowed to complete in the courtroom what he has so gallantly commenced in the field."[15]

District Attorney Newcomb invited Fountain to assist him in the Kinney prosecution, and on April 12 before a packed house, the Major, in his best histrionic form, armed with devastating evidence and incriminating witnesses, presented the territory's case against John Kinney. Despite all the brilliant attempts by Thornton to establish an alibi for the accused, Fountain returned each time with persuasive evidence. Just before four in the afternoon the jury retired with the court's charge "to pay no attention whatever to the popular clamor" against Kinney. Eight minutes later the jury returned with the verdict—guilty as charged.[16]

Leaving the prosecution of the remaining twenty-four prisoners to District Attorney Newcomb, Major Fountain, on orders from Governor Sheldon, selected a guard consisting of Captains Salazar and Van Patton to escort Kinney to the penitentiary at Leavenworth, Kansas, where he was to serve his seven-year sentence.[17]

Before ordering his cavalry to inactive status, Fountain announced that companies A and B had been invited to attend the Tertio-Millennial celebration in Santa Fe during July as guests of the territory. The arrangements committee, Fountain told his men, wanted the cavalry to participate in the parades and to compete in the drill contests. He closed on a note of warning; the Governor's Rifles, a crack Santa Fe unit, had already announced its intention of carrying off the gold medal for the best drilled unit in the territory.

The Mesilla and Las Cruces companies drilled each Sunday for two months, sharpening their formations; their repertoire included, besides the prescribed United States tactics, a variety of Mexican routines which permitted the men more colorful, dashing, wide-sweeping maneuvers. At daylight on the morning of July 6, Fountain's cavalry arrived in Santa Fe. Even at this early

[15] *Ibid.*, March 14, 1883.

[16] *Rio Grande Republican*, April 14, 1883.

[17] General Order No. 18, Santa Fe, April 27, 1883. Adjutant General's Files, SRC.

hour they found crowds on the streets awaiting the official opening of the Tertio-Millennial celebration. The throng parted and
stood in awe as the fabulous Mesilla–Las Cruces column, "trucu-
lent and fierce appearing" in rough garb, each member with carbine in hand, pistols in belt, and cartridge belts slung across shoulders, passed through the streets astride their tough little ponies
and disappeared for the time in the exposition grounds.[18]

After the men had cared for their horses, pitched their tents,
and established a tidy camp at the far corner of the grounds, they
were permitted to visit the displays. Intriguing exhibits from New
Mexico and over the nation were ready for public showing. A Boston manufacturer had set up a $5,000 soda fountain, and the
famous Studebaker Brothers occupied an acre of exhibit space
with their latest models of wagons and carriages. The troopers
paused before a display of the most modern excavating, blasting,
and milling equipment shown by a mining machinery manufacturer, before moving on to the livestock section where stockmen
were grooming prized samples from their cattle, horse, and sheep
herds, and from there to exhibits of sumptuous produce from irri-
gated farms. But they lingered longest before the domestic displays where busy women baited the hungry cavalrymen with prepared dishes, canned vegetables and fruits, and mouth-watering
bread and pastries.

Before returning to the camp, the men visited Civic Center
where the exposition committee had arranged to have constructed
a small lake with a fountain in the center and landscaped with
artistically grouped shrubs and plants. Their last stop was at the
new grandstand, with seating for over one thousand spectators
and complete with arena, athletic fields, and the running track
where by late afternoon they would begin their daily exhibitions.

While the various exhibits, athletic events, Indian performances, and horse races drew substantial crowds during the three-
week-long Tertio-Millennial celebration, the center of interest for
the entire exposition program was Fountain's cavalry. Coming
into Santa Fe with an exciting reputation built up by the Victorio-

18 *Rio Grande Republican*, July 7, 1883.

Nana campaigns and the more recent rustler wars and highly trained and rigidly disciplined by their perfectionist commanding officer, the men matched their advance billing and then some by providing new thrills for a packed gallery each day—"visitors were astonished at the exhibitions of rough riding and the horsemanship of the command."[19]

The *New Mexican* saluted Fountain's cavalry as the exposition's chief attraction and pointed out that while "these fellows, rough and desperate as they appear, and they doubtless are," still "are magnificent riders, and a better set of men for the work they are intended to do could hardly have been found in the southern country. The troop is the cynosure of all eyes when they make their appearance on the track."[20]

The climax of the Tertio-Millennial celebration was the militia drill contest, held the day before the exposition closed. Keen public interest had developed in the event, and heavy wagers were being placed on the top contenders—the crack Governor's Rifles from Santa Fe, and Fountain's cavalry. Units from all over the territory were entered in the competition, and military judges for the event were selected by General Ranald Mackenzie from regular United States Army commands stationed in New Mexico. By late afternoon, as expected, the performance brackets had eliminated all participating units except the Santa Fe and Mesilla–Las Cruces battalion. In breathless excitement the packed gallery waited for the performances which would determine the best-drilled military unit in New Mexico Territory. The Rifles drew first assignment, and, elegant in brilliant braid and blue, they were applauded time and again as they smartly snapped through their sharp routines.

An uncertain silence gripped the crowd as Fountain's troopers, slouching easily in their saddles, took the field. The Major, with Carleton-like poise, rode to the grandstand side of the track, saluted the governor's section and the judges' stand, wheeled his horse to face the column, paused, and blew a sharp blast on a small silver whistle. Instantly the mounted pack became a responsive

[19] *Ibid.*, July 28, 1885.
[20] Santa Fe *New Mexican*, July 12, 1883.

unity, performing to each command with an unexpected precision. In earlier competition, the column had adhered to textbook tactics, but for their final performance the two companies, by mixing orthodox army movements with the flaring Mexican routines, presented a fresh repertoire of maneuvers which brought a spontaneous reaction from the spectators. Thunderous ovation followed each command the Major gave. First Company A, then Company B, then combined units performed their wheeling, dashing evolutions in perfect rhythm. The gallery's enthusiastic response anticipated the judges' decision. Fountain's cavalry swept all honors, and the Major smiled proudly as the Governor presented the awards—top unit prize of $125 for proficiency in drill, with each member receiving a gold medal.[21]

The military drill contests, and especially the singular performances by Fountain's cavalry and the Governor's Rifles, inspired an upsurge of martial spirit among the citizens of New Mexico. Interest was keen all over the territory in forming new units and the Adjutant General's Office was deluged with requests for authority to muster additional companies. By August when twelve cavalry companies had been mustered, Governor Sheldon ordered a reorganization of the territorial militia. Using Fountain's Mesilla–Las Cruces cavalry, the oldest active units in the territory, as a nucleus, he created the First Cavalry Regiment, New Mexico Volunteers. Major Fountain was elevated to full colonel and made commanding officer of the new First Regiment.[22]

The new First Cavalry Regiment had to wait nearly two years for a call to active duty, but when it came, the men were ready, and the rigorous training and stiff discipline Colonel Fountain imposed upon his troops stood them in good stead.

During 1885, Apache malcontents at San Carlos, the old partisans of Victorio and Nana, found a new chief whose reckless daring and compulsion for butchery exceeded that of either of their former leaders. On May 17, the notorious Geronimo led forty-five

21 *Rio Grande Republican,* July 28, 1883.
22 General Order No. 20, Santa Fe, September 14, 1883. Adjutant General's Files, SRC.

warriors and nearly one hundred women and children away from their reservation home under the very guns of Fort Apache. On the following day, the escape was discovered by government scouts, the alert was sounded over the Southwest, and a massive search got underway. United States troops were stationed on the east side of the Río Grande at all crossings to prevent Geronimo from linking with the Mescaleros and picking up reinforcements. Government scouts watched passes in the San Andres, Caballo, Mogollon, Black, and Cooke's ranges, and patrols fanned out in all directions to protect settlers and to cut Indian trails.[23]

General George Crook, military commandant for Arizona Territory, ordered all available troops at Forts Apache, Bowie, Grant, and Thomas into the field, and a total of thirteen cavalry columns took up the search for Geronimo and his band. In addition, General H. L. Bradley, United States commander for the military district of New Mexico, pulled troops from Fort Bayard to protect settlers along the Gila.[24]

The dragnet tightened on the western slopes of the Mogollons, and it appeared that the search columns, after a punishing 150-mile chase, had Geronimo's band hemmed at Gallinas Pass. But the crafty chief split his force, sending the women and children with warrior escort into the Black Range while his men decoyed one of the columns, led by Captain R. S. Smith, into a trap at Moulton's Sawmill.[25]

Next, Geronimo moved along the New Mexico–Arizona border, cutting military telegraph lines, ambushing patrols, and deliberately luring weary columns on 100-mile marches, leaving signs so bold the pursuers dared not make camp for two or three days at a time. While Geronimo was punishing the United States cavalry, his warriors were taking a heavy toll of life and property by striking at the settlements, isolated ranches and sheep camps, and wandering prospectors. In the first ten days after leaving the reservation, the Apaches had slain fifty-seven civilians. In a radius of twenty

[23] Santa Fe *New Mexican Review,* June 15, 1885.
[24] *Ibid.,* May 19, 1885.
[25] *Ibid.,* June 2, 1885.

miles of Alma, situated in the Mogollons, twenty-four ranchmen and miners were buried. Identified victims included Nat Luce, Calvin Orwig, and Tom McKenney. Many of the bodies found were so completely mutilated and disfigured that certain identification was impossible. Near Grafton the raiders killed two men at Cantwell and Petrie's ranch; on the Gila, Charles Stevenson, foreman for the Alley and Ingersoll ranch, was shot down; and, in addition, two young boys, Harry Moreland and Frank Adams, were slain. The Moreland boy was found with an iron rod driven through his head.[26]

The Apaches made a brazen daylight raid on the outskirts of Silver City late in May and massacred a family of five. When a relief column arrived on the scene of doom, they found among the victims an infant shot through the cheek and hung by its wrists on a meat hook beside the house. Although still alive when found, the little one died in a few hours. On an adjoining ranch the column found a family of seven slain and mutilated. Searchers cut across Indian trail in all directions, which indicated that the killers had split into parties of about five each and escaped in different directions.[27]

Citizens of western New Mexico, becoming increasingly impatient with the United States Army's effort to corral the vicious, rampaging Geronimo, petitioned the Governor to call out Fountain's cavalry. Already Arizona and New Mexico cattlemen, regarding General Crook's campaign as futile since his highly touted scouts could not even find the Apache hide-outs, had organized their cowboys into a sort of ranchmen's militia and were making plans to send their men into the Mogollons to search for Geronimo. The Santa Fe *Review* reported these cowboy mercenaries, all well armed, were going forward in small squads and warned that "if they strike the Indians it means extermination. Bucks, squaws, and brats will be treated alike."[28]

Sheldon ordered Fountain's regiment to the field on May 29.

26 *Rio Grande Republican*, May 30, 1885.
27 Santa Fe *New Mexican Review*, May 29, 1885.
28 *Ibid.*, May 28, 1885.

Dog Canyon

"A third trail went northeast toward Dog Canyon."

White Sands

"*A wagon track led out from the house toward the White Sands.*"

His immediate charge was to rush to the Lake Valley vicinity and take steps to protect the people and property there from threatened Indian depredations.[29] The *Rio Grande Republican* reflected the general relief that went up at the news that Fountain's cavalry had been sent against Geronimo, noting the Colonel "should have been called out ten days earlier and many a life would have been saved. The entire uselessness of the United States troops in fighting Indians has been well demonstrated lately; they are always either 12 hours behind, or 24 hours ahead of the Indians, and are very careful not to find them. The [United States] troops are being charged with cowardice. But we have hopes that our militia boys will do some good work."[30]

Fountain set up regimental headquarters at Lake Valley, and from there scattered his companies in a thin crescent-shaped defensive perimeter from Alma on the north to the Southern Pacific tracks far to the south, placing a full company along the line to guard against an attempted crossing into Mexico. After organizing local defenses among the citizens of the tiny western settlements and mining camps, Fountain placed militia squads at secret passes and springs he had discovered years before as Carleton's scout and made every effort to close all possible outlets. Once his defenses were set, he sent scouts looking for recent Indian trails, and he himself rode over and inspected much of the desolate region. His examination disclosed that "every ranch was abandoned, chickens, pigs, dogs, etc. starving and cattle wandering . . . . The country people are thoroughly infuriated with the manner in which things are carried on by the government."[31]

Almost at once after Fountain set his defenses, the number of reports of killings and property losses began to drop, and after June 3 no casualties due to Indian raids were reported in the entire protective zone patrolled by his First Regiment. With his primary mission accomplished, the Colonel was eager to take the offensive,

[29] Sheldon to Fountain, Santa Fe, May 29, 1885. Adjutant General's Files, SRC.

[30] *Rio Grande Republican*, June 6, 1885.

[31] *Ibid.*

and on June 4 his scouts brought word that fresh Indian sign had been found near the headwaters of the Percha and Animas. This news meant something to Fountain; his Mesilla Scouts had worked the area during the Victorio campaign and found it the roughest, most inaccessible country imaginable, with confusing box canyons, precipices, and heavily timbered mesas. The sparkling waters of the Animas flowed out of a natural fortress lately called Victorio Park, a heart-shaped, spring-studded haven; at the point where the Animas issued, there jutted a high bluff which furnished defenders a natural breastworks. Victorio had lured a company of United States troops into a trap there, and Fountain's Mesilla Scouts, sent to find them, discovered the bones of fifteen men along the bluff.[32]

Victorio Park would be a likely place for Geronimo to be hiding, Fountain reasoned, and the failure of United States troops to find him could be explained by the virtually impassable access to the hide-out. Drawing fifty of his best men from the defensive perimeter and placing them under Captain Pedragon, the Colonel led his column on a night ride for the Animas. Near Hillsboro they were joined by Joe Jackson, captain of the local cattlemen's cowboy militia, with a civilian troop that doubled their force. A grueling night ride brought the column at gray dawn to what Fountain identified as the old Victorio Trail. The trace led down into the Animas canyon. Immediately Fountain's scouts discovered a fresh moccasin track in the sandy bed. From then on, as they moved up the tumbling stream, the column found Indian sign with increasing regularity.

By noon the column had reached the precipitous approaches to Victorio Park. Fountain ordered a halt, and while the men rested their weary horses in the cold stream, Jackson and he held a council of war. Fountain's report to Adjutant General Bartlett details the subsequent action: "I determined to force the enemy's stronghold. To this end a party of 23 picked men was sent ahead in charge of . . . Don Jose Trujillo, chief of scouts." The remainder of the column was divided into three parties, two sent out, one on either

[32] *Ibid.*, June 13, 1885.

side as advance flankers, working well up on the precipitous canyon bluffs, and the third held in reserve as rear guard.

Colonel Fountain, riding with the flankers right, reported that "the Indians had every advantage of position and could have made a very formidable resistance with but a few men, but they did not choose to do so. When our scouts penetrated the stronghold they discovered the enemy had abandoned its position and fled to the precipitous mountain range between the heads of the Animas. As it was impossible to penetrate this region with horses it was determined to follow them on foot. I ordered thirty-five picked men from my command, under the immediate command of Lieutenant Metcalf, and Capt. Jackson with fifteen picked men of his party, to accompany me on foot, making in all fifty-three rifles.

"In order to travel as light as possible we all stripped to our shirts, took no provisions or other impediments, the command carrying nothing but their arms and ammunition. The balance of the command was sent back with the stock, with orders to make a camp near the Victorio Trail on the divide between Cave Creek and the Animas and there await us. At 3 P.M. I started with the party on foot to climb the mountains.

"Five hours of incessant climbing over the most tremendous bluffs and precipitous mountains took us up to the summit of the range. We found the country so badly broken up as to make progress exceedingly difficult. During the night eight of my men became separated from the command. Seven of them joined me on the following day . . . . Shortly before day break . . . we discovered the fire of an Indian camp in a canon probably 1,000 feet below us. As the side of the mountain was very precipitous, the men could not avoid rolling stones as they climbed down the side of the mountain to get to the camp. These noises undoubtedly started the Indians, as they escaped down the canon. There were but three of them; they left their fire burning, also a colt they had killed for breakfast. This was probably a spy party watching the movements of my command.

"We reached our horse camp about 10 o'clock entirely ex-

hausted. The party who had separated from us during the night . . .
came in about two hours later. They reported several small trails
recently made going from the north to the south Percha . . . . A
courier just in . . . brings the report that these Indians have gone
south over very rough country. I left camp with my command . . .
en route to the Percha Pass, where it was my intention to camp
the main command and throw out scouting parties on foot across
the country on either side. During the day several small trails were
seen going in that direction.

"This with other information which I consider reliable confirms
me in my belief that the hostiles are concentrated in the vicinity
of what is known as the Carpenter district. My object in going
to Percha Pass was to assure myself of this and to proceed from
there to a point of supposed concentration where I hope to find
them. This morning Captain Chaffee, United States Army, came
in with his troops and upon consultation with me became impressed with the correctness of my views. I furnished him with a
guide and he immediately pushed on to the point mentioned. His
presence there, guarding the pass, affords me an unexpected opportunity to have my horses shod and to obtain supplies which I am
now doing and expect to leave here tonight to join Chaffee's command. . . . It is my opinion that the Indians, concentrated in the
Carpenter district, which is at the head of Tierra Blanca Creek,
will make a push for Mexico with all the stock they have and that
they can pick up en route."[33]

Fountain's cavalry had accomplished in a few hours a feat which
United States Army columns had been unable to do in two weeks.
Not only had his militia column discovered the Indian hideaway,
but, more important, it had flushed the Apache marauders from
their nearly impenetrable bastion, forcing them to begin moving
to the south where the chances for interception were much better.
The Colonel's next dispatch to Adjutant General Bartlett confirmed his suspicion that Geronimo's raiders, driven from their
Victorio Park hideaway, would strike southward for the Carpenter
district on the Tierra Blanca headwaters: "I left my main com-

[33] Santa Fe *New Mexican Review*, June 9, 1885.

mand in camp at the head-waters of Tierra Blanca on the morning of the 7th inst. and took twenty men on a scout through the range. At 10 A.M. we came across a large trail leading out of the Carpenter district and heading toward the Mimbres. We followed this trail until 3 P.M., when the Indians made a stand in a deep precipice canon on the branch of the Gavelan, in a dense thicket, and tried to check us by a sharp, but ill-directed fire. We got the hills on them, however, when they fled going over very rough country, thickly wooded. We pursued them until sundown, when they broke up into small parties going toward Cook's peak. Have been all day endeavoring to find their trail but think they have not come together. Tell the troops on the line to look out. My horses are badly used up. The traveling is terrible and a fight would be a luxury."[34]

Soon after the Carpenter district fight, Geronimo's people crossed into Mexico, and New Mexico was rid of this torment. Fountain's cavalry scoured all hideaways south to Cooke's Peak and found them vacant. Reporting to Bartlett on June 14 of his certainty that the Apache recalcitrants had at last been driven from New Mexico, Colonel Fountain was ordered to return his regiment to Las Cruces for return to inactive duty. The delirious welcome grateful citizens in every village and town along the return route accorded the First Regiment was ample reward for the hardships and hazards Fountain's crusty troopers had faced in driving Geronimo and his Apache raiders from the territory.[35]

[34] *Ibid.*
[35] *Rio Grande Republican*, June 20, 1885.

CHAPTER X

Frontier Lawyer

BETWEEN INDIAN AND RUSTLER CAMPAIGNS and supervising his cavalry regiment, Colonel Fountain carried on an extensive and, at times, lucrative law practice. By the middle eighties he had become so prominent as a trial lawyer that each term of court he had to turn clients away. As a matter of fact, the only attorneys in the entire territory who even came close to matching Fountain as a courtroom tactician were Tom Catron and W. T. Thornton of Santa Fe.

A successful practicing attorney on the New Mexico frontier had to possess, besides intelligence and training, a peculiar combination of courage, creative imagination, and physical endurance. The territory was divided into judicial districts, each with a district judge appointed under federal patronage. This officer handled both federal and territorial cases, and in addition to holding court in the towns of his jurisdiction, once each year he joined with his colleagues at Santa Fe to constitute the supreme court of the territory. Lawyers rode circuit with the judge throughout his district, facing intense heat and cold, severe storms, and crossing mountains and deserts to furnish citizens in even the most isolated communities with legal counsel.

Fountain's regular itinerary began each year with the spring term at Mesilla–Las Cruces, from there to Lincoln, Silver City, Hillsboro, and Socorro, and ended at Santa Fe with the annual supreme court session. A sample of the hardships frontier attorneys endured to keep court appointments was Fountain's near disaster in crossing the Sacramento Mountains during the winter of 1888 on his return from Lincoln court. His hard-running team plunged into a deep snow drift. The buckboard chassis was smashed and the rear axle broken, but "the Colonel being an old campaigner . . . succeeded in extricating himself from his difficulties and arrived home on Sunday, having made the 160 miles in three days, including the time lost by his smash-up."[1]

The regular term of court in each town was about the liveliest season of the year, attracting besides the judge and corps of attorneys, an army of litigants, witnesses, jurymen, interested parties, and the curious. As a matter of fact, with little else for local entertainment, the court term was matched only by revivals and the medicine shows for drawing crowds.

The most popular stop on the third district circuit was Las Cruces (having succeeded Mesilla as the district court center in 1883). The City of Crosses was a ripsnorting Anglo town, famous all over the territory as wild, wicked, and capable of indulging the most ribald tastes. This reputation spread as far as San Francisco where the famous *Chronicle* clucked: "Las Cruces is a New Mexico town with a holy name, but its people are not of a religious turn of mind. Recently they subscribed $200 for a temporary courthouse, while only $11 was raised to build a new Presbyterian Church. Here is a more promising field for the Salvation Army than San Francisco."[2]

Along the broad, dusty main street of Las Cruces was a scattering of saloons, gambling dens, and bawdy houses, which during district court term went to special pains to please the inrush of countrymen. The Senate, Centennial, and Monarch saloons, in particular, did a "roaring trade" by offering orchestras and special variety acts. The Senate featured heavyweight wrestling and boxing. Big crowds were attracted by Stonewall Whisky and bull snake and rattlesnake battles at the Centennial. But the Monarch outdid them all by offering nightly fights between bears and bulldogs. The Monarch had imported for the court season two lady faro dealers, whose tables ran wide-open night and day, and its adjunct, the Monarch Billiard Hall and Reading Room, was rated as the most stylish resort in town. The Monarch management even

---

[1] *Rio Grande Republican*, March 10, 1888.
[2] *Ibid.*, March 10, 1883.

pitched its advertising to fit the court season: "All visitors to Las Cruces during the present term of court are hereby notified that they are requested to be and appear before the 'bar' of the Honorable Dan Dameron, at the Monarch Saloon, there to show good and sufficient cause why they should not take a drink. And herein fail not at your peril." Signed: "Tom Rivers, Chief Clerk (Bartender)."[3]

Most of the cases coming before the district court were territorial cases against persons accused of crimes of violence, either against property (for the most part horse and cattle theft) or person. Of the latter, since rape was rare and assault and battery charges were hardly ever pressed (the region's folkways demanding these be settled on a personal basis), homicide was the most common offense. As a matter of fact, the docket was generally so cluttered with murder cases, little court time was left to take care of civil cases. During the 1882 term for the Third Judicial District, five murder cases were on the docket before the term began, three on change of venue from Grant County and at least twelve more were expected when the grand jury finished its indictments.

The courtroom episodes growing out of the cases tried during this particular session demonstrate Fountain's skill as a criminal lawyer and explain why defendants faced with the gallows or life imprisonment sought him out. The more hopeless and futile the prospects for the accused, the more Fountain welcomed the case. Taking it as a challenge, he left no stone unturned in developing a plausible and persuasive *raison d'être* for his client. Colonel Fountain's courtroom performances packed the gallery; spectators came from all sections to be entertained by his scintillating oratory, sharp examination of witnesses, dramatic use of evidence, and his masterful management of the jury.

The three leading cases of the 1882 term were *Territory* vs. *James Patterson, Territory* vs. *Anthony Price,* and *Territory* vs. *Chris Moesner.* It was commonly accepted that each of the accused would be hanged; Moesner's cause in particular was regarded as hopeless. Fountain was counsel for the accused in all three cases.

[3] *Ibid.,* March 29, 1884.

James Patterson was charged with the murder of John Powers at Georgetown in Grant County. Patterson, indicted at the July, 1880, term, had obtained Fountain as counsel. Claiming that strong local feeling, which presumed a verdict in the first degree, prejudiced Patterson's chances for a fair trial, Fountain succeeded in avoiding a continuance and finally managed a change of venue to Doña Ana County. When Patterson's case came up, Fountain took two days examining veniremen and finally agreed on the jury.

Testimony brought out that the crime's setting was Johnson's Saloon in Georgetown. John Powers was playing cards, and Patterson approached the table and invited Powers to drink with him. Powers refused and Patterson left. An hour later Patterson returned and invited all present to drink with him. Powers again refused, whereupon Patterson was reported to have said: "Then you don't like me, you damned son of a bitch!" Words passed and Powers started for the door saying, "You will have to take this out of me." Patterson followed him to the door, drew his pistol, and fired two shots. Powers fell in the street mortally wounded.

Fountain's witnesses testified that Patterson had previous trouble with Powers over a debt which Powers owed him. Patterson had brought suit to recover; the defense showed that Powers, after the judgment went against him, made a number of threats to take Patterson's life and that one of these had been communicated to Patterson just before the shooting. Patterson testified that from Power's language and actions he believed that Powers was about to carry out his threat, and, acting upon that belief, he fired the fatal shot.

The *Rio Grande Republican* correspondent reported that "when the testimony closed . . . the case looked very dubious for the prisoner, and the general impression among the bystanders was that the verdict would be either murder in the first degree, or that Patterson would get sentenced to imprisonment for a long term." District Attorney S. B. Newcomb opened for the prosecution "spending an hour making a forcible statement" of the case, and when he closed, the "situation of the prisoner seemed desperate. Mr. Fountain then began the argument for the defense, and it could soon be seen that he was carrying the jury with him. He spoke two and one-half hours, and frequently brought tears in the eyes of the jurors. When he concluded, it was apparent that the verdict would be for acquittal or the next thing to it. Newcomb spoke for two hours in closing the case. He made a strong logical argument, but it was plain to be seen that the jury was not of his way of thinking although he was probably right. . . . At 7:30 the jury brought in the verdict. The prisoner and jury stood facing each other."

The *Republican*'s correspondent continued:

"The clerk asked: 'Gentlemen of the jury, have you agreed upon your verdict?'

" 'We have,' was the answer.

" 'What say you?' was the question. 'Do you find the prisoner guilty or not guilty?'

" 'Guilty,' was the response, in clear tones.

"Patterson staggered as if shot. His attorney, Mr. Fountain caught his arm and whispered, 'Keep cool, you are quite safe.'

" 'In what degree do you find him guilty?' inquired the court.

" '*In the fourth degree*,' was the response. 'And we fix his punishment for one year in the county jail.'

"Paterson drew a long breath, shook his attorney warmly by the hand and in tremulous tones thanked the jury for their leniency; and so ended the most hotly contested case that has been tried at the present term of the court."[4]

A week later, Fountain's second sensational murder defense of the session came up on the district docket—the famous Price case. Anthony Price was charged with the murder of Mike McCray at Deming in Grant County. Fountain had obtained a change of venue to Doña Ana County. The Colonel required only one day in forming Price's trial jury, although he exhausted the regular panel and fifteen additional veniremen had to be summoned before he was satisfied. By six that evening the jury had been sworn and placed in charge of two peace officers.

On Wednesday morning, District Attorney Newcomb opened

[4] *Ibid.*, April 15, 1882.

the territory's case in an earnest introductory speech after which the witnesses were sworn. John Warden, principal prosecution witness, testified that in July, 1881, he was keeping a hotel at Deming. Price, accompanied by McCray and a man called Red Foss came into his dining room. The trio was drunk, but they appeared to be in good humor and roughly joked with each other, using very obscene language. Warden recalled that after Price had finished his dinner, while waiting for dessert, he began piling the dishes roughly in the center of the table. McCray told him to let the dishes alone because the owner of the house was a good man and a friend of his. Price replied that he was able to pay for all the dishes he broke and called for pie, at the time cursing the waiter. The pie was brought and eaten. Then Price attempted to rise from the table. McCray pulled him down saying, "Sit down you damned son of a bitch or you'll get killed." Price drew a pistol, cocked it and with his elbow resting on the table, and pointed the weapon at McCray who was sitting opposite.

Warden recalled that McCray asked: "Does she pop?" and he continued, "At that moment she did 'pop' and McCray fell, shot through the brain." Following a substantiating statement from another witness, Newcomb rested the territory's case.

Fountain went to work. One witness he had located, Frank Boone, testified that on the morning of the day of the shooting, Price and he had started from Deming to round up some of Price's cattle. Just before they departed, Price complained that his pistol was out of order and asked to borrow one for the trip. A Deming saloonkeeper, Sid Knox, took a pistol from behind his bar and lent it to Price, who, without examining the weapon, put it in his scabbard. Price and Boone then rode off, got the cattle, and returned to town just before noon. Price had a toothache and drank a bottle of whisky. Then he sold the cattle and started in to "have a time." He met his friend, McCray, gave him a twenty-dollar gold piece, and they both consumed fifteen to twenty drinks in rapid succession. McCray then guided Price to Dr. Keefe's office to have his tooth pulled.

Sid Knox followed on Price's behalf. He admitted that he had lent his pistol to Price. On Fountain's prodding, he explained that some time before he had filed the notches off the dog, so that the pistol would not stand at half or full cock, and that in order to discharge the pistol, it was only necessary to draw back the hammer with the thumb. When the thumb was released, Knox explained, the hammer would fall and discharge the pistol even though the trigger had not been pulled. At Fountain's urging, he admitted that he had failed to inform Price of this peculiarity about the weapon and corroborated Boone's testimony that Price and Mc-Cray were very drunk.

Next, Fountain called the defendant, who swore that McCray and he were good friends; that there had been no trouble of any kind between them; that McCray took him to the dentist where he had the tooth pulled; that he was very much under the influence of liquor; and that the doctor gave him a dose of morphine to alleviate the pain he was suffering. He remembered nothing thereafter until he found himself in irons charged with the murder of McCray. Price explained that the language said to have been used towards him by McCray prior to the shooting was such as was common between them and that he would not have considered the language offensive; but rather, he would have taken it as a joke, such as was customary between them. If he had pointed a pistol at McCray it was in a playful mood and in a joking manner and not with the intention of shooting.

Newcomb's argument for the prosecution "presented the case in a very unfavorable light for the defendant," and Fountain countered that the evidence clearly proved that the shooting was accidental. Pointing out that it had already been established that Price and McCray were very close friends, "he claimed that Price had no motive for killing McCray, and certainly no intention of shooting when he pointed the pistol." Contending that the shooting was accidental because the pistol could not stand cocked, Fountain "produced a pistol that had been altered in the manner testified to by Knox, and demonstrated to the jury how such an accident could easily occur with a pistol in that condition." He closed with a reminder that Price did not know the peculiarity of the weapon. Judge Bistol gave the charge at 4:30 that afternoon, and in fifteen minutes the jury returned with the verdict. "The courtroom was crowded with spectators when the jury filed in. It was evident from the short time required to reach a verdict that they had accepted the theory advanced by the defense. They found Price guilty of murder in the fifth degree, and fixed his fine at $1,000. Price and his attorney were the only persons in the court-room who manifested no surprise at the verdict."

The *Republican* correspondent reported Price said to his counsel, "But I can't pay the fine."

"Stay in jail three months; that will pay it," was the reply.

"Judge Bristol in passing sentence, told Price that he had made a very fortunate escape; that when the jury imposed a fine of $1,000 they were undoubtedly ignorant of the fact that under the laws of this Territory, the defendant could not be kept in jail for more than three months if he were unable to pay the fine imposed."[5]

As Fountain prepared for his third big murder trial of the session—the Moesner case, the *Rio Grande Republican* made an acid comment concerning his remarkable success as a criminal lawyer: "Give us a Mexican jury, with Fountain for lawyer . . . and we can murder any man we please with impunity."[6]

Of all the cases Fountain argued during the 1882 term, Chris Moesner's was regarded as the most hopeless; even the prisoner had accepted his fate—the gallows or, at the very least, a life term. He was charged with killing one of Lake Valley's most respected citizens, Dr. Alex Kallenberg. Local feeling against Moesner was so high that only by alert deputies slipping the prisoner away during the night was he saved from a vigilante lynching committee. Fountain had taken his case and had managed a change of venue to Doña Ana County.

As before, Fountain was very careful about the composition of his jury. The facts of the Moesner case as revealed by both prosecution and defense witnesses were that on that fatal day in May,

[5] *Ibid.*, April 22, 1882.
[6] *Ibid.*

1881, Dr. Kallenberg and Moesner were at the house of Dave Lufkin in Lake Valley. During the morning, a man named Hood and a companion identified only as "a hatchet-faced man from Arizona" came up and "kicked up a racket" with Moesner, pushed and hustled him about, poked him with a pistol, and threatened to "shoot his damned liver out." Lufkin disarmed Moesner's tormentors and ran "hatchet-face" out of camp, but Hood slunk about town waiting for a chance at Moesner. During the afternoon of the same day, Lufkin was sitting in his door, Kallenberg by his side, when Moesner suddenly burst from the house with a pistol in his hand. Lufkin then saw the reason for Moesner's alarm. Thirty feet away stood Hood, ready to fire at Moesner. Witnesses testified that Hood had prowled all over town muttering threats that he was "going to kill a damned son of a bitch," that he had obtained a Sharps rifle, and that he was seen returning to Lufkin's place. As Moesner fired, Hood dodged behind Kallenberg, and the bullet, intended for Hood, passed through Lufkin's shoulder into Kallenberg's body, killing the doctor instantly.

When Fountain announced that he had no further evidence to offer and that he was ready to argue the case to the jury, the *Republican* reported that "an honest miner in the audience whispered: 'going to try to save his neck with chin music.' The honest miner was right . . . as the result proves. Newcomb opened the argument with a clear and impassioned statement of the case; he insisted that the shooting of Kallenberg was neither justifiable nor excusable, but was a clear case of murder. During his argument, Mrs. Judge Bristol and Mrs. Bowman accompanied by a number of other ladies entered the court room and were furnished with seats within the bar. The ladies had understood that in his 'chin music' efforts to save his client's neck . . . counsel would make a brilliant display of oratorical pyrotechnics, and had come to witness the performance."

But Fountain "disappointed . . . his fair auditors by addressing the jury in Spanish, a language which the ladies did not understand." He insisted that Moesner was justified in shooting at Hood; that such shooting was in self-defense; that if Moesner had killed Hood the killing would have been justifiable; that in shooting at Hood he accidentally shot Kallenberg; and that the only question left for the jury to consider was whether Moesner exercised proper caution to avoid hitting innocent bystanders when he shot at Hood. Fountain insisted that he had, and he asked the jury not to judge Moesner's acts as they would judge those of a man unthreatened by danger and unexcited, but asked that his state of mind and the actual danger from Hood at the time of the shooting be taken into consideration. Fountain spoke an hour and thirty minutes and closed his argument with an appeal to the jury "not for mercy, not for pity, but for simple justice." The jury was out less than thirty minutes and returned a verdict "murder in the 5th degree" and the penalty, three years imprisonment.[7]

Fountain defended many celebrities in his time, but his most sensational client was Bronco Sue Dawson. Sue, probably the most generous female in all the territory, was hated by the women and loved by the men. According to local folklore, Sue "floated in from somewhere," settling first at La Luz, and was mistress to a number of cattlemen; the folk tales tell of several men dying for first place in her affections. Sue finally discovered that she could charge money for what she had been giving away for years, a change which made her a wealthy woman. Blonde and voluptuous, she was denounced for her brash, unladylike behavior, such as riding a man's saddle and throwing her leg over astride when men were around. Besides being indefatigable in sex, Sue was resourceful too; after she went into business, she rode the circuit of cow camps during roundup with a covered wagon.

Curiously, when Sue became prosperous, she became greedy and began running afoul of the law. During 1882 she lived with a man named Yonkers in Lincoln County. At first he was passed off as her brother, but when he died she claimed his property on the grounds that he was her husband. There was some local suspicion raised at the time as to the cause of his death, but, the country being sparsely settled, no investigation was ever made. For a time, Sue ran a house on the Fort Stanton–Lincoln road.

[7] *Ibid.*, April 29, 1882.

Then she took up with Robert Black, a cattleman on the Peñasco. In the spring of 1884, Black sold his cattle and moved to Socorro and started a saloon. Shortly after Sue joined him at Socorro, the pair had a vicious fight, and Sue shot him. She charmed a number of technical delays out of the court, and it appeared that she would get off scot-free. Then in 1886, an indignant local improvement committee demanded and got a warrant for her arrest and trial for murder in the first degree. The *Rio Grande Republican* crowed at Sue's predicament, claiming that "the murder for which she was arrested was as cold-blooded a deed as ever disgraced the Territory of New Mexico, and it is to be hoped that justice will at last be meted out to this woman, who if allowed to continue her murderous career will soon rank as the Lucretia Borgia of the West."[8]

Things looked bad for Sue. New Mexico womanhood could be vindicated only by the gallows or a long prison term for this "harlotrous fiend." In her darkest hour, Bronco Sue called on the one man in the territory who would defy public opinion to defend her. Mariana was indignant, humiliated, and furious all at the same time that Sue should bother her husband with her sordid troubles. But over his wife's tearful remonstrances, the Colonel answered Sue's call of distress.

On a cold November day, 1886, Fountain arrived in Socorro to begin the defense of what appeared to be the hopeless case of Bronco Sue Dawson. After all other maneuvers failed him, he filed with Judge Brinker six copies of the Socorro *Chieftain*, containing a recital of Sue's lurid past. Fountain claimed that this publicity had inflamed the public attitude toward his client and that a fair, impartial trial at Socorro was impossible and requested a change of venue to Grant County.[9]

Judge Brinker granted the motion, and Fountain set to the seemingly impossible task of building a creditable defense for Bronco Sue. Before a packed house, the prosecution presented what was generally regarded as an unshakable case. Sue, according to the district attorney, had taken Black for all that he was

[8] *Ibid.*, April 3, 1886.
[9] *Ibid.*, November 27, 1883.

Mesilla

"As the leading town in the valley, Mesilla was the judicial center for federal, territorial, and county courts."

Las Cruces

"*Las Cruces . . . drawing the commercial, political, and social leaders of the region . . . became the county seat.*"

worth; after she had taken all his money and had gained title to his Peñasco ranch and the Socorro saloon, this "despicable wretch" took even the life of Robert Black in a cold, calculated, premeditated fashion. Fountain made his points, too. Black had the reputation of being a drunkard, and in his pleading the Colonel appealed to the jury's sense of gallantry—here a weak female, attacked by a powerful, drunken fiend armed with an axe, clearly set on doing her in, did what any woman with spunk would do. She defended herself. Hammering on the self-defense theme and reminding the jurors that, regardless of the reputation of the accused, Sue Dawson was still a woman proved the winning strategy. The jury, out five minutes, returned with the verdict, "Not guilty!" The Colonel salved his conscience and compulsion for law and order by having a long talk with Sue Dawson after her trial. His persuasiveness rid the territory of a disturbing influence, for she left for Arizona the next day, never to return to New Mexico. The *Republican* noted the trial's outcome by this cursory reference, "Sue Dawson was acquitted of the murder of Robert Black by a Grant County jury; it was a great legal victory for her attorney, Colonel Fountain."[10]

Because of his overwhelming record as a winning defense attorney, Fountain was courted by the prosecution, too, and in certain difficult or sensational cases like John Kinney's trial, he joined with the district attorney to prosecute offenders. Most of his prosecution work, however, was for the federal government. Beginning in 1882 and off and on for twelve years, Fountain held the appointment of special United States district attorney. In the early years, assignments under this appointment required little effort on his part, consisting primarily of investigating violations of postal laws and prosecuting indictments against persons charged with selling liquor to Mescaleros or with thefts of stock from the Apache reservation.

Then about 1884, nesters and ranchmen entered New Mexico in greatly increasing numbers, and a furious contest developed for control of the land and water. All sorts of imaginative schemes

[10] *Ibid.*, December 18, 1886.

were used to grab huge chunks of the public domain. After appropriating the better-watered public domain ranges, cattlemen began to cast covetous eyes upon the river-bottom plots of the timid Mexican settlers. Many of these little farms had been established long before the American occupation, but the new Anglo law was difficult to understand, and few Mexicans had taken the trouble to perfect their titles under United States land laws. A bit of bullying by rough-talking, gun-brandishing cattle company riders generally was enough to flush a Mexican settler from his land, and the stockmen took it over by having their cowboys file for the property under the land laws of the United States. Some Mexicans overcame their timidity and demanded relief from this extortion and intimidation.

Since Fountain's duties as federal attorney included protecting bona fide settlers in their land claims, he was assigned to investigate and prosecute a number of these Mexican displacements— his most difficult and famous one being the Gonzales' case. For over twenty years Gregorio Gonzales had farmed a quarter section on Bonito Creek near Contrecio. He had kept the *acequias* clean and in operating order, developed a grain field, vegetable patch, and small orchard, and, in common with other Mexican farmers along the Bonito, lived in the tiny village or *placita* of Contrecio, walking out to his farm each day. When the area which included his farm was surveyed, Gonzales furnished the United States Land Office at Las Cruces with survey notes and, not understanding a word of English, thought there was no necessity of filing additional papers to prefect his title to the property.

The water on Gonzales' place made it desirable as a ranch site, and in 1885, Charley Roberts, a rider for a cattle company operating near Contrecio, filed on Gonzales' quarter section, claiming that the Mexican was not resident on the claim as required by the United States land laws. Gonzales was driven away and a herd of cattle was turned loose in his fields. Gonzales protested and Fountain was assigned to the case. His investigation showed that Roberts had not complied with the pre-emption law requirement concerning continued residence; had not constructed the prescribed house on the claim, but had simply attached a crude shed to an existing structure; and that Roberts had made no improvements or cultivated no land, instead using the claim as a pasture for his employer's cattle.[11]

Defending Gonzales' right to the claim, Fountain recommended that "the condition of the country and the habits of the Mexican people" be considered when making a decision in claim contests of this sort. His argument had weight with land office officials, for during July, 1886, the commissioner of the General Land Office ruled that "it is almost the universal custom of the Mexicans in this neighborhood and in all southern New Mexico, owing to being overrun with hostile Indians, to build small settlements where perhaps a dozen or more families reside for mutual protection, while they cultivate land at some distance from these little 'plazas' and that under such circumstances actual residence on the land is rendered almost impossible. I am of the opinion that the filing of Roberts was improperly allowed, that he has acted in bad faith, has failed to comply with the requirements of the law as to cultivating and improving the land, and that Gonzales' entry should be allowed."[12]

Fountain became so involved in land fraud investigations that his private practice suffered, and, finding the $1,800 annual salary insufficient to support his growing family, he decided during 1886 to resign as federal attorney. In asking Attorney General Garland to relieve him of his federal duties, Fountain explained that in fairness to his wife and children he was compelled to resign and devote his full time to private practice which very often provided "fees of $5,000 to $10,000 for services of far less value," and which required considerably less time than that he was putting into his federal practice which netted him only $1,800 a year.[13]

President Cleveland's Democratic administration was committed to a reform program, and one of his appointees, William

[11] *Lone Star*, February 20, 1884, and *Rio Grande Republican*, May 8, 1886.
[12] *Rio Grande Republican*, September 11, 1886.
[13] Fountain to Garland, Las Cruces, November 30, 1887. Records Relating to Service of Albert J. Fountain in New Mexico, Record Group No. 60, General Records of the Department of Justice, National Archives. (hereafter RG 60, NA).

A. J. Sparks, commissioner of the General Land Office, taking the reform pledges seriously, undertook to recapture that part of the western public domain appropriated by the "rich land grabbers" and restore it to those people whom Congress had intended to have the lands in the first place—the poor, deserving home-steaders. To accomplish this, Sparks asked the attorney general to have his district attorneys investigate and prosecute illegal entries on the public domain.

Thomas Smith, district attorney for New Mexico with head-quarters at Santa Fe, went to work on the "land grabbers" in his jurisdiction, and finding every sort of violation, he presented his investigations to a federal grand jury at Santa Fe. In reporting his failure to obtain a single indictment, Smith wrote Attorney General Garland: "I regret to report to you that the grand jury of this district has evinced the most determined opposition to the prose-cution of land grabbers and has recklessly against their oath and the evidence peremptorily refused to find indictments." Smith went on to say that he hoped for a "more favorable disposition of the grand jury at Las Cruces," but remembering the fate of the land fraud findings presented to the Santa Fe grand jury, he warned that not much could be expected since "the influence ex-erted to deter or persuade from proper action will be immense."[14]

Concerning his lack of success in obtaining indictments from grand juries, Smith explained to Garland: "You are doubtless ap-prised that the majority of the population of this territory are viciously antagonistic for palpable reasons, to the investigation of these frauds . . . . The jury system has not been regarded here with the sanctity essential to fairness and justice—and to control the juries by outside means is a practice that has prevailed so long that it is expected; a custom so continuously observed for years that it will not be easy to supplant it."[15]

As the time for convening the federal grand jury at Las Cruces approached, Smith warned the attorney general that a "strong combination has been formed to defeat the government" in its

14 Smith to Garland, Santa Fe, February 19, 1886. RG 60, NA.
15 Smith to Garland, Santa Fe, March 2, 1886. RG 60, NA.

attempt to obtain indictments against known violations of the federal land laws, and he claimed that there was only one man in all New Mexico Territory who could handle the grand jury and manage indictments for the government's case against the "land grabbers"—Colonel Albert J. Fountain. Smith was aware of the anomaly of a Democratic administration appointing a leading New Mexico Republican to high office, but he declared that this was a time of crisis and party interests should be relegated to the public good; Fountain was needed, according to the District Attorney, not only because of his earlier work on land fraud investigations, but, more important in the present instance, because his "skill as a criminal lawyer and his considerable influence with the juries of this section" were the only hope of the government in obtaining indictments.[16]

Once Smith obtained authority to appoint Fountain, he had to persuade the Colonel to accept the post he had only recently resigned. This was not easy, but after making an extended appeal to Fountain's sense of public duty and pointing to his record of suppressing lawlessness, the District Attorney won out. Fountain went to work preparing the indictments with the vigor, imagination, and precision which characterized his devastating military campaigns. Tirelessly interrogating, piecing together shreds of information gathered from all points and persons contacted, investigating every lead and relentlessly pursuing evidence and witnesses all over New Mexico, Arizona, and deep into Mexico, he was able to make stunning revelations concerning the bold schemes of the so-called San Marcial Ring, and some "unexpected frauds" besides.[17]

Fountain's investigation disclosed that a land company composed of thirteen members, headed by a Terrence Mullen, had been formed at San Marcial for the purpose of gaining title to a valuable tract of land in Socorro County. Once clear title had been obtained, the company was under contract to sell the land to Milo Smith of Denver for $40,000. Each of the thirteen members

[16] *Ibid.*
[17] Fountain to Garland, Las Cruces, October 31, 1887. RG 60, NA.

filed on a quarter section of public land in the designated tract, their entries recorded at the United States Land Office at Las Cruces. The company, Fountain showed, had an "in" with the office since two of the ring members, L. M. Lampton and Sam Biggs, were deputy United States land surveyors who lived at Las Cruces and were attached to this land office. The Colonel's report read: "Their part in it was to work the matter through the United States Land Office at Las Cruces, for which they were to receive one-sixth of the proceeds." Fountain designated Terrence Mullen as the originator of the scheme and the head of the company, who had a "small, uninhabitable log house worth about $20 built on each claim. No other improvement was made." Fountain charged that the thirteen members had never resided on the land for which they filed; some of them had never seen the land. Yet, each appeared as a witness for the other at the Las Cruces Land Office and made affidavit of continued residence, improvements made, and other requirements met, and when final receipts were issued by land office officials, the company members at once sold the thirteen homesteads to Smith for $40,000.[18]

The land company officers included a secretary, G. J. Garvin, who kept the files of company business and a set of books on fiscal transactions. Fountain especially wanted Garvin and his papers, but the San Marcial Land Company secretary had disappeared. At Deming, Fountain picked up his trail, tenaciously stuck to it, and finally located him at a small Mexican town in middle Chihuahua. The Colonel persuaded Garvin to bring his files and to accompany him to Las Cruces. Garvin became a willing prosecution witness and told all. His revelations and Fountain's evidence were so persuasive that the federal grand jury, much to the surprise of Smith, indicted all thirteen members of the San Marcial Land Company. Fifty indictments, including charges of conspiracy, perjury in making homestead entries, and perjury as witnesses for each other, were accepted as the basis for arraignment and subsequent prosecution.[19]

[18] Fountain to Garland, Las Cruces, November 30, 1887. RG 60, NA.
[19] *Ibid.*

The "unexpected frauds" came incidentally from Fountain's investigation of the San Marcial Land Company and involved the integrity of public land surveys. Lampton and Biggs, already implicated with the San Marcial Ring, held commissions as deputy United States land surveyors. Under a contract with the Surveyor General to survey large tracts of public land in New Mexico Territory, they submitted field notes describing the completed surveys, accompanied by affidavits verifying that the work had been accomplished; whereupon they were paid by the government as specified in their contract. Fountain charged that "there had never been a survey, the whole thing was a fraud, the field notes were fabricated in the office of Lampton and Biggs at Las Cruces, the chainmen and axemen were fictitious persons, their pretended affidavits were forgeries." The affidavits purported to have been executed before one Robert Mitchell, a notary public. Fountain could find no such person, and he claimed that Lampton and Biggs were "Robert Mitchell." When the Colonel dropped this bombshell before the federal grand jury, he capped his presentation by offering in evidence a notarial seal he had obtained from Lampton and Biggs's office—the device bore the name "Robert Mitchell." The grand jury brought forth eight forgery indictments against Lampton and Biggs.[20]

The San Marcial Ring indictments were prosecuted during the 1886 and 1887 terms. If Fountain had to work like a Trojan to coax indictments from the federal grand jury—thus assuring the government's day in court against the so-called "land grabbers"— once the accused were brought to trial, he had to put forth even greater effort, possibly the greatest of his entire legal career, to achieve conviction. Fountain explained to Attorney General Garland why he believed the prospects for the government's cause against the San Marcial Ring looked so bleak: "I have to contend with the ablest legal talent in the West. For nearly a quarter of a century I have practiced as an advocate in this Territory and adjacent states and territories. During that period I have tried, either for the prosecution or the defense, all the important crim-

20 *Ibid.*

inal cases, with very few exceptions, that have been tried in the Southwest. Yet, I have never before been called upon to encounter such an array of able counsel in any one case—as have been retained by the defense in these cases."[21]

This "array of able counsel" retained by the ring members included Tom Catron and W. T. Thornton, ranked, along with Fountain, as having no peers among the bar of the Southwest. These high-priced Santa Fe attorneys came into the San Marcial cases with a sustained record of having won for their clients either acquittals or greatly reduced sentences. Fountain had persuasive evidence and Garvin as witness. But he knew only too well that Catron especially was famous for literally tearing prosecution witnesses to pieces, confusing them with circuitous examination, and searching their past for embarrassing episodes which might weaken their value as a voice for the prosecution.

Facing the very real prospect that Garvin might break down or become utterly confused, Fountain decided to attempt a coup to counter the anticipated efforts of defense counsel. After he had studied the prisoner list and reflected on the character of each, he called Sam Biggs for first trial. His strategy worked perfectly. Before a shocked courtroom and chagrined battery of defense attorneys, Biggs not only pleaded guilty on all counts, including the false survey charges, but he admitted his role in the San Marcial Land Company conspiracy as well. Biggs's untimely capitulation demoralized the prisoner list, and, as Fountain had hoped, the jury did not fail to make the inference of association.[22]

Lampton and Mullen were the hardshells of the group. Their attorneys won regular continuances for them, and each succeeding session their chances of avoiding trial appeared to improve. Fountain refused to give up, and finally won a guilty verdict against Lampton at the autumn, 1886, term on the fraudulent survey charge; but before he could continue the conspiracy charge at the spring, 1887, term, Lampton died. A curious epitaph appeared in

[21] *Ibid.*
[22] *Ibid.*

District Court Clerk W. J. Joblin's docket notes: "Death of defendant suggests cause abates as to him."[23]

Only the alleged mastermind behind the San Marcial ring, Terrence Mullen, remained. His attorneys had been able to manage delays through technical questions and continuances into the fall term of court, 1887. Fountain was convinced that he would be a tough man to break. Mullen's future prospects seemed so bright that he had taken on what the Colonel identified as an almost haughty, invincible air. Fountain had been at work on Mullen's background searching for some break which might unnerve him, and on the third day of Mullen's October trial, he hit the prisoner with a line of questioning which opened the way for conviction. The incident was reported as "startling" by the *Republican*: "A startling episode occurred in United States court last Monday, during the trial of Terrence Mullen for perjury. During the progress of the trial Col. Fountain . . . propounded the following question to Mr. Mullen, who himself was upon the witness stand: 'were not you, Terrence Mullen, now testifying as a witness in this case, indicted, tried and convicted in the criminal court of Sangamon county, in the state of Illinois . . . for the crime of attempting to steal the remains of the late President Lincoln, and did you not serve a term of imprisonment in . . . the state of Illinois under sentence of said court, upon said conviction?' to which Mr. Mullen answered, 'Yes.' The sensation created in the court room by this question and answer can better be imagined than described."[24]

Mullen's attorneys won a continuance to the spring, 1888, term for their client, but the end was in sight. On April 21, the jury brought in a verdict of guilty of perjury, and Mullen was sentenced to a three-year term at hard labor and a fine of $1,000. Thus Fountain had bested the territory's most "overwhelming array of able counsel," but, though victory was sweet, it bore bitter fruit. The

[23] Docket Notes for 1886 Term, Third Judicial District, New Mexico Territory. RG 60, NA.

[24] *Rio Grande Republican*, October 15, 1887.

Colonel's vigorous exposure and prosecution of the "land grab-bers" had involved men of power, and unwittingly he added names to his growing list of enemies.[25]

25 *Ibid.*, April 28, 1888.

CHAPTER XI

The Boomer

WITH ALL HIS VARIED INTERESTS, Fountain's primary concern and greatest pride was his family. For him, Mariana continued a vivacious, satisfying young lover who inspired from him a swain's affection and attention; and her regular presentation of sons and daughters only increased his devotion. Shortly after the Fountains returned to Mesilla, Albert, Thomas, Edward, Maggie, and Marianita were joined by John; then came the adorable Fannie, fair like her father and spoiled to a sin; and Catarina, lovable and mysteriously quiet. Mariana's childbearing days ended shortly after their twenty-fifth anniversary when she presented her husband a son—Henry.

Fountain saw to it that his children received the best education the territory could offer. From the Mesilla parochial school, each child was enrolled in the Convent Academy of the Sisters of Mercy at Las Cruces. The girls continued their education at the exclusive and expensive Loretto Academy at Las Vegas, while the sons read law in their father's office and worked as clerks for other attorneys. Albert showed the greatest promise as a future lawyer and was appointed court crier for the Third Judicial District.

Whenever time permitted, Fountain camped, hunted, and fished with his sons. One of their favorite fishing spots was on the Río Grande where changes in the river bed created small lakes. On one occasion the Fountains landed a forty-pound blue catfish, and on another they scooped up four gunny sacks of fish with dip nets from these pools. Their favorite outing was the annual family camping trip to the Ruidoso, a bubbling snow-fed stream near Mount Blanco in the pine-clad Mescalero country, where fighting trout were plentiful.

The Fountain household was a happy, busy place where love and respect rather than strict discipline controlled its members. Learning was stressed, and the children took turns about the family circle each evening reading and reciting the popular poems, singing, and challenging one another in spelling and ciphering contests. Because of the Colonel's position as a leader in New Mexico affairs, Mariana was regularly called upon to entertain, and guests never ceased to wonder at her graciousness and hospitality, and the precocity of the Fountain children.

There was a lively social whirl at Mesilla and Las Cruces, and the Colonel and his wife were much in demand at the dinners, receptions, dances, and parties. At these affairs, Fountain, charming and outgoing, contrasted with shy, retiring Mariana, who was not aggressive like the Anglo wives of their social set. Her life was her home, children, and religion, and it was with the greatest reluctance that she left these for what she regarded as a frivolous evening.

Mariana took particular pains to rear the children in her faith. In fact, the entire household gravitated around her Catholic requirements. Besides devotionals each evening for the children, she saw to it that the saints' days, fast days, feast days, and every other spiritual event on the ecclesiastical calendar were observed on schedule and properly. Through the years Fountain had endured this ubiquitous observance with all the dignity he as a Protestant had been required to pledge on their wedding day. But the religious season he dreaded most was Lent. Even his Episcopal faith required certain sacrifices for this religious festival, but the elaborate specifications of the Roman Lent caused his hearty appetite to languish.

Every now and then something happened to remind the Colonel that the years had slipped by; that he and Mariana were no longer young lovers. One of these was Albert's wedding. Their oldest son had been keeping company with a Mesilla merchant's daughter, Teresa García. Right after the rustler campaign, Albert, a lieutenant in Van Patton's company, announced his intention.

It was easy for Fountain to remember that nuptial scene in detail, for it was almost in every regard a re-enactment of his marriage to Mariana twenty-one years earlier. Promptly at eight o'clock the dim aisles of the old Mesilla cathedral were illuminated; the same bells tolled the nuptial message across the plaza, and the same organ pealed forth the wedding march. Father Morin, swathed in ecclesiastical robes, stood at the altar to receive and unite in holy wedlock what the press called "the handsomest couple that has knelt there for many a day." The lovely bride, elegantly arrayed in white satin with the customary veil and orange blossoms, presented that selfsame picture of youth and innocence as his Mariana scarcely a score of years before. As the Colonel comforted his sobbing wife, he was both proud and sad; proud that Albert had selected so well in his mate, and sad, not only because this was his son's last night in the Fountain household, but also because he had suddenly made the discovery that a span of irretrievable time had passed.

Following Albert, the other children were married. One of Fountain's hardest days was giving in marriage his Marianita—the raven-haired, black-eyed image of her mother—to Carl Clausen, a hardworking local youth. Maggie stayed with the family, but her father knew it would only be a matter of time. Every young swain in the country was stricken by her, but Maggie remained independent and aloof, seemingly interested only in a nephew on her father's side, Albert Guion, of Guion and Costigan, Boatbuilders, Brooklyn, New York, who paid annual visits to New Mexico.

New Mexico was bonanza country; fortuitous mineral discoveries in the Jarillas, Mogollons, Black Range, and Organs had made some of the most poverty-stricken prospectors rich as Croesus, and the men of Mesilla and Las Cruces, living in the shadow of the Organs, were especially vulnerable to mining fever. Even before the Civil War, the famous Stephenson mines had yielded several fortunes in gold and silver. Local legends told of the rich "Lost Padre Mine," abandoned centuries before by the Spanish because of Indian attacks. Some lucky prospector, working the maze of canyons in the Organs and Jarillas, was expected to stumble onto this secret treasure trove.[1]

During the 1880's, a sustained mining boom hit the Organs. Prospecting was brisk. For months on end a steady stream of prospectors led their burros, piled high with provisions, tools, and tents, into the mountains. Mining camps and fairly permanent towns blossomed throughout the Organ Range; Cernillos, Organ, and Kelly were the liveliest camps. Chaves Hack Service did a thriving business carrying miners and excited townspeople from Mesilla and Las Cruces to the Climax, Memphis, Black Prince, Modoc, Dos Amigos, Lady Hopkins, Poco Tiempo, Uranus, Hawkeye, Oscar Wilde, and other rich strikes.[2]

Soon after returning to Mesilla, Fountain was smitten by the mining fever, and, up until 1896, whenever he could spare the time, he took his sons and walked the canyons of the Organs and Jarillas searching for favorable outcroppings, now and then washing gold from the sand with a hornspoon and canteen of water. During the boom of the eighties, while prospecting near Tularosa, he happened one evening to pitch his tent near a ledge of sandstone formation. Noting the principal ledge outcrops extended above the surface for over two miles, he broke a piece from the formation and discovered that beneath an inch or so of weathered material the rock consisted of copper ore. This was his most promising discovery yet, and after staking a claim to the area, he visited several local newspaper offices, showing samples from his claim and getting some publicity for the company he planned to form for developing the property. Seven thousand shares of stock at ten dollars a share were issued to raise money for a smelter. Fountain invested $3,000 of his own money plus much time and energy in the project. When the proposed El Paso and White Oaks railroad was surveyed to pass within three miles of his claim, a prosperous future seemed assured. Then came the rustler wars and Kinney gang prosecutions which took nearly half a year of his time;

[1] *Rio Grande Republican*, September 7, 1889.
[2] *Ibid.*, February 12, 1883.

a local depression ruined his capitalization scheme; and the project collapsed, costing Fountain all he had invested.[3]

Fountain continued his prospecting and mining ventures through the years and found enough placer gold in the gulches to pay expenses, but that was about all. In 1890, he made a strike near Fillmore Pass so promising that he hired six men to drive a tunnel to bisect veins which he calculated cut through the pass side of the mountain. As late as 1896 he was still pouring money into development work at this location, his assay scarcely high enough to pay expenses. A vein his crew struck in 1893 assayed so rich that a *Rio Grande Republican* correspondent visited his camp and reported: "We saw some of the ore panned out. A very considerable amount of gold could be seen with the naked eye. It looks very much as though the Colonel is to be well rewarded for his labor of many years in this country." A week after this glowing report, the vein petered out.[4]

Fountain moved his family to Las Cruces in 1885. He had been considering this change since 1881 when the railroad, long expected by Mesilla, built to Las Cruces instead. With this strategic advantage, Las Cruces quickly eclipsed its neighbor, drawing the commercial, political, and social leaders of the region, when it became the county seat. In 1883, the Third Judicial District center was transferred from Mesilla to Las Cruces, followed shortly by the United States Land Office and other important public operations. The Colonel moved his law office to Las Cruces when the Third District headquarters changed, commuting from his home at Mesilla for two years before changing his residence.

Right away Las Cruces benefited from having the Fountains as residents. The Colonel threw himself into a civic improvement campaign to cleanse this wicked town and bring it culture. One of his first projects was to organize the Las Cruces Dramatic and Musical Club.[5]

There was no fit place in town to present plays. Van Patton's

---

[3] *Lone Star*, February 24, 1883.
[4] *Rio Grande Republican*, August 25, 1893.
[5] *Ibid.*, March 20, 1885.

Hall had a seating capacity of fifteen hundred, the largest in the territory, but it was set up for prize fights and wrestling. Fountain leased the hall and designed and supervised the construction of a stage. He had heavy curtains installed, and then he went to work creating the sets.[6]

While workmen were converting Van Patton's Hall into a suitable theater, the Las Cruces Dramatic Club members rehearsed their first play, a new version of *Pocahontas* by Fountain. "The scene is the Mescalero Reservation; Chief San Juan is substituted for King Powhatan; Captain John Smith is a dude mining expert; the fair Pocahontas, Miss Hattie Bailey, sings operatic airs; the three acts are full of original choruses and local hits. Magnificent real Apache costumes have been furnished from the Mescalero Apache Agency, and Fountain, who plays and sings the part of San Juan, chief of the Mescaleros, will wear the state trappings of that noted chief. The hit of the performance is a song, chorus, and march by the . . . ten little Indians led by Miss Sadie Bowman. The Club Orchestra furnishes the music."[7]

The production was extensively advertised, and culture-starved theatergoers from all over southern New Mexico, some even coming by train from as far away as Albuquerque and Santa Fe, streamed into Las Cruces for opening night.[8] *Pocahontas* was a sustained hit. After several showings at Las Cruces, Fountain's troupe was invited to other southwestern towns, including El Paso and Albuquerque. A scouting party from the Albuquerque Fair Association, after watching the first performance at Las Cruces, had invited the players to appear in October as the leading attraction for the Albuquerque exposition.[9]

The biggest ovation received by the Las Cruces troupe outside their home town was at Albuquerque. The fair association provided a special railroad car and every comfort for the players' stay in their town. Exposition crowds flocked to their performances,

[6] *Ibid.*, March 7, 1885.

[7] Abstract from *Pocahontas* manuscript. Fountain Papers, University of Oklahoma Library.

[8] *Rio Grande Republican*, March 28, 1885.

[9] El Paso *Times*, May 1, 1885.

and the local newspaper declared: "The *Journal* does not feel that Colonel Fountain has as yet received merited praise for the splendid entertainment given by his *Pocahontas* in this city. The citizens of Albuquerque are highly appreciative."[10]

Encouraged by the enthusiastic reception of their first effort, the Las Cruces players continued as an active dramatic organization until the turn of the century, presenting a regular schedule of plays each year and furnishing entertainment not only for Las Cruceans, but for theatergoers in many other towns of the Southwest. Earnings of the Las Cruces Dramatic and Musical Club were donated to charitable and civic causes, one of the favorite club projects being the organization and operation of a public reading room at Las Cruces (ancestor of that city's modern public library). Following the *Pocahontas* hit, Fountain directed and played the lead in "Faint Heart Never Won Fair Lady," a comedy set in the Spanish court of Charles II.[11]

While no effort of the Las Cruces players ever seemed to match their first in *Pocahontas*, their polished performances continued to attract crowds and acclaim by critics. Their presentation of *Among the Breakers* in 1889 was rated by some veteran theatergoers as the equal of *Pocahontas*. In its critique of this play, the *Republican* observed that: "The leading role, David Murray, was assumed and masterly rendered by A. J. Fountain. It is a character that calls forth the most subtle, strong, and artistic powers of an actor. While Colonel Fountain is before the audience, one becomes oblivious to the fact it is but a play, so realistic and natural is his acting. This alone is the true measure of the actor. In voice, action, and expression he was the tragedian rather than the low villain. Had Colonel Fountain adopted the stage for his profession we could have prophesied for him as successful a career as has characterized his distinguished brother."[12]

Next to the theater, the most popular social events for the

---

[10] *Ibid.*, May 3, 1885, and Albuquerque *Journal*, October 14, 1885.

[11] El Paso *Times*, July 17, 1886.

[12] *Rio Grande Republican*, September 14, 1889. Fountain's brother, Edward, was a prominent Shakespearian actor.

Anglo aristocracy at Las Cruces centered around the activities of Aztec Lodge No. 3. The regular weekly Masonic meetings were highly secret and closed to the public, but at least once each month the lodge opened its doors for an installation or other special program.[13]

The most eagerly awaited event on the Masonic calendar was the annual Aztec Ball where, amidst all the traditional pomp and pageantry of the Order, elegantly dressed couples danced until dawn. The Masonic Order at Las Cruces was regularly called upon to officiate at cornerstone laying ceremonies, dedications and memorial services, and funerals for distinguished citizens, and Colonel Fountain generally was the featured speaker for these events. His sparkling oratory could inflate the most insignificant event to an occasion of importance; in funeral orations especially did he excel, coming up with phrases like "Gone across the dark river and into the land of shadows."[14]

Another organization which embellished Las Cruces' social life, especially in the observance of Memorial Day and Independence Day, was the local post of the Grand Army of the Republic. Colonel Fountain had taken the initiative years before in organizing a territory-wide association of California Column veterans, and, alert to the establishment of a national organization for the Grand Army of the Republic, he promoted the creation of posts throughout New Mexico, including Phil Sheridan Post No. 14 for Las Cruces in 1889.

In the days before the Grand Army of the Republic and before Memorial Day had been set aside as a special commemorative period for the Civil War dead, the big patriotic event of the year at Las Cruces was Independence Day. Fountain's cavalry made the Fourth of July a colorful, noisy, martial celebration. Beginning at midnight and continuing until dawn, rifle squads, stationed on the plaza, fired series of salutes. The famous Mesilla band arrived at daylight, and by nine o'clock a military parade, featuring the highly publicized First Cavalry Regiment, had

[13] *Rio Grande Republican*, December 26, 1885.
[14] *Ibid.*, October 17, 1885.

formed. After a gigantic picnic at noon, Colonel Fountain entertained the officers and men of his regiment with a full dress reception at his residence. Speeches at the bandstand during late afternoon, featuring Colonel Fountain, were followed by fireworks that night and a grand ball at Van Patton's Hall.[15]

When the Grand Army of the Republic post was organized at Las Cruces in 1889, Colonel Fountain was elected post commander, and in 1891 he was selected Departmental Commander for New Mexico, a position he held for a number of terms. As the officer in charge of all Grand Army posts in the territory, he organized heavily attended annual encampments at Deming, Santa Fe, and Las Cruces, and in 1891 he traveled to the Grand Army National Encampment at Detroit.[16]

As the Grand Army increased in popularity, the organization's special observance, Memorial Day, came to eclipse the Fourth of July for patriotic expression. Phil Sheridan Post No. 14 made Memorial Day remembered throughout the year. The 1892 program typifies the enthusiasm of an observance at Las Cruces.

All business stopped. The Stars and Stripes floated from all shops, stores, and residences. Post Commander Fountain had scheduled his gunners to fire an anvil salute of forty-four guns at sunrise, to begin firing one hundred minute guns at high noon, and to fire a national salute at sunset. At ten o'clock sharp, the military and citizens' procession formed in front of the Grand Army Hall, the parade consisting of Fountain's cavalry, members of Phil Sheridan Post No. 14 in full Civil War uniform dress, smartly tailored Women's Relief Corps units, the Mesilla Cornet Band, Sons of Veterans, and a flashy drum and bugle corps which gave sparkle to the parade. The procession marched to Van Patton's Hall where a deeply impressive memorial service was conducted. Just before the service concluded, the Sons of Veterans presented to Fountain a gavel made of wood from the flagstaff at Fort Thorn on which the Union flag was raised by the California Column on July 4, 1862; in one end was a bullet which killed

[15] *Ibid.*, July 3, 1886.
[16] *Ibid.*, July 31, 1891.

Captain McRae, who commanded a battery at Valverde, and, in the other end, a button worn by Colonel Kit Carson; the handle was formed from a beam on which Union men were hanged at Doña Ana by the Confederates.

Following the memorial service, the procession marched to the plaza and paused before the Memorial Cross, erected to the unknown dead of the Grand Army, while the Commander, assisted by the ladies of the Women's Relief Corps, decorated the shrine. Then the column moved on to the cemetery to decorate graves. That evening at eight, all persons collected at Van Patton's, which had been transformed from a religious sanctuary for the memorial service to a gala party hall, artistically decorated with evergreens, wreaths, garlands, and buntings. "The ladies were in splendid attire and lent a pleasing as well as impressive aspect to the scene." Fountain called for order and entertained the crowd with a description of the hardships of his march across the desert in 1862 with the California Column, subsisting on "hard tack, salt pork, and coffee," and even going without this for twenty-four and thirty-six hours at a time. Refreshments, furnished by the Women's Relief Corps, included ice cream, cake, and lemonade. At the stroke of midnight, the Colonel ordered "break ranks," the bugle sounded tattoo, then taps, and "lights out."[17]

With all his opportunities for accumulating great wealth, Colonel Fountain was generally in debt most of the time. This was due to many things. He loved to entertain and his house was regularly the scene of sumptuous dinners, champagne receptions, and social parties. His many public services took valuable time and attention from a potentially lucrative law practice. Over the years he invested substantial sums in ill-fated mining schemes. He indulged his children in their every want. He was generous to a sin with public causes; during 1886 when Father Lassaigne decided to replace his ancient rambling adobe building with a new church, Colonel Fountain headed the Padre's subscriber list with a gift of $250.[18]

[17] *Ibid.*, June 4, 1892.
[18] *Ibid.*, October 16, 1886.

Next to his family, Fountain's greatest concern was the settlement and economic development of the territory to such a level that statehood could no longer be denied by the Congress. To this end he had helped tame the southern frontiers of New Mexico, driving the Apache bands onto reservations and suppressing lawlessness through extended militia campaigns. As a newspaper editor he had advertised New Mexico and especially the Mesilla valley, literally, to the four corners of the earth. To his dying day he gave unstintingly of himself to achieve this goal.

Beginning in 1880 and for sixteen consecutive years, Fountain served with the New Mexico Bureau of Immigration as commissioner for Doña Ana County. The primary purpose of this agency was to promote and publicize New Mexico to encourage immigration and development of the territory. Commissioner Fountain wrote and published a thirty-four-page pamphlet on Doña Ana County and had it distributed to state governments and libraries over the country. In his typical indefatigable style, he sent boomer literature and letters to the Santa Fe, Southern Pacific, and Denver and Río Grande railroads for dissemination through their advertising bureaus. He headed citizen committees formed to write laws for the territorial legislature which would encourage settlement and development of New Mexico. Fountain prepared and published maps showing the extent of public domain available for settlement. Commissioner Fountain wrote the Santa Fe Railroad president urging excursion rates for land buyers coming to New Mexico, and he communicated with the secretary of the interior and the President requesting that they urge Congress to settle the private land grant question in the territory. All of these services he performed gratuitously, and the *Republican* observed, "Colonel Fountain has expended more time and labor than any other member of the Bureau."[19]

Commissioner Fountain entered exhibits from New Mexico Territory in every state fair and national exposition that would give him space. The Missouri Horticultural Society permitted him to show New Mexico products at the Missouri State Fair at Lex-

[19] *Ibid.*, May 29, 1886.

ington, and reporters judged that the most "notable exhibit came from Las Cruces, New Mexico Territory, consisting of corn (black, white, and red ears), quinces, wheat, wine, vinegar, and brandy."[20]

At the Denver Exposition in 1889 his Mesilla valley exhibit was rated as the most exciting and illustrative showing from all states and territories. It was housed in a Santa Fe baggage car, "filled end to end and from roof to floor with delicious fruit, golden grain and produce of all kinds from the Mesilla Valley."[21]

Because of his knowledge of immigration matters and interest in the territory's development, Fountain was regularly appointed by the various territorial governors to represent New Mexico at the many irrigation and transportation conferences held during the 1880's and 1890's. One of these was the Trans-Mississippi Congress, which convened at Denver in May, 1891. The subjects discussed included commerce, transportation, finance and markets for western products, irrigation and reclamation of arid lands, and Indian lands. The delegate from New Mexico played a leading role in this congress, chairing several of the discussions and presenting papers on irrigation and Indian lands.[22]

A full-fledged boom hit the Mesilla valley during 1887, and Commissioner Fountain decided the time had come for the region to put its best foot forward through a fair. At his prodding, delegates from Doña Ana, La Mesa, Mesilla, Colorado, Rincon, Tularosa, Organ, San Augustine, La Union, Bosque Seco, Brunswick, San Miguel, and Chamberino came together at Las Cruces in May and organized the Southern New Mexico Fair Association. Fountain drafted the articles of incorporation and sent out invitations to all towns in the southern four-county area to participate. The fair was scheduled for early September, so Fountain and other board members traveled over the Southwest speaking on behalf of the exposition. When he stopped at Silver City, the *Enterprise* identified him as the "gentleman who has done much towards

20 *Ibid.*, December 18, 1886.
21 El Paso *Times*, September 28, 1889.
22 *Rio Grande Republican*, May 31, 1891.

bringing on the boom in the Rio Grande Valley . . . . The fair will eclipse anything yet held in the Territory."[23]

The executive board had premium lists for fruits, grain and grain products, flowers and shrubs (Fountain was chairman of this section), native wines and brandies, minerals, and needle and fancy work. Special halls, temporary buildings, and animal shelters were erected at the fairgrounds, and for days before the opening, countrymen traveled the dusty roads to Las Cruces in wagons, on horses and burros, and afoot, bringing fowls and small animals in crates, driving horses, sheep, and cattle, and carrying the treasures of their fields and kitchens for display at their first fair.

Fountain, as chairman of the entertainment committee, was determined to provide a variety program the fair visitors would not soon forget. The Fort Bliss military band, rated "best in the West," was engaged; he collected $200 prize money for the winning baseball team; a cowboy tournament (forerunner of the rodeo) was organized; and he planned to stage a "Tableaux Vivants" by Apache Indians with war dances, music, and "all the fantastic paraphernalia peculiar to these descendants of the Aztecs." He engaged the Sisters of Charity to run the dining tables and feed the visitors. His entertainment schedule excited so much interest that one newspaper observed, "The Colonel would have made a great showman if he had not been bred a lawyer."[24]

Opening day for the Southern New Mexico Fair was an event the likes of which had never occurred in Las Cruces. Crowds from all over the Southwest and the East, brought in by a special train from St. Louis, thronged the pavilions and exhibits. Governor Ross came down from Santa Fe to open officially the exposition.

The official program for first day included a reception for visitors and an address by Colonel Fountain. At three in the afternoon the New Mexico Bureau of Immigration held its quarterly meeting at the fairgrounds. The second day was designated "Col-

23 Silver City *Enterprise*, July 2, 1887.
24 Albuquerque *Citizen*, July 18, 1887.

onists' Day," to honor those persons who had come on the excursion trains from the East to look New Mexico over as a future home. Special hack service carried visitors out to Mesilla Park and to other farm and real estate developments where a free lunch awaited all. The highlight of the third day was the cowboy tournament, headed by the famous Joe Nations. Ten wild Mapula steers from Chihuahua challenged all comers in the roping contest. Frank Wallace of the Mothersill Ranch roped and tied his steer in one minute and nineteen seconds, winning first prize, a saddle. The fourth day brought the baseball tournament; El Paso and Las Cruces were the finalists. El Paso drubbed the host team and carried off the $200 prize money. The fair closed that evening with a promenade and grand ball. The next day Fountain and other exposition stockholders met and decided that, since Las Cruces' first fair had been a smashing success, the exposition should be an annual affair.[25]

Any frontiersman who worked as hard as Colonel Fountain in taming and civilizing the southern New Mexico wilderness, could be expected at times to have considered monuments and other enduring mementos which would testify to future generations his daring, sacrifice, and great personal effort expended on their behalf. The Colonel has many monuments of sorts, the most conspicuous of which is New Mexico State University. With his unbounded vision, intense local pride, and personal knowledge of what an institution of higher learning would mean for the youth of his region, it was but natural that he should promote the establishment of a public college at Las Cruces.

As the Mesilla valley boom continued into 1888, Fountain called a meeting of prominent Las Cruceans to discuss the formation of a college, his argument being that statehood was near, that the youth population of the valley was increasing at a rapid rate, and that no student could be sent away to school for less than $500 a year. Soon he had persuaded Numa Reymond, George Bowman, W. L. Rynerson, and Eugene Van Patton to serve with him as a committee to prepare the articles of incorporation and

25 *Rio Grande Republican*, September 10, 1887.

to search for ways and means to carry their project forward. In about six months, Fountain's college committee had, by making substantial pledges themselves and raising cash and promises from others, raised enough money to buy and donate land at nearby Mesilla Park for the proposed Territorial Agricultural College.[26]

By early autumn, 1888, it was apparent to Fountain's college committee members that they had done all that could be accomplished locally and that their next step was to approach the territorial legislature for the charter and legislation placing the institution on the list of public operations receiving sustained support from legislative appropriations. The Las Cruces committee, realizing the need for a key man in the legislature to push their college bill, picked Fountain.

The Colonel, though active in territorial politics from the days of his return to Mesilla, remembered his hard times as a Texas senator and studiously eschewed elective office. This cause, however, was too great. He agreed to stand for election and won a house seat. Many new public honors came to him as legislator, including selection as speaker of the house (unheard of for a first-termer), but his primary concern was the Las Cruces college bill which he shepherded through to final passage. While the Colonel was in Santa Fe pushing the college bill, his committee at Las Cruces moved ahead. Las Cruces College, a subscription school, was organized as a pilot project for the proposed agricultural college, and seventy-seven students enrolled for the first term.[27]

Under authority of the Las Cruces Agricultural College bill, a board of regents was named. This governing body selected Hiram Hadley as college president.[28] September 13, 1890, the first cornerstone was placed on the new Las Cruces campus. Colonel Fountain, in charge of arrangements for the ceremony, invited the Fort Bliss band. The parade to celebrate the occasion included Aztec Lodge No. 3 in full regalia, units from Phil Sheridan Post No. 14,

[26] *Ibid.*, April 28, 1888, and May 5, 1888.
[27] *Ibid.*, July 27, 1889.
[28] *Ibid.*, August 23, 1890.

his own First Cavalry Regiment, and a colorful processional of the Knights Templar, El Paso Commandery. Special trains brought in guests from all over New Mexico and western Texas. Governor L. Bradford Prince came from Santa Fe to assist in the dedication ceremonies. Fountain's college committee had set up fruit stands on the college grounds where "tons of luscious grapes, melons by the wagon-load, and other fruits were served free to all." As the crowds gathered for the occasion, the *Republican* prophetically observed, "This day will be one which will always be remembered and noted as a land-mark in the history of the Mesilla Valley."[29]

It was fitting that Colonel Fountain, having been the prime mover in bringing the agricultural college to Las Cruces, should preside over the dedication and make the principal address: "This is the most momentous occasion in the history of the Valley. For the first time in history the granite peaks which have stood through the ages like sentinels looking down upon it, see the end of a great struggle approaching. Education is the corner stone of all free government and in the interest of such government Congress has arranged for the organization of agricultural and mechanical colleges in all the states and territories. Las Cruces is to be congratulated upon this prize it secured from the last Legislature. The citizens hardly realized what had been won, not an ordinary common school but a grandly endowed institution. This means that our children will be able to obtain the highest education."[30]

[29] *Ibid.*, September 12, 1890.
[30] Las Cruces College Dedication Speech Manuscript. Fountain Papers, University of Oklahoma Library.

CHAPTER XII

Mr. Republican

POLITICS SEEMED TO HOLD a mystical fascination for Colonel Fountain, and, despite scars and bad memories from his late Texas political venture, he became deeply involved in territorial Republican party affairs soon after returning to Mesilla. This time, however, he concerned himself more with party machinery and organization and studiously shunned elective office, satisfied for the time to dominate southern New Mexico political life as a party leader, building his personal influence and power to the point that by 1880 he ruled Republicans in that region with an iron hand.

For several years preceding Fountain's return to New Mexico, political activity had been almost nonexistent in Doña Ana County. More than anything else, this apathy was due to the bloody Mesilla riot of August, 1871. Colonel J. Francisco Chaves, Republican candidate for territorial delegate to the United States Congress, and his Democratic opponent, José Gallegos, happened to make campaign appearances in Mesilla on the same day. Each candidate's partisans held a lively rally in the course of which parades were formed by armed-to-the-teeth marchers, and, when the rival columns met on the plaza, the inevitable happened. Nine demonstrators died outright from the point-blank firing; fifty suffered serious wounds; and politics was shunned as a conversation topic in that town for years.

When Fountain returned to Mesilla in 1874, he found that the Democratic party had faded to oblivion and Republicans were inactive. But after a year of energetic organizing, the former Texas senator had resurrected enough partisan interest among local Republicans to call a county convention. When the delegates convened at Mesilla on August 12, 1875, and unanimously elected

Colonel Fountain's Domain, 1866–96

him president of the Doña Ana County Republican Convention, his political career in New Mexico was underway.[1]

Fountain held this county post continuously for the remaining years of his life, astutely building a loyal personal as well as party following, becoming the patron of the Mexican voters, and developing a power bloc which had to be reckoned with in the party councils at Santa Fe. No local party matter was too small for Fountain to consider, and his attention to detail paid off in the political power he could muster in his domain. Republicans were organized into tightly knit precincts from tiny La Mesa and Colorado to more heavily populated Las Cruces and Mesilla. For years his slate of candidates (probate judge, county clerk, treasurer, assessor, county commissioners, superintendent of public schools, sheriff, river commissioners, and coroner) swept every office in the sprawling Doña Ana County; and as regional political czar he handled all patronage and party benefices for southern New Mexico. As perennial head of the Doña Ana County delegation, Fountain regularly served on the powerful Territorial Central Committee and often was selected as a delegate to national Republican conventions.[2]

Once he had perfected the party organization, Fountain attended to his law practice, militia campaigns, and dramatic performances, directing his highly disciplined machine behind the scenes. All went well for about ten years. Then a series of developments began to unfold which more and more forced him into the open politically, compelling him to play a more direct role as party leader and finally reaching the point that in order to retain the favored position of his party, protect the interests of his region, and preserve his personal power, the Colonel was forced to run for elective office.

The first of these developments took place in 1884, and, curiously, rather than the Democrats causing the difficulties, it was a certain element in the territorial Republican party known as the "Santa Fe Ring," a cabal of Republicans at the capital city, led by

[1] Mesilla *News*, August 14, 1875.
[2] *Rio Grande Republican*, March 29, 1884.

Tom Catron and bent on various mischief, particularly that of monopolizing party benevolence for clique members. For a year or so the "Ring" had neglected southern New Mexico interests, ignoring Fountain's demands for public buildings and roads, passing over his nominations for political appointments, and dominating the selection of the only national elective office in New Mexico, territorial delegate to the United States Congress. The legislative assembly just ended, dominated by "Ring" members, had added insult to injury by appropriating $200,000 for new capitol buildings, $150,000 for penitentiary construction, $5,000 for a school in Santa Fe to be under the direction of the Sisters of Charity, and a larger sum for a new hospital in Santa Fe for another religious order. To gain the key Las Vegas vote, the Assembly had appropriated $150,000 for a new courthouse at Las Vegas. The requests for projects in the other counties were completely ignored, and worse for Fountain's bailiwick, the legislators had carved out a chunk of western Doña Ana County to create a new county called Sierra.

Incensed at the legislature's action, especially the partition of Doña Ana County without his prior consent, Fountain declared war on the Santa Fe Ring. He circulated protests throughout the territory charging that the "buildings they now have in Santa Fe are good enough" and claiming that if the program was carried out it would "impose a heavy and unnecessary bonded debt upon our people, and an enormous increase of taxation . . . for the benefit of the few."[3]

For some time the capital city clique had hand-picked the delegate to Congress, and the biennial territorial convention, its delegates cowed by the Ring's oppressive power, traditionally endorsed the manager's choice. Encouraged by southern New Mexico partisans, Fountain decided to challenge the Ring's candidate at the upcoming Santa Fe convention. He introduced his insurgency plan to the Doña Ana County Convention in mid-August and proposed William L. Rynerson, a prominent Las Cruces attorney as candidate for delegate; his plan received solid local backing.[4]

[3] *Ibid.*, April 12, 1884.   [4] *Ibid.*, August 23, 1884.

Next he visited Republican conventions over the territory and won a surprising number of pledges of support for Rynerson. As the Santa Fe convention neared, it appeared that his rebellion stood a chance of succeeding. The day before the convention opened, the powerful Central Executive Committee, of which Fountain was a member, met at the Governor's Palace, and the Ring candidate, L. Bradford Prince, was offered for endorsement. The Doña Ana County Republican chief refused, demanding instead that open nominations from the floor be allowed for selecting the delegate candidate. This question was hotly debated, Tom Catron attempting to table it, Fountain fighting back each time with vigor; so persuasive was he, that the question finally carried. The Colonel emerged from the session late that evening, wearied but delighted in his victory, little knowing the web of strategy that the Ring members already were spinning to nip his rebellion.

The next day the convention opened with formal ceremonies and party pageantry. As the chairman moved through the order of business, Fountain on several occasions sought recognition, and each time he was studiously ignored. Finally, when the Grant County chairman received the floor, he yielded to the Doña Ana County leader. Fountain's speech began tamely enough, praising the arrangements committee for the accommodations and courtesies provided for the delegates and assuring in high-sounding phrases the success of Republicans generally in the November elections. But once these mild introductory remarks were made, he launched a blistering denunciation of the Santa Fe Ring, charging it with "party frauds" and "fixed nominations." He revealed to the delegates how he had "fought the dirty work of the Ring," and he invited them to join him in his fight against the clique's "bogus candidate" by exercising their right as Republicans to nominate a candidate in a free and open convention. Then he offered Rynerson's name in nomination.

At first his outburst stunned the delegates; then it stirred them to excited demonstrations; and it appeared that Fountain had captured the convention. But on the balloting, the work of the Ring to thwart his efforts became evident. As the roll was called, two delegations claimed to represent San Miguel County. According to Fountain, the Romero group, pledged to Rynerson, was the bona fide delegation, while the rival López delegation, committed to Prince, was a creation of the Ring to confuse the convention and to thwart an open election. Since the fourteen-vote San Miguel delegation would be vital for Rynerson's nomination, Fountain made a terrific floor fight for recognition of the Romero group. But when the vote was taken the powerful Bernallilo, Santa Fe, and Taos county delegations held together, and with a substantial number of abstentions—due, Fountain claimed, to Ring intimidation—the count showed forty-eight to forty-three in favor of accepting the vote of the López delegation. When the result was announced by the Chair, Fountain led the Rynerson supporters from the convention and set up an insurgent Republican headquarters at nearby Mottley Hall. There they worked all afternoon composing and printing protest circulars captioned "The majority must and shall rule," and "Republicanism is founded on principle, and does not subserve the purpose of selfish men." These were distributed throughout the city, special pains being taken to place copies in the hands of the Prince delegates. The insurgents hired a band, complete with corpsmen carrying revolt banners, and kept it on parade around the plaza all afternoon.

Fountain's Mottley Hall convention increased in strength throughout the day, and by evening it had pulled 105 delegates, a majority of the convention, into the insurgents' camp. That night, while Prince's partisans met at his home and nominated him as their candidate, after which they were entertained by a lavish banquet, Fountain's rebel Republicans opened their convention with beer, demonstrations, singing, and speeches. Rynerson was the convenion's unanimous choice. The Santa Fe Ring managers, appalled at Fountain's daring and his unexpected show of power, called on him in his hotel room the next morning to make peace, agreeing to withdraw Prince's candidacy and pledging themselves to fight for Rynerson's election.[5]

It was well that New Mexico Republicans closed ranks and

[5] *Ibid.*, August 30, 1884.

made peace, for hard times were in store for them. The territory's population had increased substantially during the 1880's, and many of the new settlers were Democrats. Long inactive Democratic cells, strengthened and encouraged by the newcomers, were taking on fresh life. In the 1884 election, the Democrat Grover Cleveland won the Presidency, the first time this had occurred since 1856. New Mexico Republicans, long accustomed to their party winning national elections and thus to monopolizing top positions in the territory, were forced to retire and submit to a flock of new Democratic appointees from the governor down.

Even in Doña Ana County, long a certain Republican province due largely to Fountain's management, the Democrats showed some signs of life. Fountain's machine checked their resurgence for the time being, however, largely because the opposition party lacked a leader able to tackle the Colonel. Then came 1887—a year that marked a turning in southern New Mexico politics and a year that marked the crest of achievement and success for Colonel Fountain, for thereafter, to his dying breath, he had to fight for every day he lived. This was the year Albert Bacon Fall came to Las Cruces.

Born in Kentucky in 1861, Fall had drifted west in his early life, settled for a time in Texas, and then moved to New Mexico. In the Kingston diggings Fall worked for several years as a hard-rock miner and took on all the noisy, blustery, uncouth qualities of his craft. With all his crudeness, Fall was compulsively ambitious, and, after reading a few law books, he decided to move to Las Cruces to practice as an attorney.

Law and politics were inevitable concomitants, and in no time at all he organized the Democrats at Las Cruces and established a paper, the *Independent Democrat*. Fountain took little notice of the newcomer until the *Democrat* announced that Fall would run for Doña Ana County's seat in the territorial legislature. Republican precinct leaders warned that Fall was popular with the Mexican voters, and the only man who could turn the tide was the Colonel himself.

Fountain reluctantly agreed to run for the post, not only because he wanted to beat "this contemptible upstart" and his renascent Democrats, but also because two significant developments for New Mexico were a-borning and he wished to have that directive influence over these which a legislative seat would provide; one was the territorial college for Las Cruces and the other was legislation to authorize calling a convention to write a constitution preparatory to applying for statehood for the territory.[6]

Fountain whipped Fall in the November election by a two to one margin, and was happily surprised shortly after he arrived in Santa Fe to learn that he had been elected speaker of the house.[7] In that position, Fountain appointed all committees, and, as head of the powerful rules committee, he moved his legislative program with deliberate precision which harkened back to the old days as majority leader and president of the Texas senate, when he had rammed the Davis Radical measures to passage. Although he gave special attention to his pet projects—the territorial college for Las Cruces and the constitutional convention—he did not neglect the broader needs of the territory. The manner in which he worked for the general welfare drew praise even from the *New Mexican*, which had been bitterly anti-Fountain since the Colonel's revolt against the Santa Fe Ring: "Colonel Albert J. Fountain made an excellent Speaker and a remarkably fine record during the past session. He was alert, intelligent, well-posted, and impartial. He worked hard, very hard, for his constituents in the good of the Territory. His influence was great and exercised on the right side. He is a very fine parliamentarian and besides is a very able lawyer. His decisions and rulings were universally sustained."[8]

Fountain pushed the territory's legislative business to completion by late spring, 1889, so he could be free to help lead the statehood movement. His constitutional convention measure provided for fifty-one delegates, apportioned among the counties of the territory, to be selected by popular ballot during the August elec-

6 Santa Fe *New Mexican*, September 27, 1888.

7 Legislative Assembly of the Territory of New Mexico, Twenty-eighth Session, *House Journal*, 8.

8 Santa Fe *New Mexican*, May 15, 1889.

tion. Fountain won one of the convention seats assigned Doña Ana County and joined the other delegates at Santa Fe on September 3 for the opening session of the constitutional convention.[9] Spurred by promises from leaders in Congress of certain and prompt statehood if they wrote a constitution acceptable to the voters of the territory, the delegates happily set to their task, first electing J. Francisco Chaves president of the convention. Before Chaves turned the various committees loose on their special constitutional writing assignments, he reminded the delegates that "this was liable to be the greatest epoch in the history of New Mexico, resulting in the admission of New Mexico into the sisterhood of states." He recalled for them "the trials and adversities which had befallen the people of New Mexico; their long and gallant warfare with the savages; their isolated position and their hard struggle to attain the present peaceful and prosperous footing." It was "the railroad and the telegraph which came only about nine years ago," which he credited with having "brought the light of American progress." No longer, he declared, were the miner, the ranchero, and the farmer required to keep "two men to stand guard against savage Indians in order to perform their work, and there was abroad a spirit of enterprise among our people that justified in demanding admission into the Union."

Chaves praised Fountain and other territorial leaders, who, at great personal risk and sacrifice, had tamed the territory, advertised its resources, and brought it to this happy state, and he vowed "that the constitution framed by this body would be in every respect a credit to every member who has a hand in it; such a one as would refute the charge that the people of New Mexico are incapable of self government." He closed with the observation that "the success of the people of New Mexico in the past under the most adverse circumstances was a sufficient guarantee of the future, and with such a constitution as would be framed, he believed Congress would welcome New Mexico into the Union with open arms."[10]

[9] *Rio Grande Republican*, November 3, 1889.
[10] Constitutional Convention, Territory of New Mexico, *Proceedings*, 4.

It took hard work and many long night sessions, but by September 21 the convention had produced a document which fairly well conformed to the traditional American constitutional pattern—three co-ordinate departments of government (executive, legislative, and judicial), separation of powers, defined functions, and a bill of rights. The proposed constitution was printed in both English and Spanish and distributed to citizens over the territory with the request by the convention that their work be reviewed and suggestions for changes given. Approval seemed so certain that Governor Prince appointed Fountain and twenty other New Mexico leaders as statehood commissioners and sent the delegation to Washington to report to Congress on New Mexico's progress in meeting statehood requirements.[11]

The statehood commissioners were assured that the only remaining requirement for admission to the Union was approval of the constitution by a territory-wide referendum. With this highly optimistic report Governor Prince reconvened the convention to prepare the final draft before submitting it to the voters. Once their revision work had been completed, the delegates returned to their home districts to campaign for adoption. Fountain worked hard to stir interest for the constitution in his district; but in every town in Doña Ana County he met indifference and sometimes hostility toward the attempt to end what Fountain called in his speeches "territorial vassalage."

At first he was puzzled by the lack of response. Persons who in years past had jumped at the chance to serve him could not be depended upon; it was a sad day for the Colonel when he discovered that his long-standing power and influence no longer had a magical hold on the voters of southern New Mexico. Then it came to him how his old following had been undercut. He had been away nearly a year with the legislature, constitutional convention, and statehood commission, and, during his absence, Fall and his Democratic henchmen had busily poached on his domain; his erstwhile highly disciplined machine had been scuttled by Fall's

11 *Rio Grande Republican*, July 13, 1889.

proselyting; and the issues used to accomplish this mischief were the constitution and statehood.

Fountain and all other New Mexico Republicans well knew that the Democrats opposed the constitution, for, when the call went out for delegate elections, the Democrats "under the peremptory orders" of Fall, W. B. Childers, H. B. Fergusson, and other party leaders had "refused to nominate candidates for the convention or participate in the convention," claiming they were dissatisfied with the apportionment of delegates "which they said gave advantages to the Republicans."[12]

Once the convention got underway, Fall, Childers, and other opposition leaders organized a bold anti-statehood movement with party newspapers, broadsides, special conventions, rallies, and traveling speakers scattering dire warnings about what would happen to New Mexico and her citizens if the constitution were adopted and statehood achieved under the proposed constitution. Democratic propagandists reminded the voters of the baneful influence of the old Santa Fe Ring, that mysterious and powerful Republican clique which the general public still held in awe and feared, and warned that Tom Catron and other Ring members would write the constitution and dominate the state once New Mexico was admitted to the Union. When the preliminary draft was circulated among the people by the convention for suggested changes, each section, clause, and phrase was dissected by Democratic speakers who interpreted the organic language to show their impressionable audiences that a Republican tyranny was implied. Democratic quarreling with such provisions as suspending the governor during impeachment, making judgeships appointive, and limiting the state tax to 1 per cent really made little difference to most of the voters. But when Democratic agitators charged that the proposed constitution would validate the claims of land barons to 10,000,000 acres of land, much of it already settled and improved by farmers and small ranchmen, or when they made the claim that religious rights would suffer under the new constitution their audiences paid close heed to every word.

[12] L. Bradford Prince, *New Mexico's Struggle for Statehood*, 48–59.

As a matter of fact, Fall and other Democrats, by callously injecting the religious issue and mixing it with the constitutional question, did more to confuse and frighten the Mexican voters (Spanish-Americans comprised three-fourths of New Mexico's 150,000 population) and thereby assure defeat of the constitution and statehood than all their other efforts combined. One of the most insidious pieces of anti-constitution propaganda produced by the opposition was a circular that Fountain discovered had been passed to every Mexican family in Doña Ana County. Captioned "In Confidence," it read: "All faithful members of the Holy Catholic Church, and especially all of our people of Mexican blood, to whom this sign shall come, are invoked to read with care and to weigh well its contents. We ask of you to respect all that is contained in this paper as something told in strict confidence. . . . A Convention to make a constitution of the new state of New Mexico will be held in the town of Santa Fe September 3rd. It is the declared intention of the enemies of our religion to send delegates to that convention who will so form the organic law so as to force you to deny your children all kinds of education excepting that of the world. The plan is to provide in that constitution that you be obliged to pay taxes to sustain public schools, notwithstanding you cannot on account of conscientious scruples permit your children to be educated in said places. No faithful son of the church, nor any man of the Mexican caste, who understands what he owes to himself and to the traditions of his fathers will submit to this. . . . Great is the danger that this execrable, wicked education will be forced upon us . . . . What they call progress is progress to perdition. Their boastful energy is what they are relying on to take our houses and possessions from us."[13]

Two weeks before the territory-wide referendum on the constitution, statehood forces had become so apprehensive over the effect the Democratic-sponsored distortion campaign was having on the voters that the statehood commission appointed Fountain, Catron, E. S. Stover and Miguel S. Otero of Bernalillo County, and William Caffrey of Lincoln County as a special committee to

[13] *Rio Grande Republican*, July 13, 1889.

launch a massive answer campaign. Setting up headquarters in Santa Fe, the committee drafted answers to each charge made against the constitution and statehood. These were published in newspapers and on circulars and handbills and distributed throughout the territory. Samples of their work included the claim that the constitution was "fair to all parties, liberal and progressive in its provisions, and one which compares favorably with that of any of the states. We do not claim for it perfection. In it provision is made for its amendment at any future time, when it may be determined by experience that any of the provisions are not in the best interests of the people or that it may be bettered in any particular."[14]

But of all the counterpropaganda the statehood committee got together the most persuasive was an appeal by J. Francisco Chaves, president of the constitutional convention. His challenge went beyond the eloquence of his sparkling phrases, for Chaves was respected by people in both parties, and the committee believed that his words would gain a hearing in circles closed to all others. Fountain had thousands of copies of Chaves' appeal printed, attached them to published drafts of the constitution, encased the documents in handsome covers, and had them broadcast to the four corners of the territory. Titled an "Address to the People," Chaves' statement declared: "Forty-two years since, New Mexico became a part of the United States by treaty stipulations with Mexico; that treaty guaranteed that . . . the Territory should be incorporated into the union of the United States . . . at the proper time to the enjoyment of all the rights of citizens of the United States. . . . It is only in a state that you can have the enjoyment of all the rights of citizens according to the principles of the constitution. During all these years the people of New Mexico have patiently waited and constantly petitioned Congress to declare that the 'proper time' had arrived. . . . Everything indicates that the 'proper time' has arrived, and if you desire to enjoy the rights guaranteed by the constitution, and be free and independent, and not servile, you

[14] Statement of the New Mexico Statehood Commission, Santa Fe, July 22, 1890. Fountain Papers, University of Oklahoma Library.

can do so by adopting the constitution framed for that purpose. We ask you to abandon a territorial form of government, and assume that of a state, because a territorial government is contrary to the spirit and genius of American institutions. . . . The Territory of New Mexico has always been made the dumping ground for the political debris of the states . . . . A territorial government means weakness, instability, wrong, oppression, and outrage to the people. It means that you are not complete citizens, are incapable of self government, and not entitled to enjoy the rights of American free men. . . . For forty-four years, you, as the pioneers from the states and as the descendants of those gallant Spanish conquerors who first occupied New Mexico, have, hand in hand, stood as a barrier against the savage Indian, submitted almost to exile from friends and comforts of civilization, and endured unexampled privations and sufferings to advance this land to an enlightened condition, produce prosperity and prepare it for a sovereign state. . . . If you elect to remain as a territory hereafter, your condition will be self-imposed slavery. Your position today is that of peons of the eastern aristocrat. You work and toil to enrich and fill his coffers. He does not wish you to become a state. By becoming a state you diminish his power and add to your own. . . . The opportunity to divest yourselves of this sub-ordinate position and state of semi-slavery is now before you . . . . By voting against the constitution you admit the slanders which have been fulminated at your reputation and against your capacity for self government. No wrong was ever righted by silent submission. No right was ever obtained without insisting upon it. If you possess manhood, if you prefer prosperity to poverty and misery, if you believe yourselves capable of self-government, if you believe liberty is a blessing, if you desire to enact your own laws, and select your own rulers, without reference to those who do not know or care for you or yours, give this constitution a fair consideration and ratify it by your vote. Insist on, demand your right! God helps those only who help themselves."[15]

[15] *Address to the People*, 47–55; and Republican Party, Territory of New Mexico, Constitutional Campaign Papers. Fountain Papers, University of Oklahoma Library.

As the statehood campaign drew to a close, a point that Fountain incessantly hammered on, a note of warning, was "New Mexico leaders labored for nearly half a century to bring the Territory to the threshold of admission to the Union. A favorable vote on the constitution will assure prompt statehood; rejection means possibly a ten, twenty, or even thirty-year delay of this cherished goal."[16]

As election day, October 7, neared, reports from over the territory told of an upsurge of support for the constitution, and the statehood committee became more and more optimistic that they had checked the Democratic avalanche. The day before the election a great statehood procession, complete with bands and described as the largest and most brilliant public demonstration ever held in New Mexico, formed at Fountain's headquarters on the plaza in Santa Fe and demonstrated throughout the night. Similar displays were staged in all the leading towns of the territory, and so enthusiastic was the response from all quarters that Fountain and his co-workers faced election day with a certainty that their cause would carry.

The *Rio Grande Republican*, Doña Ana County's leading paper, was not as optimistic. It pointed out that the Democrats favored statehood but only under their own terms and that their strategy was to delay admission to the Union until the party was strong enough to overrun the dominant Republican party. The stakes were high—two United States Senate seats, one Congressman, maybe more, the governorship, and many other elective offices. Until the Democrats were sufficient in number and power to carry these posts, the *Republican* warned that they would do anything and everything in their power to thwart statehood, including exploitation of the religious issue, confusion through misrepresentation, and free drinks—"The Democrats of Doña Ana

[16] Fountain Statehood Speeches, March to October, 1890. Fountain Papers, University of Oklahoma Library. The Colonel's prescience was confirmed. New Mexico was not permitted to enter the Union until 1912, twenty-two years after Fountain's campaign.

County offer obstruction to all enterprise; a race issue; free whiskey for votes from now until election day; and Anarchy."[17]

On the evening of October 7, 1890, when the votes were tabulated for the most bitterly fought election in New Mexico's history, the certain work of the Democrats in frightening the Mexican voters by raising the religious issue (warning, without basis, that the Catholic religion would be erased by the new constitution) and in alarming farmers and small ranchers concerning their land titles (by claiming, again without basis, that the new constitution favored the land barons who would be enabled to recover huge grants, thus displacing the small freeholders) was evident. The total vote showed 7,493 for the constitution and statehood and 16,180 against, the issue carrying only in Grant and Valencia counties. Even in certain Santa Fe County only 1,068 declared for the issue while 1,549 voted against it. In Colonel Fountain's own Doña Ana County, the voters, intimidated by Fall's chicanery or won by his whisky, polled only 669 for the constitution, while 1,010 declared against it; and in neighboring Lincoln County, where there were many small ranchmen, the vote was 379 for and 710 against the constitution.[18]

This defeat went especially hard with Colonel Fountain. He was in the habit of winning; for nearly twenty-five years he had been victorious in virtually all things; any cause that won his attention seemed assured of success—on the battlefield, in the courtroom, on the stage, and in the legislative halls, he had been invincible. The constitution reversal was his first setback since the Texas senate days. But no defeat could have struck him a harder blow than the present situation.

When he wed Mariana in 1862 and decided to cast his lot on the Río Grande, he had turned his back on assured success, either with family connections in the East or in a lucrative law practice with Greene Curtis in California. Fountain had invested his productive years, years of hard work, sweat, blood, and great energy and intellect to tame this southwestern wilderness, develop and adver-

[17] *Rio Grande Republican*, August 23, 1890.
[18] *Ibid.*, October 9, 1890.

tise its resources, promote its settlement, and guide the territory to a point that statehood was justified. Through the statehood commission he had convinced the Congress that New Mexico was mature enough and ready to govern herself, and he had been assured that statehood would come as soon as the constitution was approved.

But with all his lofty motives, the Colonel had a personal stake in what would have been his greatest victory, for approval of the constitution and statehood would have created a host of new political opportunities and rewards for New Mexico's leaders. So certain was victory that the Republican Central Committee had fairly well divided the top offices among Fountain, Catron, Otero, and other high party members. The Colonel had set his cap for one of the United States Senate seats. Now, all was lost. Fall, Childers, Fergusson, and other Democratic leaders had, by their rabble-rousing, distortion, and misrepresentation, demonstrated to Congress and the world that New Mexico was not ready to enter the Union.

Already fifty-two, Fountain was tired and, unusual for him, despondent. But a few days of Mariana's soothing care and playing about the house with his youngest son, four-year-old Henry, enabled him to overcome the bitter, gripping disappointment of defeat, and he was ready to seek fresh victories.

CHAPTER XIII

The Fountain-Fall Vendetta

NEW MEXICO POLITICAL HISTORY has no peer for intrigue, assassination, cabals, and general conniving. Certain of its periods are conspicuous for strong leadership; others for trickery and subterfuge; the 1890's must rate as the era of violence. The focus of this turmoil was Doña Ana County; according to a truism among party leaders, he who controlled this populous heartland not only held dominion over southern New Mexico, but enjoyed a respected, powerful voice in the total affairs of the territory as well.

Colonel Fountain had discovered the strategic nature of Doña Ana County; from 1875 to 1890 he had been undisputed Republican czar of the region, his party dominating southern New Mexico political affairs. Albert B. Fall's arrival in Las Cruces during the late 1880's provoked a change. The former miner from Kingston, determined to challenge Fountain's Republican monopoly of southern New Mexico politics, pumped new blood into the decadent Democratic party. Fall declared: "My ambition is to see this a Democratic state, with two Democratic senators. . . . With judicious appointments, we will send, as soon as admitted, two Democratic Senators to the United States Senate. Unless a great deal of care is exercised . . . the Territory will be very close, as we have a population which is influenced, not so much by political considerations as by the old Mexican idea of following a certain leader, or leaders, in whom they have confidence."[1]

The defeat of the Republican-sponsored constitution-statehood issue made it clear to Fountain that local Democrats had found a driving leader in Fall and that he could no longer take his follow-

---

[1] Fall to Carlisle, Las Cruces, March 6, 1893. Selected Records Concerning Albert Bacon Fall. RG 60, NA.

ing in Doña Ana County for granted. The Colonel attempted to check Fall's rebuilding efforts and, in doing so, became involved in a feud which saw both leaders vigorously proselyting voters, making political loyalty a highly personal matter, their intense competition producing hotly contested elections, intrigue, civil war, and a score of new graves in the Las Cruces cemetery. The bitterness of the Fountain-Fall political war led one contemporary writer to observe that these two party titans had made Doña Ana politics "a thing apart and of its own kind. Except in party names, it has no connection with the politics of the states. Here it is merely a case of 'follow your leader,' of personal loyalty to some man who has run, or who expects to run for office. Being so personal, of course it is more virulent."[2]

The first episode in the Fountain-Fall vendetta, coming hard on the heels of the constitutional referendum, was the November election for county and territorial offices. Even though Fountain's Mexican following had abandoned him to vote against the constitution and statehood—primarily, he believed, because of the Fall-inspired fear campaign—the Colonel was confident that he could, by appealing to their common sense and long-standing loyalty to him, win them back to the party fold. To achieve this, just before convention time, he visited every precinct in sprawling Doña Ana County; besides conferring with local *jefes políticos,* the Colonel delivered fighting speeches in Spanish to the townspeople, reminding them of the peace, order, and beneficence of Republican rule and warning his audiences that Fall and his Democrats were political adventurers intent on using their vote for personal aggrandizement rather than public good.

The response to Fountain's recouping efforts was enthusiastic; he seemed to have regained his old magic; and by the time the Doña Ana County Republican Convention met, the Colonel was certain that his work had restored Republicanism to pre-eminence in southern New Mexico. When he learned that the Democrats had nominated Albert Fall for the territorial legislature, he accepted his party's nomination, eager to inflict upon the Demo-

[2] Florence F. Kelly, *With Hoops of Steel,* 29.

cratic chieftain a defeat more devastating than the 1888 election which had led the Colonel to the speakership of the House of Representatives.

Before the convention closed, Fountain, Rynerson, and other party leaders framed a daring manifesto which claimed the Republicans to be the defenders of right, decency, and progress, and which indicted Fall and his Democrats as corrupters: "We charge that the Democratic Party of Doña Ana County under its present leadership has become a party of obstruction to progress, a corrupter of morals of our people, an enemy of good government, a foe to law, a disturber of peace and a standing menace to the lives, the property, and the prosperity of our people. We charge that the Democratic Party of this country has fallen under the control of a corrupt and dangerous ring and clique composed of men who have no regard for the rights or interests of our people. That if the public assertions of these men are entitled to credence, defiance of all law, public disorder, confusion, and anarchy would be the inevitable result of their elevation to power. To effect their objects, they have resorted to methods that are abhorrent to all good citizens. We call every law-abiding citizen of this county without regard to his former political affiliation to join with us in defeating the dangerous and revolutionary designs of these men and thus secure the public safety."[3]

Fountain had this declaration printed both in Spanish and English, and copies were posted on buildings, nailed to telegraph poles, and hand delivered to voters all over the county. Hammering on these charges, the Colonel campaigned throughout his constituency, and with the help of a Mexican band, parades, fireworks, and other crowd-getters, he was met by receptive throngs at every town in the district. Victory seemed assured.

So certain were the Republicans of sending the Democrats to defeat that the *Rio Grande Republican* published a pre-election victory statement, advising why the county was going for Fountain and referring to the Colonel's opponent, A. B. Fall, as "a

[3] *Rio Grande Republican*, October 21, 1890.

pigmy and baby beside Colonel Fountain." The *Republican* declared that Fall would be a "nonentity in the legislature—absolutely worthless to anybody. Whereas Colonel Fountain has large experience; in fact almost everybody having business before the legislature endeavors to obtain Colonel Fountain's assistance on account of his experience. He can prepare his own bills and fight hard for them. Such a man is very valuable to have in the legislature."[4]

Wearied by the campaigning, Fountain rested at home the day before election, and as pledges of support for returning him to the speaker's chair poured in, he made plans for Mariana and little Henry to accompany him to Santa Fe for the legislature's opening day. After the polls closed on November 4, runners kept the Colonel informed throughout the evening on the count—every precinct in the populous sections of the county was reporting majorities for Fountain. During breakfast next morning a courier delivered a note to Fountain's kitchen door which told that Fall had carried the county by forty-five votes! The Colonel was stunned, but recovered to attend a viciously contested recount session that evening with the board of county commissioners sitting as a canvassing board, Fall appearing as attorney for the Democrats, and Fountain for the Republicans. With all the verbal jabbing, snarling, and traded insults, elementary arithmetic confirmed the original tally.[5]

Fountain was disappointed, but rather than brooding over his defeat, he looked about for an explanation. First of all, he reasoned that the election coming so close to the constitution-statehood referendum may have affected his margin some, although he ran strong in the predominantly Mexican precincts which only a few weeks before had voted down his constitution proposal. As he studied the returns, the Colonel found that Fall had swept all precincts in the mountain country north and east of Las Cruces. A few years before, hardly a voter could be found in the rough

[4] *Ibid.*, November 1, 1890.
[5] *Ibid.*, November 13, 1890.

Sacramento-Jarilla region. Of late, however, small cattlemen from Texas, reportedly "all good Democrats," had moved in and established ranches in the spring-fed canyons.[6]

As the Fountain-Fall feud became hotter, Fall's most comforting and enduring support came from these settlers, who besides being voters, were, many of them, also gunmen of some reputation. Since their needs were simple and few, there was little that Fall could do to repay their intense loyalty to him. But there was a way Fall could and did reciprocate. These clannish, high-tempered, proud mountain people were eternally in trouble—homicide and rustling stock from the big ranches being the most common complaints against them. Fall became their acknowledged defender, generally on a complimentary basis. In later years, Fall bragged that he had defended five hundred rustlers and not a single client ever went to prison. A common combination in the mountain rustling and murder cases was Fountain for the prosecution and Fall for the defense; and the bitter courtroom battles these rival partisan chiefs waged helped bring their contest for political primacy in Doña Ana County to a bloody climax.[7]

But with all the power that came to him from the blind support of his mountain mercenaries, Fall was not satisfied. He wanted the Mexican vote too, and his victory in 1890 emboldened him to woo the Spanish-Americans away from their historic attachment to Colonel Fountain and the Republicans. And he succeeded. Fall won a smashing victory over Fountain in the 1892 legislative race, and his hand-picked candidate was victorious again in 1894.

As Fountain's political world came crashing down, he fought back as best he could through grand jury investigations which exposed Democratic campaign methods, which he published in the *Rio Grande Republican*. Fountain's revelations of Fall's tactics show that the Democratic chieftain was determined to win at any cost and that he was prepared to destroy all persons and things that stood in his way; that if he lacked finesse, he had abundant

[6] *Ibid.*, November 14, 1885.

[7] David H. Stratton, "New Mexico Machiavellian? The Story of Albert B. Fall," *Montana—The Magazine of Western History*, Vol. VII (October, 1957), 9.

imagination; and most important—that his methods worked.

One tactic which never failed to get a substantial Fall vote was for Democratic managers to sponsor dances in key precincts on the night before election. The voter-guests were plied with "free Democratic whiskey." Dead drunk by midnight, they were locked up at Democratic headquarters, guarded until daylight, then, in a drunken stupor, were marched to the polls to cast their ballots.[8]

At Bosque Seco, Fountain discovered that just before election time the Democratic-dominated school board brought suit against a number of Mexicans for back poll tax. The delinquent taxpayers were arrested and docketed for trial. Attorney Fall suddenly appeared to defend the Mexicans free of charge, "telling them that he was the friend of the poor Mexicans." Bosque Seco went Democratic for the first time in history. Grand jury probing of Democratic methods disclosed that a Fall worker, Manuel Nevares, went about the county telling the Mexicans that "Boss Fall" would have charge of hiring men on the water projects and that "if they did not vote the Democratic ticket they could not expect to have employment on the dams and canals."[9]

Fall's Democratic workers found that of all their artifices, the rumor was the most effective. A few well-chosen insinuations dropped in the market and on the plaza among the impressionable Spanish-Americans in a matter of hours became full-blown gospel fact. One rumor which cut Fountain's 1890 margin in the populous Las Cruces and Mesilla precincts was to the effect that if elected, "his first act would be to pass a bill disfranchising every voter who could not read and write the English language." The timing of this rumor had been perfect for the Democratic cause. Coming on the eve of the election, the Colonel had no opportunity to answer it.[10]

Fall's *Independent Democrat* carried Spanish language sections before each election. The lead article in each issue explained why Fall was "the faithful friend of the Mexican Race." The *Rio*

[8] *Rio Grande Republican*, October 18, 1890.
[9] *Ibid.*, October 30, 1892.
[10] *Ibid.*, November 13, 1890.

Grande Republican challenged this claim, charging that the Democratic campaigns had become under Fall's direction, "from beginning to end an appeal to passion, prejudice, ignorance, and bigotry." The *Republican* added that Fall "now spells his name Alberto B. Fall," and reported that the Democratic chief planned to prefix the "letter 'O' to his surname to catch the Irish vote." Furthermore had he been "running for office in Texas he would have announced himself as the faithful friend of the Negro race, or if his lot was thrown in China he could as easily adapt himself to the occasion and be the faithful friend of the Chinaman."[11]

The damage Fall had done, not only to Fountain and the Republicans, but to southern New Mexico generally was epitomized in a *Republican* editorial on the eve of the 1892 election: "Among the benefits (?) A. B. Fall has conferred upon the residents of the Mesilla Valley during his brief residence here has been to stir up strife and array against each other old friends and old residents by his cunningly devised innuendoes and insinuations. Those who should work together for the common interest of the valley and without whose mutual cooperation we cannot hope to prosper, are now hardly on speaking terms. When the blessed Redeemer uttered that great humanitarian doctrine: 'Blessed are the peacemakers' he evidently did not refer to A. B. Fall. What surprises the *Republican* is that sane men and men of intelligence should allow themselves to be drawn into his Machiavellian schemes by this stranger, a mere bird of passage."[12]

But the thick-skinned Democrats were little concerned with community welfare, good will, and regional harmony. Their preoccupation was winning elections, holding key political posts, and building power. Fall and his associates regarded Fountain and other local Republicans as sanctimonious and impractical, and with the 1892 election, it appeared the world was their oyster. Not only did they swamp the Republicans, but, more important, their party won the national election; Grover Cleveland captured the Presidency for the Democrats. A new set of territorial officers,

11 *Ibid.*, October 7, 1892.
12 *Ibid.*, October 14, 1892.

from the governor on down, all Democrats, took over the management of New Mexico's affairs. For his good works on behalf of the party in New Mexico, Fall was in line for one of the choice appointments, his name regularly mentioned in connection with the post of judge for the Third Judicial District.

This prospect held dreadful implications for Fountain, Rynerson, Catron, and other prominent New Mexico Republicans, for besides being party leaders, they were also attorneys whose livelihood depended upon their law practice which for the most part was conducted in courts on the Third Judicial Circuit. For Fountain and other Republicans, Fall was bad enough as a private citizen and Democratic leader; if he had dealt them untold misery already, then, cloaked with the authority and sanctity of the bench, he could be expected to make their lot little less than bearable.

Thus economic necessity exceeded even political expediency in the movement which Colonel Fountain organized to oppose Fall's appointment. President Cleveland, Attorney General Olney, and leading United States senators were deluged with letters, telegrams, and petitions denouncing Fall's nomination and warning of the dire results if their appeals were disregarded. Republican Governor L. Bradford Prince awaiting the installation of his Democratic successor, William Thornton, wired Senator Platt, "Fall's nomination for Judge is worst possible." Prince begged the Senate Judiciary Committee to "hold for investigation" Fall's nomination.[13]

The office files of Attorney General Olney and members of the Senate Judiciary Committee bulged with anti-Fall correspondence. One of the prize efforts was a candid communication from Tom Catron to Senator Carey: "I see by the telegrams that President Cleveland has this day sent in the recommendation of A. B. Fall to be judge of . . . this Territory. A worse appointment could not have been made. Mr. Fall is wanting in every element of honesty . . . . He is a partisan who would not shrink to do anything. His being allowed to occupy that position means persecution for

[13] Prince to Platt, Santa Fe, March 28, 1893. RG 60, NA.

Republicans and immunity for Democrats. It means judicial interference in political matters to further political ends. I think you
should see that he is not confirmed. . . . If Mr. Cleveland's other
appointments for New Mexico should be the same as this one the
Republicans will have to leave the Territory anyhow."[14]

Fountain wrote each member of the Senate Judiciary Committee, President Cleveland, and Attorney General Olney, sketching
for each the activities of Fall since his arrival at Las Cruces and
protesting his appointment. His most damning report was directed
to Olney. In it the Colonel described Fall as "an absconding
debtor from Texas, leaving a large number of unsatisfied judgments against him in that state." Fountain explained that he had
been retained by several of Fall's creditors to collect the amounts
due and that his efforts in this regard had increased Fall's enmity
toward him. The Colonel added that about the time he was pro-
ceeding against Fall in the local courts for recovery, Fall had defeated him in the legislative elections and that the first measure
Fall introduced in the legislature, and which he drove through to
passage, was a statute "reducing the period within which suits
might be brought on foreign judgments to seven years. When Mr.
Fall came to New Mexico the statute law of this Territory provided that suits on foreign judgments might be brought within
fifteen years. As a result of this legislation the unsatisfied judgments against Mr. Fall in Texas became barred by the laws of this
Territory."[15]

Certain New Mexico Democrats, embarrassed by Fall's roughshod methods, opposed his nomination, too. William L. Jenkins
of Victoria wrote the Senate Judiciary Committee that Fall had
"defrauded his clients of monies" at Lexington, Kentucky, and
that at Las Cruces he was "a ward politician and not fit for the
position of judge," who "acted as deputy sheriff at the polls and
had a large force of armed men under his command in violation
of the election laws of the Territory of New Mexico and the
United States." Jenkins offered other reasons for believing Fall

[14] Catron to Carey, Santa Fe, March 27, 1893. RG 60, NA.
[15] Fountain to Olney, Las Cruces, March 24, 1893. RG 60, NA.

unfit for the judgeship: "In the fall election in Doña Ana County, New Mexico, on November 8, 1892, one Pedro Enojos, a Mexican who was not a citizen of the United States and who was not entitled to register or vote, made application and made an affidavit that he was a citizen, that he had applied for registration, and had been unlawfully refused. He voted on this affidavit for which he was indicted for perjury and illegal voting at the . . . 1893 term of United States Court. . . . The defendant stated in open court . . . that he was not a citizen, that he had not applied for registration, and that his affidavit was false and that he had made the affidavit and voted at the solicitation of A. B. Fall who was a candidate for the legislature, and that he told Fall that he was not a citizen and had no right to vote, but still Fall induced him to vote and to make the affidavit and vote."[16]

Another Democrat and a practicing attorney who was apprehensive over the manner in which New Mexico's courts might be conducted should Fall be appointed, Frank W. Clancy, also lodged a protest with the committee. In his estimation Fall was "entirely destitute of the natural qualities which the holder of a judicial position should have. . . . He is violent in temper and vindictive towards his enemies, and would, I believe, be a tyrant upon the bench. . . . I am quite sure that he ought not to be a judge."[17]

The heavy anti-Fall mail caused the Senate Judiciary Committee to waver on recommending the appointment, but with Fergusson, Childers, and Fall himself pushing for action, the Doña Ana County Democratic chief finally was confirmed in April, 1893. The new judge, whose official duties included serving as associate justice of the territorial supreme court, was not long in matching and, in some instances, even exceeding the expectations of his critics.

One of Fall's first acts was to manage deputy United States marshal appointments for Oliver Lee, Jim Gilliland, and Billy McNew, all lusty young gunmen and Fall's leading partisans

[16] Jenkins to Senate Judiciary Committee, Victoria, March 18, 1893. RG 60, NA.

[17] Clancy to Chandler, Albuquerque, April 5, 1893. RG 60, NA.

among the mountain people. Up to this time, this trio had come down to Las Cruces only at election time to bully and intimidate local citizens on Fall's behalf, to go on a periodic spree, or to answer recurring summonses to homicide and rustling charges, the latter a vexing formality since defense attorney Fall's eternal changes of venue, continuances, and missing prosecution witnesses lent a sort of immunity to their deeds. After Fall's appointment, the trio moved down to Las Cruces more or less permanently to serve as a bodyguard for his judgeship.[18]

Next, Judge Fall turned to Colonel Fountain. Fall's friends in Washington had kept him posted during the confirmation hassle, and he was well informed on the Fountain-led effort to sabotage his appointment. Shortly after Fall's elevation to the bench, the roster of United States attorneys for New Mexico Territory was published. The judge was shocked and chagrined to find that the list included the name "Albert J. Fountain"; he was enraged that regardless of the party in power, Fountain always seemed to receive his federal appointment.

Fall began his own letter-writing campaign to undercut Fountain, and he had his friends write, too. Every official in Washington who might possibly have influence in bringing about Fountain's removal was treated to a recital of the Colonel's past, especially his El Paso troubles, the Mills scandal, and the federal court trial at Austin. But regardless of Judge Fall's claim that he was bringing Fountain's record into the open to show his unfitness for the federal position of district attorney, his real purpose was revealed by a laconic passage in one of his letters to Attorney General Olney in which Fall admitted that Fountain should be removed because he "conducts all the United States business in my district . . . and he is exceedingly obnoxious to myself."[19]

As it turned out, Fountain attempted to resign his federal appointment during 1893, not because of pressure from Washington, but due to the press of his private practice. Several years

18 Deposition of Thomas Brannigan, Las Cruces, November 13, 1894. RG 60, NA.
19 Fall to Olney, Las Cruces, May 18, 1893. RG 60, NA.

earlier he had assisted in organizing the Southern New Mexico Stock Growers' Association. This combination of big operators, of cattle syndicates, absentee owners, and local managers backed by eastern and foreign capital, retained Fountain as chief counsel and paid him well to look after their interests. More and more of Fountain's time was taken up in drafting and lobbying legislation favorable for the association through the territorial legislature and in investigating and prosecuting depredations on association herds, and he had reached the point where it was necessary to give full attention to these affairs.[20] But Olney prevailed upon him to continue for at least a year, and, more than anything else, to spite Fall, Fountain did so, finally resigning his federal position in 1894. But Fall's raking up Fountain's past, adding his own brand of insinuations, and broadcasting this to the world through letters and newspaper articles only intensified their differences and inspired the Colonel to watch for an opportunity to avenge himself. This was not long in coming.[21]

President Cleveland was very sensitive about his appointees, especially judges, becoming involved in politics. He had issued an order forbidding federal officeholders to participate in nominating conventions, political campaigns, and elections.[22] Judge Fall did not regard this rule with any seriousness. It was not long before he had verified the charge made by those opposing his appointment to the bench that "he is a partisan who would not shrink to do anything. His being allowed to occupy that position means persecution for Republicans and immunity for Democrats. It means judicial interference in political matters to further political ends." Fall continued as chief of the Doña Ana County Democrats and played a leading role in territorial conventions, his speeches as virulent and partisan as ever. Each election he was out promoting his candidates and serving as Democratic challenger at the polls; he was ever ready to recess court for a day or so if a

[20] Las Vegas *Optic*, February 15, 1895.

[21] Appointment File. Records Relating to the Service of A. J. Fountain in New Mexico, RG 60, NA.

[22] James D. Richardson, *A Compilation of the Messages and Papers of the Presidents, 1789–1908*, Vol. VIII, 494.

Democratic convention or other party business happened to conflict with his judicial schedule. The Judge sensed his new power and let no opportunity pass to assert it. Fountain endured many a blistering harangue from the bench.

But the Colonel held his peace, making no rebuttals, and the lack of opposition was taken as license by Fall. He became more daring than ever; his indiscretions mounted as Fountain hoped they would. In the 1894 legislative race, Fountain ran his son Albert against Fall's hand-picked Pinito Pino. The Colonel worked hard for Albert's election, not only because he wanted his son to win, but also, because he wanted the contest for this important post to be so close that Judge Fall, desperate for victory, would be forced to make his big play. Things worked out exactly as Fountain had planned. Young Albert ran a good race and had a first-count majority of over two hundred votes. In the postelection battle, which included a power-politics recount session presided over by Judge Fall, his man Friday, Deputy Marshal Oliver Lee, persuasively stationed by the ballot boxes with Winchester poised, young Albert lost—but the Colonel won.

On January 7, Judge Fall rushed a hasty letter of resignation to President Cleveland. This was face-saving; friends in Washington had sent out a warning that Attorney General Olney had a deskful of evidence against Fall from which he was preparing a report to the President with the recommendation that Albert Fall be removed immediately.[23]

The work which Fountain, Catron, and other New Mexico Republicans had exerted on Fall's behalf was substantial. Most of the evidence on Olney's desk came from the Colonel's office in Las Cruces and included several score affidavits describing Fall's use of his judicial power for partisan and personal advantage, centering around the election of 1894.

Ben Michelson's affidavit advised Olney that while he was serving at the polls as a judge of election, Judge Fall "unlawfully entered the ropes surrounding the polling place" and informed

---

[23] Fall to Cleveland, Las Cruces, January 7, 1895, and Olney to Fall, Washington, January 30, 1895. Selected Records Concerning Albert Bacon Fall, RG 60, NA.

Michelson "in violent, angry, and excited manner, that if any one created any disturbance there, it was the right of the Judges of Election to have them removed and arrested." Michelson told Fall he "had not asked for his advice, and that he had no more right inside the ropes surrounding the polling place, than any other citizen." Fall roared back "that he would mash Michelson's damned mouth all over his face." Michelson assured Olney that at the time of Fall's outburst "there had been no disturbance whatever at the polling place, nor was there any disturbance during the election."[24]

Michelson added that later in the day Judge Fall returned with Bart Cohen, led him under the ropes surrounding the polling place, and helped him vote. Michelson pointed out that Cohen had lived in Doña Ana County less than two months and was "not a duly qualified voter at the election, and that it was a matter of notoriety in . . . Las Cruces, that . . . Cohen was not a legal voter, and entitled to vote."[25]

Thomas Brannigan, a Democrat, in his notarized statement declared that, while serving as judge, Fall had participated actively in the campaign for Democratic candidates, that he attended the Territorial Democratic Convention where Brannigan heard the Judge speak several times, and that Fall had managed the Doña Ana County Convention where he served as presiding officer. Brannigan recalled that on election day Fall acted as one of the challengers at the polls, and he heard the Judge "use threatening language toward the challenger on the opposite side of the door . . . and also saw him during the day taking an active part and managing the affairs of the campaign." Brannigan swore that later in the day Judge Fall and Deputy United States Marshal Oliver Lee, both heavily armed, rode in a buggy to the town of Doña Ana to superintend the election there. During the recount which took the legislative seat away from the Colonel's son, "Fall was present at the courthouse with the recount committee," where, assisted by Lee, Gilliland, and McNew, "he was overlooking the counting

[24] Ben Michelson's Deposition, Las Cruces, November 27, 1894. RG 60, NA.
[25] *Ibid.*

of votes and had charge of the deputy United States marshals."[26]

Herman Wertheimer's deposition explained Fall and Lee's buggy ride to Doña Ana. According to him, by noon eighty-four ballots had been cast at this village, about equally divided between Democratic and Republican candidates. While the election judges were at their homes eating dinner, the ballot box was taken from the polling place, the ballots removed, and eighty-four new ballots, all marked for Democratic candidates were substituted. Early that afternoon the switch was discovered, and county election officials were notified. The eighty-four Democratic ballots were later tallied in the Fall-Lee supervised recount.[27]

Francisco Parra told Olney that he was awaiting trial for killing a calf. Pablo Sanches and Pomposo Sandoval, two Democratic workers, came to him just before the election and warned that if he "did not vote for the political party of which they were members . . . that Judge A. B. Fall . . . would send him to the penitentiary for said charge, and that if he would vote the ticket of their said political party that Judge Fall would dismiss said cause."[28]

Fountain reported to Olney that over fifty fraudulent registrations, all Democrats, had been entered on the voting lists for a single precinct in Las Cruces. He submitted two affidavits to illustrate Fall's role in these registrations. Antonio F. García swore that he had been approached by a Democratic worker, Francisco Barela, just before the election and solicited to vote for the Democratic candidates. García advised Barela that he was not a citizen of the United States. "Barela thereupon replied that he would have Garcia naturalized," and took him "before A. B. Fall." When Barela told Fall that García would "vote the Democratic ticket if given his naturalization papers . . . he was thereupon sworn, and his certificate of citizenship (final) was thereupon given him. At the time said proceedings were had, the court was not in session.

26 Thomas Brannigan's Deposition, Las Cruces, November 13, 1894. RG 60, NA.

27 Herman Wertheimer's Deposition, Las Cruces, November 27, 1894. RG 60, NA.

28 Francisco Parra's Deposition, Las Cruces, December 4, 1894. RG 60, NA.

Affiant further says that he was not charged any fees for said certificate of citizenship."[29]

The other affidavit came from Andreas Chaves who swore "I never had any intention of becoming a citizen of the United States and never declared my intention to become a citizen until Monday, the fifth day of November, A.D. 1894, being the day preceding the late election held in the county of Doña Ana when I was taken before Hon. A. B. Fall. . . . Judge Fall made me a citizen of the United States and the clerk . . . issued me a certificate of naturalization."[30]

The Colonel furnished Olney with instances of Fall using his judicial power to protect his personal interest, too. From Sam Sherfy, county superintendent of schools, he got a statement that Fall was engaged in mining ventures in the Organ Mountains, employing from forty to seventy men in his various diggings. Sherfy charged that Fall had "become indebted to large numbers of persons for work and labor done and for material furnished, and refuses and neglects to pay said indebtedness, that his numerous creditors are left without recourse as they cannot sue in the court over which . . . A. B. Fall presides and that is the only court having jurisdiction."[31]

Fountain and the Republicans were jubilant at Fall's surrender of the judgeship, for not only had a strategic Democratic advantage been lost, since Fall could no longer promote partisan interests and protect his hirelings from the bench, but, equally as important, there had been the loss of prestige to both Fall and his Democrats. The Colonel had his vengeance, too, and he pressed this victory for all that it was worth.

Fountain still smarted from the Democratic steal of 1894 in which, through Fall's intervention as territorial judge, Democratic candidates had swept all offices. But with the new judge, Gideon Bantz, Republican grievances would at last receive a hearing, and the Colonel organized a contest suit. While the legislative seat,

---

[29] Antonio F. García's Deposition, Las Cruces, December 4, 1894. RG 60, NA.
[30] Andreas Chaves' Deposition, Las Cruces, November 17, 1894. RG 60, NA.
[31] Sam Sherfy's Deposition, Las Cruces, December 3, 1894. RG 60, NA.

county commissioners, assessor, and other local positions were important, the most stategic office, because of the methods used by Fall to play the game, was that of sheriff. Fall's mountain gunmen, Lee, Gilliland, and McNew, besides carrying United States deputy marshal commissions under Fall's regime as judge, also held deputy sheriff appointments from Fall's puppet, Sheriff Guadalupe Ascarate. Their dual commissions, plus the backing of Fall's court, had imparted an immunity to their depredations— on the range as well as in town. As officers of the law, they prowled the streets of Las Cruces, armed to the teeth, regularly disarming and arresting Fountain partisans, intimidating any and all opposition, bullying citizens who dared protest the Fall despotism, and generally protecting the party's interests. There was one man in Las Cruces they left alone. Colonel Fountain's cold-steel courage and his reputation as a deadly marksman deterred Fall's men from meeting him in an open fight. Recently the trio had been joined by Fall's brother-in-law, Joe Morgan, also a gun fighter and reportedly a fugitive from a Texas killing. Fall's removal from the bench resulted in his partisans losing their marshal commissions, but the Democratic sweep had occurred before Fall's removal. Thus, Ascarate was still sheriff. One of his first official acts had been to renew the deputy sheriff appointments for Lee, Gilliland, McNew, and Morgan.

Fall's method of operation was based on brute force. The Colonel realized that since Fall could no longer legitimatize political brigandage from the bench, the sheriff's office with his gunmen as deputies was Fall's last remaining prop—yank out this foundation stone and his power would crumble, for, without Lee, Gilliland, McNew, and Morgan to bully, harass, and intimidate, Fall was nothing.

Thus, Fountain lodged a contest suit in district court, concentrating on the seat of power—the sheriff's office—charging, with the evidence already furnished Olney and the President on the basis of which they had booted Fall, that the Democrats had won the election of 1894 by fraudulent and coercive methods and claiming that the Republican candidate for sheriff, Numa Reymond, should be permitted to take over the law enforcement office.[32]

The prospect of losing this last source of power made Fall more desperate than ever. It was bad enough to have to face the embarrassment that came with his loss of the federal appointment. The *Rio Grande Republican*, Las Vegas *Optic*, and other leading territorial papers were giving him an incessant censuring, reminding readers in each issue of the circumstances surrounding his firing. Returning to his law practice at Las Cruces, belligerent, bitter, and dangerous, Fall prepared to fight the Fountain-inspired contest case for Doña Ana County sheriff.

Through continuances and other delaying tactics, Fall was able to frustrate the Republican effort to take over the sheriff's office until March 13, 1896, nearly a year and one half after the election. Meanwhile, Sheriff Ascarate continued in office; Fall's henchmen retained their deputy commissions; and an ugly net of conspiracy drew tighter.

Fall well knew that the person responsible for his misery was Colonel Fountain; the Republican was in the ascendancy again, and he had to be stopped, not only to satisfy Fall's personal vengeance, but also because the future success of the Democratic party seemed at stake. To know better the Colonel's plans and to dredge for any bit of scandal which might embarrass Fountain or his family, Fall planted a network of spies in Fountain's office, on the streets, and even in Mariana's household. Her servants and the stable boy were on Fall's payroll, reporting every move the Fountains made, every word they uttered. Chief of spies was a colored Las Cruces barber, Nigger Ellis. Fall's operatives reported through him.[33]

With ghoulish invention, Fall conjured Fountain's fate. Through his *Independent Democrat*, Fall set abroad the idea that his own life was in danger; assassins lurked in the shadows awaiting

[32] *Rio Grande Republican*, December 15, 1894, and March 13, 1896.
[33] Pinkerton Reports, March 6, 1896.

the opportunity to do him in; deputies Lee and Morgan were always at his side, heavily armed, supplying a paid-for-by-the-county bodyguard.

During the dog days of the summer in 1895, matters nearly reached a roaring climax. The *Rio Grande Republican* had not relented one iota on the blistering anti-Fall editorials. The choleric former judge threatened "to exterminate the editor" should his name appear again in the *Republican* columns. The newspaper took the dare and claimed that it had "consternated the six-shooter brigade. For several days a dark cloud loomed over our peaceful horizon, scouts were sent to the Sacramentos and in due time the bodyguard appeared on the scene; the people laughed; our peaceable citizens saw groups of six-shooter laden men congregating about the headquarters of the chief; the citizens looked on, and they positively declined to be frightened. Something had to be done to redeem the situation."[34]

Fountain watched and smiled. There was sardonic humor in these desperate efforts by Fall and his crowd to preserve their favored position. Clearly, their lack of poise in crisis was accelerating their downfall. The people had taken heart. No longer were they cowed. Worse, they had laughed; now, added to the public shame of loss of high position was ridicule. The *Republican's* observation that "something had to be done to redeem the situation" was prophetic. Fall struck back with calculated harassment.

One of Fountain's most loyal supporters was Ben Williams, a constable. Courageous and conscientious, Williams had served over the Southwest as a peace officer, holding commissions at various times as deputy sheriff and United States deputy marshal. Williams was vulnerable on three counts: he had furnished President Cleveland one of the affidavits of Fall's partisanship on the bench which had led to the Democratic chief's loss of that high office (Fall was privy to this); Williams, through Fountain's influence, held an appointment with the Southeastern New Mexico Stock Growers' Association as a brand inspector, and as such had been closely watching the growing herds of Lee, Gilliland, and

[34] *Rio Grande Republican*, August 6, 1895.

McNew; and worst of all for Williams, he was unremitting in his loyalty to Fountain.

Fall sicked Oliver Lee on Ben Williams. Obtaining a warrant from a justice of the peace at Mesilla, Lee arrested Constable Williams for carrying firearms. The prisoner was "vigorously prosecuted" by the Democratic prosecuting attorney. Even though Williams showed his commission as law enforcement officer which authorized him to carry weapons, the judge ordered him remanded over for trial at the next session of district court.[35]

Williams made bail and the harassment continued. Deputy Lee arrested him again on August 16 on the same count, possession of firearms.[36] Out on bail again, Williams, on the night of September 14, was walking along Main Street. As he fronted Desseur's Building three men stepped from the shadows—Albert Fall and Joe Morgan he recognized immediately; the poor light prevented him from identifying the third party. Morgan put his pistol in Williams' face and fired. The constable moved at Morgan's motion; the bullet whined past his temple, but the point-blank blast gave him a bad powder burn. Williams staggered back, threw his left arm over his face, drew with his right, and fired twice at Morgan, one bullet hitting his arm. Fall's shot passed through the crown of Williams' hat. As he returned Fall's shot, Morgan fired again, the bullet entering Williams' left arm at the elbow and passing out the shoulder. This shot spun the constable around. He fired twice at Morgan, hitting him again, then as he turned and ran for cover across the street, two additional shots were fired at him by the third party still hiding in the shadows.[37]

Williams recovered from his wounds in time to face, with Colonel Fountain, indictments issued by a Doña Ana County grand jury composed of sixteen Democrats and five Republicans. Neither Fall nor Morgan was ever called to task for the ambush.[38]

---

[35] *Ibid.*, August 9, 1895.

[36] *Ibid.*, September 20, 1895.

[37] *Ibid.*, August 23, 1895.

[38] *Ibid.*, October 4, 1895, and November 8, 1895.

CHAPTER XIV

The Ninth Life

DURING THE MID-EIGHTIES, the nation's range cattle industry underwent a phenomenal expansion. High beef prices and growing markets attracted eastern and European capital, and small cattlemen raced with the big, powerful corporate enterprises for more grass and water. As the ranching industry spread northward from Texas into the Great Plains, into the Rockies and Great Basin country, and the Indian Territory in search of new ranges, New Mexico came to share in this expansion.

Stock raising had been an important activity in New Mexico from earliest times, but until the 1880's markets had been local, consisting primarily of supplying government contractors with beef for army posts and Indian reservations over the Southwest and, lately, feeding rail construction crews. Railroads came to the territory during 1881 connecting local ranches with eastern markets, and southern New Mexico became an important outpost on the far-flung ranchman's frontier.

Most of this stockman's paradise was public domain, which was a sort of nature-run-riot of rough upland (the San Andres-Jarilla-Sacramento cordillera) linked by ridges and tilted hogbacks to the higher Blanco and Capitan ranges, expansive tablelands, desert flats, and pine-clad mountains. Springs seeped from sandy canyon floors and broke out on the wide plateaus, furnishing, with the snow-fed Ruidoso, Hondo, Bonito, Eagle, and Peñasco, adequate water for livestock if the peripheral range was wisely used and not overstocked.

Businessmen at Las Cruces, Mesilla, Tularosa, and Lincoln quickly saw the profit-making opportunities of this close-to-home bonanza and formed cattle companies. The Felix Cattle Company, operating on the Río Felix, had as its incorporators Numa Reymond, William Rynerson, and James J. Dolan. With a capital stock of $300,000, this enterprise was rated as most promising. Dolan managed the company's 5,000 head of stock.[1]

This was a small operation, however, compared with the neighboring Lea Cattle Company with 28,000 cows and the El Capitan Cattle Company with 12,000. These early cattle companies brought thoroughbred bulls from Missouri to improve their herds and regularly reported an astonishingly low 2 per cent loss of stock. When reports went abroad that the Lea company branded 6,000 calves and El Capitan company 4,000 all in a single roundup and that Peñasco grass produced for the Ganz-Llewellyn Cattle Company three-year-olds dressing out between 550 and 675 pounds, cattlemen in other sections took notice.[2]

By 1885, a fairly steady stream of Texas cattlemen, most of them small operators, was passing through the sleepy little towns of lower Doña Ana County en route to the new ranges in the San Andres, Sacramento, and Ruidoso country. Herds of from 200 to 600 head passed several times each week near Mesilla; the cattlemen who could afford it shipped their stock by rail to El Paso, then drove the animals overland to their New Mexico ranges; the poorer ranchmen walked the herds all the way. In what seemed no time at all these public domain pastures were stocked; one estimate was that 700 immigrants had settled in the Ruidoso-Hondo basin between January and September of 1885; and in the decade from 1880 to 1890, Lincoln County grew from 2,500 to 6,800.[3]

Wherever they went, be it the Kansas cow towns, Indian Territory, or New Mexico, these Texans, a special breed—insolent, high tempered, and intensely loyal—raised hell. They brought to New Mexico their curious folkways, open range ranching, community roundups, and abundant trouble for anyone who dared cross them. A fairly typical settlement of Texans grew up near

[1] *Rio Grande Republican*, March 19, 1887.

[2] *Ibid.*, October 22, 1887.

[3] El Paso *Times*, September 10, 1885, and *Rio Grande Republican*, August 3, 1891.

Tularosa; the leader of this colony was a young man named Oliver Lee.

Lee and his half-brother, Perry Altman, both of them Taylor County ranchmen, arrived in New Mexico during 1884 in search of a new range. The western slopes of the Sacramentos in Doña Ana County suited them, and the following spring they moved their families and herds to the new location. Lee's spread was situated on the edge of Dog Canyon; the choice site in the famous canyon, its sheer, forbidding walls thrusting upward 2,000 feet, was already taken by a Frenchman, Frank Rochas. Lee-Altman clan members settled nearby, they wrote friends back home in Texas, and soon they had neighbors. These included the McNews, who settled near Cloudcroft, the Raleys, whose ranch was on the southern end of the Jarillas, and the Gillilands who took up a range next to the Lees.

These mountain folk were clannish, proud, and poor, but ambitious, the most driving one in the group being Oliver Lee. He readily saw that if his spread—the Circle Cross brand for cattle and Double S for horses—was to grow in this new country, he must face the facts of nature; that while the grass was good, water was scarce; thus the Tularosa country power equation: control of water equals control of peripheral range.

Lee's leadership attracted a following from the Texas families at Tularosa. Young Billy McNew and Jim Gilliland formed the hard core of Lee partisans, and at various times they included Bill Carr and Tom Tucker. The latter had been a rider for the Aztec Cattle Company and the Hash Knife outfit of Arizona Territory. Homicide indictments in Arizona and Texas caused him to flee to indulgent New Mexico Territory, where he was given deputy sheriff and deputy United States marshal commissions. Deadly when sober and dangerous when drunk, Tucker went on one spree at Silver City, New Mexico, which ended with the killing of an Anglo and several Chinese or "Celestials," as they were called. The brutish attitudes of the time considered "Celestials" and, in certain courts, even Mexicans as of no importance, and Tucker easily beat the Anglo-killing charge on that old reliable plea, "self defense."[4]

Tucker drifted into the Tularosa country just before the Lee-Good range war erupted. John Good, backed, some claimed, by capital furnished by Tom Catron and John Riley, was moving good-sized herds on the Lee ranges. The scarcity of water and grass on account of a drought made it necessary for Lee and his cronies to hustle just to keep their own herds in any kind of shape. This pressure on the Lee community, even though the land was open range, made a touchy situation.

Community roundups brought the Good riders and Lee partisans together; inevitable disputes flared over certain calves; and bitter words were exchanged. George McDonald, a Lee neighbor and supporter, was the first man to die in the Tularosa range war. McDonald had been conspicuous in his opposition to the Goods; he was cut down from ambush at the spring near his cabin. A short time later, John Good's son, Walter, received word that Perry Altman, Lee's half-brother, had found a stray Good horse. Walter was invited to pick the animal up in Altman's horse pasture. Walter's remains were found a short time later in the White Sands, a curious gypsum-dune desert southwest of Tularosa, twelve miles from Altman's place. George McDonald had been avenged.[5]

Good's cowboys went after Lee and Altman. When the Lee pack, strengthened by Tom Tucker and a character named Cherokee Bill, fought off the Good attacks, John Good gave up trying to settle his score by private means and turned to the law. Indictments were issued by a Doña Ana County grand jury for the arrest of Lee, Altman, and Tucker. Colonel Fountain was called in to prosecute the trio, and he ruthlessly built his case against the alleged killers of Walter Good. Fountain even came up with an eyewitness, a Negro boy employed by the Lees, who declared that he was at Altman's ranch when Good rode up to claim his horse. Lee, Tucker, Altman, and Cherokee Bill, all heavily armed, had

[4] *Lone Star*, October 7, 1882.
[5] *Rio Grande Republican*, June 29, 1889.

been waiting at Altman's corral for a day and a half. The witness claimed that he heard these men discuss their assassination plan and that Altman had agreed "to undertake the task of getting Good to the right place." As Walter rode up, "Altman and Tucker went out to greet him, and as soon as they had hold of his hands pulled him off his horse. They then carried him back of the corral, tied him to the fence, spoke a few minutes to him, and then stepped off about ten steps and emptied their pistols into his body. The body was untied, wrapped in a wagon sheet, and carried into the house."[6]

Altman's house burned to the ground shortly after this incident. Fountain claimed in his prosecution that the killers did this to destroy the blood splotch on the pine floor. His investigation also revealed that two large spots of blood, covered with dry manure, were found back of the corral. With the blood was considerable hair which was identified positively as being that of Walter Good. Back of the bloody ground stood the board corral punctured with bullet holes. A wagon track led out from the house toward the White Sands.[7]

Lee, Altman, and Tucker made bail, their sureties all Doña Ana County Democrats. As their trial approached, Fountain had his witness closely guarded, but, three days before the proceedings began, "the defendants and their friends captured him" holding the poor devil prisoner until the day of the trial. Prosecutor Fountain was heartsick at the outcome. His star witness under oath "denied the truth of all he had before sworn to."[8]

Oliver Lee had won his first big victory, for continuances and other delays, plus a change of venue to Socorro County, resulted in the eventual dismissal of all charges against Altman, Tucker, and himself insofar as Walter Good's murder was concerned. Old man Good, broken and beaten, left the country.[9] Thereafter, Lee cut a wider swath, and since his immunity from legal process seemed to extend to his cohorts, they were not a bit slow in arrogantly pushing this privilege for all it was worth. Gilliland and

[6] *Ibid.*   [7] *Ibid.*   [8] *Ibid.*
[9] Sonnichsen, *Tularosa,* 39–52.

McNew "treed the town" every time they came down to Las Cruces. Old-timers remembered that Gilliland especially "never was in town that he was not drunk, and he could get drunk the nastiest way of any man . . . he not only smelled bad—he was always doing something he shouldn't."[10]

But Tom Tucker was the bully, strutting the streets of Las Cruces "looking like a traveling arsenal." On one occasion he "made an assault on Ed Brown, bartender at the Arcade . . . and threw a rock that shattered two of the handsome glasses. . . . Brown says Tucker threatened to shoot him, the trouble growing out of the refusal of the bartender to give him liquor." Albert Fall intervened and Sheriff Ascarate "promptly arrested Brown and let Tucker go home."[11]

While his cronies played every now and then, Lee stuck to business, ruthlessly extending his range and increasing his herds. People who dared to challenge him ended up on a lonely trail with a bullet in the back. Ralph Cornell, a Tularosa rancher, and Lee had a quarrel over water rights; one dark night a bushwhacker blasted Cornell off his horse. When the Southern Pacific sought water rights in the Sacramento Mountains, Lee was hired to buy them up. Old-timers say that those ranchers who refused to sell Lee ran out of the country. One Sunday morning in February, 1893, Mat Coffelt and Charlie Rhodius were driving a herd of fifteen cattle to El Paso. Lee, McNew, and Tucker rode up, claimed some of the cattle, and proceeded to cut them out. When Rhodius objected, Lee shot him from the saddle, then quickly turned, and cut down Coffelt. Fall rushed to Lee's defense with the usual results—the two killings were ruled justifiable homicide.[12]

The big obstacle to Lee's push up spring-fed Dog Canyon was Frank Rochas. This tough little Frenchman seemed determined to hold onto his orchard, garden, and small herd of cows. During 1886, a rifleman, screened by the rocks above the Frenchman's

[10] Biographical Sketch of Jim Gilliland. Fountain Papers, University of Oklahoma Library.

[11] *Rio Grande Republican*, September 9, 1892.

[12] El Paso *Times*, February 14, 1893, and *Rio Grande Republican*, February 17, 1893.

cabin, pumped several well-aimed slugs into the unsuspecting Rochas. Crawling inside, he barred the door, drove his attacker away with some well-placed shots of his on, and eventually recovered from his wounds.[13]

But the day after Christmas, 1894, the gritty little fellow was gunned down on his threshold. The tracks of three horses distinctly marked the Frenchman's dooryard. Rochas had never taken the trouble to file for his homestead. In no time at all Oliver Lee obtained title to Rochas' claim in Dog Canyon. The Lee legends grew as he and his partisans, Gilliland and McNew, sometimes with Tucker, rode roughshod over the countryside. One tells of a nameless grave near the old Coe ranch, its inscription simply stating "He called Oliver Lee a liar." Another Lee story was, "Everyone was afraid of him. He was a crack shot and never missed. He could shoot the eye out of a bird in the air and never miss. He was a fine looking man; always a gentleman . . . very quiet and would just appear from nowhere without a sound. . . . It was the damndest thing I ever heard of. We had dogs to give us warning when anyone was approaching the place. We did not hear the horses hoofs; the dogs didn't whimper and all of a sudden Oliver Lee was at our front gate."[14]

With his "to the death" followers—Gilliland, McNew, and Tucker—and attorney Albert Fall ever ready to defend him from prosecution, Lee truly seemed invincible. Fall and Lee supplemented one another; just as Fall was building a political dynasty at Las Cruces, based on the terrorism Lee's gunmen could evoke, so Lee was building a range dynasty with the same coercive tactics. It is curious that the chief obstacle to the full realization of both Fall's and Lee's objectives was Colonel Fountain whose role resulted less from a studied interference on his part and more from a curious concatenation of fate. On the one hand Fountain was high mogul of the Republican party in southern New Mexico and thus naturally committed to thwarting Fall and his ascendant

[13] *Rio Grande Republican,* July 3, 1886.
[14] Letter to the author from Margaret Behringer, Oklahoma City, Oklahoma, February 18, 1961.

Democrats, and, on the other, the Colonel was chief investigator and prosecutor for the Southeastern New Mexico Stock Growers' Association, holding this lucrative and powerful position because of his reputation as a pitiless, unremitting enemy of lawlessness. As events developed, in this capacity, Fountain was brought headlong into the aspirations and operations of Oliver Lee. Thus it came to both Fall and Lee that Fountain must go if their respective dreams of power and success were ever to be realized.

By the early 1890's, corporate ranching dominated southern New Mexico. Stock-raising syndicates, backed by eastern and European capital and managed by astute businessmen, pushed up the Hondo-Ruidoso basin, across White Mountain, and into the Tularosa, buying up nesters' claims for water rights and flooding the public domain ranges with their herds, inevitably—but always legally—crowding the small ranchmen. Many old-timers sold out to the big companies; others stuck it out, sulking on the small canyon spreads, and got their revenge by poaching on syndicate herds.

Range losses had become so great by 1894 that the corporation managers decided to take action. In March of that year twenty-one representatives of the great and powerful cattle companies, whose brands ranged over a territory greater in extent than some states or even some nations, met in the law office of Colonel Fountain at Las Cruces and established the Southeastern New Mexico Stock Growers' Association. Fountain drafted a constitution and bylaws for the new organization, and the members met later in the month at Lincoln courthouse to ratify the Colonel's work. The preamble read in part: "Realizing the present and growing necessity of concert of action among stockraisers, we . . . associate ourselves together for the purpose of giving our united effort and influence to the general advancement of the live stock interest and to the special protection of our joint and individual interests." A sop was thrown the small ranchmen by making them eligible for membership, the reasoning behind this being that within the organization they could be watched more readily, and membership carried responsibilities—perhaps some might be constrained to shorten their ropes.[15]

At the first association election, W. C. McDonald, manager of the Carrizozo Land and Cattle Company, was elected president; James Cree, head man for the V Pitchfork V Land and Cattle Company of Ruidoso, was named secretary; and Fountain was placed on retainer as special investigator and prosecutor. His contract with the association obligated him "to faithfully perform and discharge all the duties to said association which may be required of him as an attorney and solicitor, and at all reasonable times to give such advice in regard to matters properly belonging to said association that may be required of him by its executive committee or its officers, and to attend all terms of court in the counties of the district in which said association exists and to prosecute all offenses growing out of any violation of the stock laws of the territory of New Mexico, and to prosecute all offenders and all offenses incidentally connected with the violation of said laws." When the Colonel signed this agreement, he in effect signed his death warrant.[16]

While Fountain's most spectacular work for the association was the vigorous, relentless rustler roundup which he set in motion almost immediately after receiving his appointment as association counsel, he also gave considerable attention to the long-range needs of the organization he served and, in so doing, was instrumental in developing a basic and much needed stockgrowers' code for the territory. He had already made a start on this as counsel and lobbyist for the Doña Ana County association; to such earlier Fountain-promoted reforms as hide control and inspection and quarantine laws, the Colonel in his new position worked for a tighter bill-of-sale measure, and a territory-wide brand law. Stock brands in New Mexico Territory were on a county basis. Ranchmen in adjacent counties might have iden-

15 *Rio Grande Republican*, March 31, 1894.

16 Southeastern New Mexico Stock Growers' Association Contract with Albert J. Fountain, Las Cruces, March 20, 1894. Fountain Papers, University of Oklahoma Library.

tical brands, and, consequently, ownership of livestock was disputed, which was ideal for the rustler. Fountain drafted a proposal which provided for brand registration through a territorial board. This agency would be vested with authority to assign a single brand for each stockman which would be his exclusive identification throughout New Mexico; only by special permission of the territorial board could a ranchman have more than one brand registered in his name. Fountain, aided by McDonald, Cree, and other association leaders, lobbied this proposal through the legislature to adoption.[17]

Fountain's experience with local law enforcement officers in Doña Ana County had made him doubtful of the reliance honest ranchmen could place on sheriffs and their deputies in protecting the ranges against stock depredations. At the quarterly meetings of the association, the Colonel recommended that a company of rangers with jurisdiction throughout the territory be organized along the lines of the famous Texas Rangers. Association members favored his proposal and directed him to draft a ranger bill and have it ready to submit at the next legislative session.[18]

But it took time, energy, and money to push a bill to passage in the New Mexico legislature, and Fountain needed immediate help in policing the association ranges. In six months over 2,000 head had been plundered from member herds. When the association executive board appropriated a substantial expense account for Fountain's use, he hired a staff of special investigators. His top men were Ben Williams, the Las Cruces constable, and Les Dow. The latter, a Texas-born cattleman, had trailed a herd into the Seven Rivers country during the mid-eighties and lately had held appointments as United States deputy marshal and special agent for both Texas and New Mexico stockraisers' associations.

Dow and Williams rode the southern ranges checking brands, watching for diseased cattle, and turning immigrant herds back at the border if local ranges were overstocked or the water supply was low. But their most important work for Fountain was stock-

17 *Rio Grande Republican*, October 14, 1894.
18 *Ibid.*, July 28, 1894.

theft investigations. Their reports to the Colonel showed that many cattle thieves were altering branded stock by blotting old brands and then burning on their own brands. This additional step further confused ownership, and the only way to determine the original brand was to skin the animal and examine the flesh side.[19]

Fountain's investigators discovered that two distinct rustler gangs were at work on association herds. One group they reported was headquartered near Socorro, and the leader they identified as Eli "Slick" Miller, alias Jim Rose. His followers included Lee Williams, Abram Miller, Doc Evans, and Ed Brown. Besides plundering association calf crops to build their own herds, these men were reported to be gathering up sizeable horse and cattle herds from the far-flung member ranches and driving them to anonymous markets in Mexico or east into the Indian Territory. Fountain's operatives fixed the location of the other rustler gang in the Tularosa and claimed it was headed by Oliver Lee. Fountain wasted no time in moving in. While Dow and Williams visited butcher pens collecting hides, the Colonel went about gathering depositions and lining up witnesses. In planning his strategy, Fountain considered moving in on both the Socorro and Tularosa bands at once or taking them singly. Well remembering past difficulties in prosecuting the men at Tularosa because of Albert Fall's singular ability to get them off the hook, he decided to go against the Socorro gang first, hoping for convictions there, which would, he believed, improve his chances for a successful prosecution of the seemingly invincible Tularosa band. By late July, scarcely three months after the organization of the South-eastern New Mexico Stock Growers' Association, warrants were issued for the arrest of the Slick Miller gang. Fountain reported to the association directors that "evidence of the most conclusive character has been obtained of the operations" of this gang.[20]

Warrants for the Socorro band were issued in Lincoln County, but defense continuances and a change of venue to Chaves County

[19] *Ibid.*, June 21, 1895.
[20] *Ibid.*, July 28, 1894.

delayed prosecution until late November, 1894. When Miller and his gang turned up at Roswell for trial, one member, Ed Brown, was missing, and the court declared his $1,000 bond forfeited. Fountain's evidence and relentless prosecution cut down the Socorro gang one by one. By December 1, his work was nearly completed. Slick Miller received a ten-year sentence in the territorial penitentiary, Doc Evans got off with a two-year sentence, and Lee Williams was sentenced to one year, these three having plead guilty to the prosecution's charges.[21]

Fountain's investigations and prosecutions of stock theft netted ten additional convictions from the Socorro gang, and by the end of the first twelve months of operation, the Southeastern New Mexico Stock Growers' Association declared in its annual report that the Colonel's work had sent fifteen men to prison.[22] This clean-up campaign, while generally approved, had its critics too, the noisest one being Fall's *Independent Democrat* at Las Cruces. Besides castigating Fountain for his alleged high-handed prosecution methods, it claimed that the syndicate cattlemen he represented "could give points on stealing cattle too." The Las Vegas *Examiner* answered that the Southeastern New Mexico Stock Growers' Association was "one of the best and strongest organizations in the Territory," having "accomplished an untold amount of good," and added that it could be said for the section where the association "operates what cannot be said of hardly any other section of New Mexico; that cattle stealing since the inception of the association has gradually become a thing of the past."[23]

James Cree, association secretary and manager of the V Pitchfork V Cattle Company, gratified by Fountain's work on the Socorro rustlers, was eager for him to close in on the Doña Ana County ring. The Colonel urged the association to go easy until the sheriff's contest case had been decided, pointing out that as long as the gang's operations were within the county and as long as Fall's puppet, Sheriff Ascarate, and his deputies—Lee, Gilliland,

21 *Ibid.*, December 1, 1894.
22 *Ibid.*, March 29, 1895.
23 Las Vegas *Examiner*, December 19, 1894.

McNew, and Tucker—were in power, their efforts would be wasted. On the other hand, Fountain argued, once the contest case, which he was pushing to a decision by attempting to overcome Fall's incessant continuances and technical delays, had been decided, the Republicans stood an excellent chance of winning. Then they could install their candidate, Numa Reymond, who, Fountain was convinced, would appoint reliable deputies to go after the county rustlers. Cree was impatient and pushed Fountain for immediate action, urging "We must try and get at that Sacramento gang some way or other. Probably when I see you we can talk the matter over and arrange a plan."[24]

Fountain was doubtful of his chances of gaining a conviction for any of the Fall crowd under present conditions, but pressed by Cree, he sent Williams and Dow into the Tularosa. Williams came up with the first definite evidence. Fountain's report to Cree shows that at La Luz and Tularosa, Williams "obtained positive evidence" that a butcher shop at Tularosa was slaughtering association stock. The owner of the shop was induced to talk. His statement declared that "Oliver Lee and others of the Fall Party were connected with the thieves. . . . Sufficient evidence was obtained to secure the indictments of all the parties by any unprejudiced grand jury, especially in one case of the killing of a V Pitchfork V animal" by the butcher shop owner. Williams even came up with an eyewitness to testify. "We were also able to prove that in a small valley over 100 animals had been killed by these parties. It being impossible to prevent these facts from obtaining publicity, the gang . . . became desperate, threats were made against Williams, myself, and all others connected with the proposed prosecutions." Fountain went on to tell Cree that this "culminated in the shooting of Williams by Fall and Morgan on the streets of Las Cruces. I was anonymously notified that if I attempted to prosecute these parties I would be killed. Of course I paid no attention to these threats. When the Grand Jury convened we found that a large majority were tools of Fall." Williams

[24] Cree to Fountain, Fort Stanton, September 12, 1895. Fountain Papers, University of Oklahoma Library.

had brought in and jailed the butcher shop owner and nine other persons. "Prosecution witnesses were present and waiting to testify . . . . Instead of investigating these cases, the Grand Jury proceeded to investigate Williams and myself. Fall went before the Grand Jury and swore that the Stock Association had paid men to assassinate him, and sixteen of his satellites on the Grand Jury did as he wished. There was no investigation of any of the jail cases. Williams was indicted for murder (killing a criminal he was attempting to arrest about a year ago). I was honored by an indictment charging me with forging a private telegram to myself from Major Tell of El Paso some years ago. . . . The indictment was immediately dismissed by Judge Bantz when it came into court and he read (the jury foreman) a stern lecture on the subject." No bill came forth on any of the alleged rustlers or the Tularosa butcher Williams had jailed. Fall moved for a discharge which was granted. "Williams is still in bed seriously wounded. Fall admits he shot him; the grand jury reported they could not find the time to investigate this shooting." Fountain was furious over the outcome. He closed his report to Cree with the promise to "begin to fight this gang in earnest. I require funds and immediately upon receipt of your check . . . I shall start in person for Tularosa and begin the work of corraling the entire gang. . . . The present condition of affairs cannot long exist." His final line is ominously prescient: "I anticipate a hard contest, one perhaps to the death."[25]

Les Dow had better luck in his search for evidence. About the time he took to the field, the fall roundup was getting underway. He joined the roundup crews and drifted with them northward into Lincoln County. Lee and McNew were partners and he watched their roundup wagon. One of his informants was riding with Lee's crew, so Dow did not join in, but waited for reports. Among the small ranchmen there were rumors that inspectors were watching for burned cattle. Jeff Ake claims he was the first to learn of this, and he sent out word "for God's sake go out and

[25] Fountain to Cree, Las Cruces, October 3, 1895. Fountain Papers, University of Oklahoma Library.

shoot every burned cow you got. There's going to be hell a-popping and you'd better get clear."[26]

Dow's informant kept him posted on when the cut would be made just before the participating cattlemen took their herds and headed for the home ranches. Dow was told that a burnt steer, formerly an **H** (H Bar) had been blotted and a **Ħ** (pigpen) brand (Lee and McNew's brand) burned on, was in the main herd; Dow also was told that McNew was cutting for both since Lee was absent. Dow moved in. The wagon cook showed Dow to McNew's bedroll. The inspector took McNew's pistol, figuring thereby McNew would have only his Winchester in his saddle scabbard. Shortly McNew rode up with the Lee-McNew cut. First Dow arrested McNew, took him to the chuck wagon, and handcuffed him to the wagon wheel; then he roped the altered steer, shot it between the eyes with his six-shooter, and calling on the cook and two cowboys, George Bunting and Lee Green, for help, he skinned the steer. Then, with McNew and the steer hide, Dow headed for Lincoln, turning down McNew's plea that they first stop by the ranch and see Oliver Lee. At Lincoln, Dow turned the prisoner and evidence over to Sheriff Sena.[27]

One phase in the dramatic aftermath of Les Dow's daring occurred at Mesilla. McNew made bond at Lincoln and turned up a few days later in a posse which included deputies Lee and Gilliland. These officers had just returned from the Sacramentos with two prisoners—Bunting and Green. A Mesilla justice of the peace heard the charge against them of unlawfully killing and skinning a steer belonging to Lee and McNew on orders of Les Dow and released them on $1,000 bond each.[28]

Dow's timely work gave Fountain hope, for at long last the Tularosa gang, which, with attorney Fall's help, had been able to defy Doña Ana County justice so well for so long, faced a grand jury in a foreign county. Once New Mexico Territory was finished

[26] James B. O'Neil, *They Die but Once—The Story of a Tejano,* 199.

[27] Biographical Sketch of Les Dow. Hiram Dow MS, University of Oklahoma Library.

[28] *Rio Grande Republican,* November 15, 1895.

with the Lee band, Fountain understood from Dow, Texas Rangers would be waiting with warrants to answer for their alleged depredations on West Texas herds. Cree was delighted with the turn of events. Bidding Fountain good fortune in the Lincoln County cases, he wrote, "Really the leader of the gang ought to get justice at the hands of long-suffering honest citizens whom they have robbed for so long. I sincerely trust you have corroborative evidence and will send the whole lot to the pen and break up this gang of thieves and murderers."[29]

In preparing for the Lincoln trip, the Colonel found it easier to complete his thick file of corroborative evidence than to assuage Mariana's apprehensions. She was grief-stricken over the recent death of her mother, which made her more emotional than ever, and it seemed that Fountain could keep nothing from her, no matter how hard he tried. She had heard the servants talk of the threats abroad to kill her husband; she knew of the anonymous notes—death messages warning him to drop the prosecution of the rustler cases. Christmas brought little joy to the Fountain household. The air of melancholy, of doom inside contrasted strangely with the happy Yule spirit about the town—the parties, carols, and church festivals; even the Santa Fe locomotives carried garlands of mistletoe. Only Fountain's youngest son, eight-year-old Henry, seemed oblivious to the anxious goings on; his mother pleading with his patient but unyielding father, older brothers and sisters calling at the house, and they too talking in low guarded tones, urging, pleading. Fountain tried to make it clear that duty demanded that he go, and, finally, when she saw that no appeals could dissuade her husband, Mariana proposed that he take little Henry for company. Fountain saw her motive. Mariana was sending a small boy as his companion, confident that even the most depraved assassins would do him no harm with a child along. Fountain attempted to avoid this desperate step, but at last to allay her fears he gave in. On a cold January morning, 1896, Jack Fountain helped his father load the buckboard with food, blan-

29 Cree to Fountain, Fort Stanton, December 4, 1895. Fountain Papers, University of Oklahoma Library.

kets, oats for the team, cartridge belt and Winchester, and his carefully guarded dispatch case.[30]

While they worked away, the Colonel told his son, "I don't want to live in a place where I have to carry a gun all the time. It was that way when I left El Paso, and it is getting to be almost as bad here now. One thing keeps me alive and keeps me going is the assurance that if I am killed I have three sons who will avenge my death."[31]

Despite hardships of low temperatures and biting wind, Henry enjoyed the trip to Lincoln, especially camping along the way, interesting landmarks like Chalk Hill and the restless, mysterious White Sands, and stops at La Luz, Blazer's Mill, and Tularosa for visits with friends. Their first camp was at Parker's Well, about twenty-five miles out from Las Cruces on the eastern slope of the Organ Mountains. When Fountain and his son awoke at dawn next day, their horses were missing. All signs indicated that the team had turned back over the road toward home; their lines had been cut; and in a draw near the spot where Henry and he had slept, the Colonel found fresh boot tracks.[32]

Fountain and Henry walked back to the main road and waited. Shortly, a miner named Dan Huss rode up, and Fountain sent a note by him to his son Albert. About midnight Albert and his father-in-law, Antonio García, arrived with the runaway team. The Colonel's son explained that the horses' arrival at the home corral caused great alarm until Huss came with the note. Albert pleaded with his father to allow him to accompany the pair to Lincoln, pointing out that he knew the horses had escaped, not because of panic caused by a prowling mountain lion as explained by the Colonel, but because the lines had been cut and claiming, "I don't think it is safe for you to go alone for I fear something is going to happen to you." The Colonel laughed, insisted there was

[30] *Rio Grande Republican*, January 10, 1896.

[31] Recollections of Jack Fountain. Fountain Papers, University of Oklahoma Library.

[32] El Paso *Herald*, May 31, 1899.

Lincoln

"Fountain had the feeling of being closely watched—in the court-room, on the streets of Lincoln."

Pat Garrett

"Well remembered [was] the work of Sheriff Pat Garrett in erasing a reign of terror in Lincoln County."

no danger, and directed Albert to return home and assure his
mother that all was well.[33]

Lincoln was crowded for the convening of the grand jury. The
streets and saloons buzzed with excitement over the imminent
indictment of the famous Oliver Lee and his partisans. Les Dow's
steer hide, spread flesh side up on the floor in old Lincoln Courthouse, Colonel Fountain's file of corroborative evidence—depositions, letters, affidavits, brand registration documents—and his
persuasive presentation of the cause of the association he represented were enough to convince the veniremen. A total of thirty-
two indictments were handed down. The most important were
Cause No. 1489—*Territory of New Mexico* vs. *William McNew
and Oliver Lee*; Charge—Larceny of cattle and Cause No. 1890—
Territory of New Mexico vs. *William McNew and Oliver Lee*;
Charge—Defacing brands.

Throughout the proceedings Fountain had the feeling of being
closely watched—in the courtroom, on the streets of Lincoln, and
in the hotel lobby at night as he visited with friends. During a
recess on the final day of court an anonymous messenger handed
him a crudely written note. It warned "If you drop this we will be
your friends. If you go on with it you will never reach home
alive."[34]

His business finished on Thursday afternoon, January 30, the
Colonel loaded the buckboard, picked up Henry, bade friends
good-by, and headed for home, stopping after a brisk eighteen-
mile ride at Mescalero for the night. Friday morning near the
agency an Apache friend presented him a pinto pony. Fountain
tied the wiry little beast to the tail of the buckboard and set out
on the Tularosa road. He met a number of vehicles and horsemen.
Several of the travelers he knew and he pulled up a number of
times for a chat. All during the day he noted two men on horseback; sometimes behind him, sometimes ahead of him, and never

[33] Recollections of Albert Fountain, Jr. Fountain Papers, University of Oklahoma Library.
[34] Sonnichsen, *Tularosa*, 117.

on the road but off to the side as if trying to avoid recognition.

The Colonel and Henry spent Friday night in La Luz. Henry had a sweet tooth and his indulgent father gave him a quarter to spend at Myer's store. The boy made a ten-cent purchase and tied the remaining dime and nickel change in the corner of his handkerchief. By an early start Saturday they were far down the Tularosa–Las Cruces road by midmorning. One of the friends they met was Santos Alvarado, the stage driver. He shared the run between Tularosa and Las Cruces with Saturnino Barela. Luna's Well was the midway point, where they exchanged mail and passengers. Alvarado told Fountain he had seen three riders down the road; when he reached a point one-half mile from them they galloped off toward the Sacramentos. Shortly Fountain saw the mysterious trio, one of them on a big white horse. Throughout the day the three riders clung doggedly to the horizon, sometimes ahead, sometimes behind the buckboard. At noon Fountain drove into the yard at Pellman's Well on the edge of the White Sands. After watering and resting the team and fixing Henry a quick dinner, Fountain turned back on the main road. By three that afternoon he was approaching the long cut through Chalk Hill; just beyond, his team would be on the rise which led into San Augustin Pass; from there it was a downhill grade into Las Cruces and home. Three miles from Chalk Hill he met Saturnino Barela, the other stage driver. As they visited in the road, Barela saw the three stalkers reined up on the rim of a hill a mile or so behind and pointed them out to Fountain. The Colonel told Barela that he had been followed since leaving Lincoln, at first by two and now today by three riders. Barela encouraged Fountain and Henry to ride back to Luna's Well, spend the night with him at the stage station, and then ride together into Las Cruces next morning. Fountain thought this over, then thanked Barela, but declined, explaining that Mariana was expecting them and that Henry had caught a cold and needed his mother's care. Barela watched the pair move down the road toward Chalk Hill and then turned to go to Luna's Well.

A chill wind whipped up. Handing Henry the reins, Fountain

wrapped the child in the Indian blanket and stuffed Mariana's quilt under the seat and around Henry's legs; then he buttoned his heavy overcoat around his throat and pulled his wide-brimmed hat down over his forehead to check the icy blast. He looked in all directions searching for the outriders. They had disappeared. He had not been too concerned as long as he could see them. As he entered the Chalk Hill cut, he reached for the Winchester, flexed his chilled hands, and jacked a shell into the chamber; holding the stock against his hip with one hand, he urged the team to a faster gait with the other. On the approach to the west side of the hill his eye caught a movement in a clump of weeds bordering the rutted road. In the gathering dusk he strained his eyes. Alert, ready, his fighter's sense aroused, he told Henry to lie flat under the spring seat. Just as the child cuddled beneath him, a burst of fire erupted from the weed patch. A staccato roar filled his ears. Before he could whip the Winchester into line, heavy slugs tore through his thick chest and vitals. The old warrior's last sensation was that of helplessness, the sound of Henry's shrill scream, and the surge of the runaway team tearing wildly down the sandy trace.

CHAPTER XV

Dead Men Tell No Tales

AFTER MASS, Mariana bustled about the kitchen. Albert and Henry were expected to drive up to the corral gate any minute, for the Colonel's letter from Lincoln, posted the day before court closed, told that they would arrive home sometime Saturday night or by Sunday noon at the latest. The entire family was there to celebrate the homecoming. Henry was the family favorite, and he had been missed by all during his nearly month-long stay at Lincoln.

When the travelers had not arrived by noon, the Fountains, each determined to keep from the others the deadening fear that gripped his heart, made a hollow effort at the meal they had planned to share with their father and Henry. During that gray, gloomy afternoon as each leaden hour was tolled by the giant hall clock, Albert tried his best to cheer his mother, who had become tensely silent.

Just before dark a wagon rattled into the back yard and stopped at the corral gate. Rushing to the kitchen door, Mariana, Albert, and the others stood straining their eyes to make out the familiar, powerful, comforting figure of Fountain reaching to lift Henry to the ground. A single person, stooped and walking with a shuffle, approached the dooryard. It was the mail carrier, Saturnino Barela. When he inquired if the Colonel had arrived from Lincoln, Mariana fainted. Albert and Jack carried her inside to be cared for by the women, and they returned to Barela.

He explained that the evening before, he had met the Colonel and Henry on the road east of Chalk Hill and that while visiting, Fountain had pointed out three mysterious riders lurking on the horizon and had said that he had been followed for days. Barela told the boys that he had urged their father to drive back to the stage station at Luna's Well and spend the night with him. The grizzled old stage driver explained that the Colonel had thought this over, then decided that since Mariana was expecting them and Henry had a cold and needed his mother's care, he must go on. Barela had watched them drive off and then had turned up the road to Luna's Well. As he approached the three riders, one mounted on a great white horse, they galloped off, their course forming a circle which would bring them back to the road several miles ahead of Fountain's buckboard.[1]

On his return run Sunday morning Barela told the boys that he had carefully watched the road. Just beyond Chalk Hill he saw where a wagon had swerved off the road. He got down and studied the ground. Strange horse tracks surrounded the spot where the buckboard had stopped. Anxious over this discovery, he had pushed his team on to Las Cruces.

At once Albert organized a search party and raced off into the cold, dark night for Chalk Hill. Barela sounded the alarm over the town and another posse, led by W. H. H. Llewellyn and Eugene Van Patton, set out behind the Fountains.

The two parties had joined by dawn; then dividing into small groups they cast about for sign over the rolling plains on either side of the road. The calmest men in the posse were Van Patton and Captain Thomas Brannigan, chief of Mescalero Scouts. Their coolness was rewarded, for they found the most significant clues.

Their first discovery, made at the western base of Chalk Hill behind a clump of weeds, consisted of two empty cartridges and the prints of knees and high-heeled boots in the sand where a sharpshooter had taken up position. Tracks across the road and behind the hill indicated that two men had held three horses. Indications were that they had raced about 150 yards down the road to catch the runaway team. Van Patton walked back and forth across the ground where the buckboard had first swerved. His sharp eyes picked up a reddish-brown stain on the sand; step-

[1] El Paso *Herald*, February 4, 1896.

ping off its location, he noted that it was exactly 424 paces south of the Chalk Hill and just off the main road near the spot where the buckboard had left the highway.[2]

This dried pool of blood measured seven to eight inches deep "and twice or three times as large as a spittoon. The blood had spattered around for a distance of six feet." It appeared that a blanket had been spread on the edge of the pool and a heavy object placed on it. Van Patton and Brannigan reasoned that the "blood had collected in Fountain's overcoat and when he fell to the right as the buckboard swung around, the blood spurted out making a long spatter." Nearby Van Patton found a blood-soaked handkerchief and two powder-burned coins, a five-cent piece and a ten-cent piece.[3]

The grim path was plainly marked. The buckboard had been led off the road about one hundred yards to the east. There a stop of some duration was indicated by boot tracks around the wagon, by the hoofprints of restless horses, and by cigarette papers scattered about on the ground.[4] Sign indicated that six horses had moved directly east toward the Jarillas, two of them pulling the buckboard and the pinto pony being led. With Brannigan in the lead, the posse tracked east five miles, until they reached a blind trail that crossed from Black Mountain to Dog Canyon; from this point the trail swung north through clumps of tall grass. Toward evening the weary searchers entered the red sand dunes near the mouth of a canyon at the north end of the Jarillas. Brannigan sighted a familiar hulk and halted the posse. Moving in close, he identified the Colonel's buckboard. He set its location about twelve miles due east of the main road. While Van Patton and Llewellyn held the posse back, Brannigan measured the tracks and checked the ground for additional sign. Harness was scattered over the red sand. An investigation showed only the two long straps were missing, and after discovering the imprint of a blanket on the sand, caused, he believed, by a heavy weight resting on it,

2 *Rio Grande Republican*, February 14, 1896.
3 El Paso *Herald*, June 1, 1899.
4 *Ibid.*, May 31, 1899.

the Mescalero scout surmised that the killers had used the straps as girths and ties to secure the bodies on horses.[5]

The buckboard had been plundered. Contents of the boxes and the valise were scattered over the ground. The blanket, quilt, and Fountain's sheath knife and Winchester were missing. Twelve cartridges had been removed from his shell belt which was on the seat. The Colonel's cravat, tied to a wheel spoke, flapped grotesquely in the evening wind. His dispatch case was flat on the ground, lid back and empty, his papers strewn about.

Llewellyn directed the posse to circle the buckboard and pick up the trail again. When they reached the point where the led horse had been released, one detachment tracked the animal to Luna's Well on the main highway. The main trail continued east for five miles to an abandoned campsite. Near the charred remains of a campfire, the searchers found sign indicating that the party had cooked a meal—bacon broiled on sticks and coffee. In the same area Albert found a broken whisky bottle. Studying the high-heeled boot tracks about the campsite, Brannigan identified them as belonging to the same three men whose tracks he had found around the buckboard; one set had the same telltale run-over heel. Brannigan made notes concerning the prints of both the men and the animals and broke sticks to measure the length and width of the impressions. Again he found in the sand the imprint of a blanket, containing a heavy weight. Leading out from the campfire were the tracks of a child's shoe. Albert identified these as Henry's; but Brannigan noted that the child's tracks were all made by the right shoe. The Mescalero scout speculated that the shoe had been attached to a stick and pressed into the sand; and he inferred from this deduction and from remnants of Henry's clothing and his bloody handkerchief found along the route that the child was dead before his captors reached the campsite; that the weight of his body had added to the weight of his father's remains to produce the blanket imprint on the red sand.[6]

Just east of the campsite, the trail branched. One trace turned

[5] El Paso *Times*, February 4, 1896.
[6] El Paso *Herald*, June 1, 1899.

southeast toward a low-lying pass in the Jarillas. Another set of tracks bent north and then west; a third trail went northeast toward Dog Canyon. Carl Clausen was assigned to the Jarilla pass trail, Van Patton headed a party over the west trail, and Llewellyn kept the main party moving toward Dog Canyon. At dawn Llewellyn's posse divided; the leader selected the five best-mounted men, sending the remainder back to Las Cruces, and pushed up the well-marked trail. Three miles from Oliver Lee's Dog Canyon ranch, the posse was blocked off the trail by a fast running herd of cattle, driven across Llewellyn's line of march by two of Lee's cowboys. All sign of the trail had been erased, and Llewellyn ordered a return to Las Cruces.

Van Patton's party trailed west across the main road and finally near San Nicholas located a white horse, identified as one of the Colonel's buckboard team. The posseman reported that the brute was jaded; dried blood was matted on its left side; and its back was sore, but not bleeding, from carrying a heavy burden. Van Patton shaved the patch of bloody hair and added it to the blood-soaked sand samples he had gathered at Chalk Hill.[7]

Clausen, on the Jarilla trail, fared better than all the rest. He picked up a trail which included the tracks of a large, shod horse. He surmised that the horse had been ridden at night because the trail showed that the animal had plowed into mesquite bushes and backed off. The tracks led him to Wildy Well, Oliver Lee's southernmost ranch. It was broad daylight when Clausen rode up to the house. The sand padded his approach, and a group of men at the corral did not see him until he was quite close. When they caught sight of Clausen, "they ran pell mell around the house as if frightened." At first no one re-appeared. Then a Negro came out the door, "stepping sideways, in his hand a sixshooter; he stepped slowly until he was past me," Clausen related, "and then made a dash behind the water tank; another man then came out. He came forward in a surly manner. I spoke to him. He did not answer. After he had taken his place another man, Oliver Lee, came out. I spoke to Mr. Lee and asked him if I could fill the

[7] *Ibid.*, June 2, 1899.

water kegs. He agreed and told me to get water. He asked me about the searching party and I told him we were searching for Fountain. I asked him why he and his men could not go out and assist us. He said he hadn't time and 'what the hell are those sons of bitches to me?' I asked him if he was the owner of that ranch and he said no. I asked him where I could find the owner and he said possibly he might be at his home ranch. Oliver Lee mounted his horse and taking my back track went straight toward the Jarillas. I soon lost sight of him. I examined the tracks of his horse and found them to be the same that I had followed. After getting a supply of water I returned to the house to pay for it and on opening the door, three men within hastily sprang up with their hands on their guns and confronted me."[8]

As each section of the posse returned, curious townsmen plied the searchers with questions, and the anxiety which had gripped Las Cruces since Saturnino Barela's arrival on Sunday evening with the news of his fearsome discovery was succeeded by hysteria, especially among the Mexicans. Their Anglo patron and defender, *El Coronel*, the indestructible one, was dead. Llewellyn, Van Patton, and Brannigan declared that from the evidence they had gathered on the initial search, there was but one inescapable conclusion—murder. These three friends of the Colonel organized fresh posses to scour the country for the bodies. Brannigan brought in a squad of Mescalero Apache scouts, headed by old Peso, to trail for the posses. The original course to Dog Canyon, now barely distinguishable and in spots hard to find because of the many search parties casting over it, was examined again by Peso's Apache squad. These Indian trailers sifted sign all the way to Dog Canyon and offered to search across the broad band of cattle tracks. The Anglo possemen would not follow, which led Peso to conclude that they were afraid that they would find the murderers if they followed his braves beyond the cattle tracks.

Newspapers all over the Southwest gave wide coverage to the so-called Fountain mystery. Every returning posse had a fresh story to tell, and their findings, imaginary or real, were described

[8] *Rio Grande Republican*, April 15, 1898, and El Paso *Herald*, June 7, 1899.

in lurid detail. Editorial speculation was offered for what had happened. One of the most perceptive reports came from a Santa Fe *New Mexican* article captioned "Dead Men Tell No Tales." "There can be no motive for murdering the child except to put a dangerous witness out of the way."[9]

Indignation extended far beyond Las Cruces. Citizens' meetings at Roswell, Las Vegas, Santa Fe, and other towns drafted resolutions condemning the murders, charging the foul deeds to a band of Dog Canyon rustlers the Colonel was prosecuting, demanding the early arrest and conviction of these killers, and collecting purses for a reward to hasten their capture.[10]

The Masonic lodges of New Mexico sent resolutions of regret to the Fountain family, hired detectives to gather evidence, and offered a cumulative reward of $10,000 for the arrest and conviction of the Fountain killers. The Doña Ana County commissioners offered a $500 reward; and Governor Thornton issued a proclamation: "Owing to the gravity of the crime I offer a reward of $5,000 for the arrest and conviction of such criminals." And he promised "a full and complete pardon to any party connected with the crime—except the principal—who may first turn state's evidence and furnish the testimony for the arrest and conviction of his associates."[11]

The Republican party of New Mexico and every other organization in the territory with which the Colonel had connections eulogized his mighty efforts to promote the better interests of the territory and condemned his killers. The Southeastern New Mexico Stock Growers' Association, through secretary James Cree, added a reward and placed the total resources of its powerful membership at the disposal of the authorities in the efforts to find the killers of their chief agent, Colonel Fountain. Cattlemen all over New Mexico joined in statements of appreciation for what Fountain had done for the stock-raising industry and made offers of assistance. A. J. Tisdale of the giant Bell outfit requested that his

9 Santa Fe *New Mexican*, February 5, 1896.
10 *Ibid.*, February 13, 1896.
11 *Rio Grande Republican*, February 21, 1896.

company be assessed for any sum which might be its proportionate share.[12] The aggregate bounty by February 22, 1896, totaled $20,000, perhaps the richest reward ever offered in the annals of Western crime and, for the times, a king's ransom.[13]

Stockmen throughout the West, from Texas to Arizona Territory, Wyoming, and Colorado offered assistance. The Denver *News* noted that "Cattlemen of Colorado have been appealed to. The appeal should receive prompt response. The cattle interests of New Mexico and Colorado are so closely allied that range men have a mutual interest in hunting down and punishing their assassins. If they are allowed to escape, it may be that they will next execute their vengeance on some Colorado cattlemen. All law abiding citizens have a common interest in suppressing this kind of crime, and nothing should be left undone to accomplish this end."[14]

Immediately Albert Fall got into the act. His *Independent Democrat* published stories that Fountain had been seen in St. Louis, San Francisco, Chicago, and New York, that he was on his way to Cuba to join the revolutionists, and that he had positively been seen in Mexico City. Fall and his cronies dropped rumors here and there that Mariana and the Colonel had become incompatible, and Fountain had run off with a younger woman, the Colonel taking his favorite son with him to a secret lover's rendezvous in Denver.[15]

Fall and the Democratic faction at Las Cruces did nothing to assist in the search for the killers and the location of the bodies. Sheriff Ascarate remained in town. When Fall and his followers received biting criticism from local newspapers and when the heavy finger of evidence pointed more and more to Oliver Lee and his gunmen, Fall screamed that the whole deal was political; that the Republicans were using the Fountain issue to crucify innocent Democrats.[16]

[12] Las Vegas *Examiner*, February 26, 1896.
[13] El Paso *Herald*, February 22, 1896.
[14] Denver *News*, March 18, 1896.
[15] Pinkerton Reports, March 18, 1896.
[16] *Rio Grande Republican*, February 28, 1896.

Fall and the *Independent Democrat* were challenged by ringing rebuttals from all over the territory. The Eddy *Argus* charged Fall with attempting to make political capital out of this dreadful event. "That Dona Ana County is a political hot-bed, as warm as it is corrupt, is well known; but the efforts made by unscrupulous parties there to make political capital of the murder of Colonel Fountain is disgusting in the extreme. The ghouls who at moments like this pry open and ferment political feuds are not above wielding the knife that did the deed."[17]

The neighboring El Paso *Herald* declared "the Las Cruces political war which has been dragged into the Fountain murder case has become a territorial scandal and to such an extent that adjoining states and territories are beginning to look askance at New Mexico and especially the southern part of it as a country where life and property are unsafe."[18]

According to the Springer *Stockman*, the *Independent Democrat* was "a blot and blur on New Mexico Journalism," for "Judge Fall and his paper had set their foot down on every enterprise with reference to its own locality and the territory at large; such newspapers have a tendency to further crime instead of doing a share toward the enforcement of law and order and building up morality. Its contemptible slurring remarks last week making sport of the disappearance and supposed murder of Colonel Albert J. Fountain and child should be enough to rise up the people of Doña Ana County and Las Cruces to the fact that tar and feathers with an urgent request that he leave town, county, and territory in twenty-four hours."[19]

The Fountain murders had immediate and long-range effects on the general reputation of New Mexico. The territory was not admitted to the Union until 1912, and, while many factors influenced the delay in statehood, a principal one was the widespread attitude that the territory was unfit for statehood as long as lawlessness abounded, as long as the perpetrators of crimes were

17 Eddy *Argus*, February 18, 1896.
18 El Paso *Herald*, February 22, 1896.
19 Springer *Stockman*, February 21, 1896.

allowed to roam the territory with impunity. Certainly the Fountain assassination caused a further decline in New Mexico's reputation. The Las Vegas *Optic* urged that "the press should speak out and encourage the public officials. It will be an everlasting stain on the territory if this should go unpunished."[20]

The *New Mexican* implored, "God grant that the dark mystery that shrouds this awful, this hideous, this unspeakably cowardly crime be lifted, and that the fiends incarnate who perpetrated it may be discovered and punished in accordance with the enormity of their offense." The editor added that "it certainly is not creditable to New Mexico that such things can happen within her borders. . . . For the credit of New Mexico as well as for the sake of the afflicted family in Las Cruces and the cause of common humanity these efforts should be redoubled and never relaxed till the facts are brought to light and the guilty ones adequately punished."[21]

Fountain's old defender, the *Rio Grande Republican,* demanded that territorial officials do everything in their power to "wipe this ugly stain from New Mexico's escutcheon. . . . Our community has been under the shadow of this dark crime, almost unparalleled in its awful brutality. The news of it traveled to every part of the country, and the horror of it has made people fear for the lives of peaceable citizens; people who would locate here go farther on, and we are constantly receiving anxious inquiries from the outside world about the matter, showing the light in which is viewed the locality where such deeds could be perpetrated."[22]

At Denver the *News* declared "there should be no return to the era of Billy the Kid,"[23] and the El Paso *Times* informed its readers that "the situation in Doña Ana County, our neighboring county in New Mexico, is deplorable and a disgrace to that territory. The eastern and northeastern part of the county seems to be infested with a gang of cattle thieves who value the life of a man less than

[20] Las Vegas *Optic*, February 9, 1896.
[21] Santa Fe *New Mexican*, February 5, 1896.
[22] *Rio Grande Republican*, June 25, 1897.
[23] Denver *News*, February 10, 1896.

that of a dog and lose no opportunity to boldly display their utter disregard of the law. They maintain and shield themselves from outraged justice by creating in honest and law abiding citizens a fear for the safety of their lives and property, and many have appealed to justice at the expense of both."[24]

Governor Thornton felt the sting of these sharp comments and spared nothing to solve the murders. Shortly after offering the $5,000 territorial reward, he issued a proclamation calling on the citizens of Doña Ana, Lincoln, Chaves, and Eddy counties to turn out and join the search. His statement reflected his official concern for New Mexico's reputation: "The crime perpetrated is so grave and heinous that it behooves all good citizens who wish to see crime stopped and the guilty punished to turn out and do their whole duty, and as far as possible protect the honor and reputation of our territory by promptly discovering and bringing to punishment the guilty parties."[25]

It was ironic that in face of the demands of indignant newspaper editors that "it is the duty of officers of Doña Ana County to find out the murderers of the Fountains and bring them to justice at the earliest possible moment" Sheriff Ascarate and his deputies had done nothing. The Sheriff was Fall's man; his chief deputies were Oliver Lee, Jim Gilliland, and Billy McNew. All the searching parties had been private citizen groups, and their three weeks of searching had added little to the grisly evidence that the initial Llewellyn–Van Patton–Brannigan posse had found.

The citizens who yearned for law and order well remembered the work of Sheriff Pat Garrett in erasing a reign of terror in Lincoln County. A similar situation now existed in Doña Ana County, and respectable citizens longed for a strong man to take over the sheriff's post and apprehend the Fountain assassins. Before his death, the Colonel had carried on a fight in the courts to unseat Fall's sheriff, Ascarate, and have the Republican candidate, Numa Reymond, installed. As attorney for the Doña Ana County Democrats, Fall had managed, by continuances and various tech-

24 El Paso *Times*, February 10, 1896.
25 Santa Fe *New Mexican*, February 8, 1896.

nical delays, to stall a decision in the Fountain-led contest case. Fall's strategy was evident. Already the case had lagged in the courts for nearly two years; it was nearly time for another election. All the while Fall's lackey, Ascarate, had occupied the all-important sheriff's office, thus assuring that any action not receiving Fall's endorsement would meet delays and indifference. In addition, Fall's power was protected, inasmuch as Ascarate's chief deputies, the Sacramento gunmen, were always near at hand ready to pistol-whip opposition into silent submission.

Governor Thornton was aware of the impasse in Doña Ana County and was conscientious in urging prompt local official action. The Fountain murders made an early decision in the election contest case all the more necessary. Doña Ana Republicans, hopeful that the New Mexico judiciary would decide in their favor, declared that Fall's vigorous fight against a final decision was due to his fear that, in face of the overwhelming evidence, he would lose his puppet sheriff and his seat of power.

The law-and-order faction did not expect much in the way of vigorous pursuit of the Fountain killers by the mild-mannered, wealthy Las Cruces businessman, Numa Reymond, but they did believe that he would appoint deputies of courage who would go after the killers. Anticipating a decision in the contest cases fairly soon, leading Las Cruces citizens called on Governor Thornton and proposed that Pat Garrett be approached as a possible deputy appointee.

Curiously, the maudlin sentimentality of many New Mexicans for Billy the Kid had made his killer, Sheriff Garrett, one of the most hated men in the territory. After writing a book on the Billy the Kid episode, which attempted to vindicate his actions, Garrett settled in obscurity on a ranch near Uvalde, Texas. At Governor Thornton's invitation he came to El Paso and met with a party of New Mexicans. Fall had been screaming "dirty politics," so Thornton was careful that his delegation was bi-partisan, the group including Republican Llewellyn and Democrats Fall and Ascarate.

During the El Paso meeting, Numa Reymond offered to drop

the contest suit if Ascarate would resign, thus opening the way to the appointment of Garrett as sheriff. This caught Ascarate off guard and, it is reported, "that gentleman placed himself in the hands of his friends," principally Albert Fall, who belligerently declared Doña Ana County Democrats "were not willing for him to resign because they thought that political motives were at the bottom of the scheme."[26]

Then Thornton proposed that Garrett be hired as Ascarate's chief deputy at a salary of $500 a month, to which "Ascarate . . . flatly said that he was able to take care of the Sheriff's office and would not let anybody dictate who his deputies should be." Fall clearly feared an intrusion into his bailiwick and discouraged any effort to obtain an immediate appointment for Garrett; so the meeting broke up, "nothing accomplished as Judge Fall objected to the whole proceedings saying that there was some political scheme in it."[27]

Fall was roasted editorially for opposing Garrett's appointment, one of the strongest statements coming from the Roswell *Record*: "Fall objected on the grounds that Garrett's appointment would be an admission that the sheriff was unable to cope with the law-lessness now rampant in that county. There was another objection which did not come to the surface, but which can be seen, and that is, Garrett would probably unearth the murderers of Colonel Fountain and his little son. The last objection is the real milk in the cocoanut, and the legal objection was only a blind."[28]

The result of the El Paso meeting was that Garrett moved his family to Las Cruces, and Thornton assigned him to the Fountain case as a private detective until the sheriff's contest was settled. But there was really very little that Garrett could do in this capacity since it was well known why he was at Las Cruces; each day the trail of the murderers got colder, and the Governor finally decided to bring in additional outside help. Shortly after the El Paso meeting Thornton wired James McParland, head of

26 El Paso *Herald*, February 28, 1896.
27 *Rio Grande Republican*, February 21, 1896.
28 Roswell *Record*, March 4, 1896.

Thomas B. Catron

"Tom Catron . . . for the prosecution."

Albert Bacon Fall

"Local Democrats had found a driving leader in Fall."

the Denver office of the Pinkerton National Detective Agency. McParland assigned operative J. C. Fraser to the Governor. It had been worked out ahead of time by James Cree, Colonel Fountain's old friend, that the cost of the Pinkerton investigation would be paid by the Southeastern New Mexico Stock Growers' Association.[29]

Fraser arrived at the Governor's Palace in Santa Fe on March 3, and Thornton briefed him on the Fountain case. The Governor drew a sketch map of the Tularosa road, the trail followed by the searchers, the location of the abandoned buckboard and the campsite, the three sets of boot tracks, one with the run-over heel, and the curious markings from a child's shoe. Thornton closed the interview with the comment that Colonel Fountain "had many enemies, owing to his position as attorney for the stockgrowers' association; he had always been a bitter prosecutor of cattle thieves, and was a fearless man . . . . The men who are suspected of this crime are Oliver Lee, William McNew, and James Gilliland."[30]

Fraser arrived at Las Cruces on March 4, carrying letters of introduction from Thornton to Llewellyn, Van Patton, and Garrett. With typical Pinkerton thoroughness Fraser scrutinized the town, posing as a representative of the Fraser and Chalmers Mining Machinery Company. Each night he made the rounds of Las Cruces saloons, or "resorts" as he called them, and spent many hours in the hotel lobby listening, watching, orienting himself to the town and its people.

In less than three days, operative Fraser was well into his investigation. Bits of information sifted from bar-room conversations, interviews, and official statements from Llewellyn, Van Patton, Brannigan, and all other informants whom he could induce to sign an affidavit provided the Pinkerton agent with a preliminary list of suspects. First of all Fraser was intrigued by Albert Fall and his role in the affair. "This man Fall has always been the attorney

[29] Cree to Thornton, Fort Stanton, February 17, 1896. Fountain Papers, University of Oklahoma Library.
[30] Pinkerton Reports, March 4, 1896.

for these cattle thieves and is said to be tied up with them now,"
Fraser reported. He was impressed by the fact that Joe Morgan,
Fall's brother-in-law, Oliver Lee, Jim Gilliland, and Billy McNew,
"all of whom are said to be controlled by ex-Judge Fall," walked
the streets of Las Cruces "armed to the teeth." When they were
in town Fraser noted that while McNew and Gilliland hit for the
"resorts," Lee hung around Nigger Ellis's barber shop and Fall's
office. "Joe Morgan, the ex-deputy marshal . . . and who is now a
deputy sheriff . . . has openly threatened some of the best men in
town, claiming that they have been talking too much about this
Fountain case."[31]

In commenting on the fear that gripped the town, Fraser reported, "I find everybody very timid about here and for this reason
my work is going to be very slow. No one wishes to be connected
with me or the case openly, so you can see how the feeling stands."
Old Saturnino Barela had been pushed around by the Fall crowd
and warned not to put out any more talk about the Fountain
matter. Yet, Fraser believed he needed the stage driver's statement, so finally, through secret arrangements, he had a midnight
interview with Barela in the back of Freudenthal's general store
while Van Patton and Brannigan served as lookouts.[32]

After a few days on the job, Fraser wrote McParland: "Things
are certainly in a very bad shape around Las Cruces . . . . We have
had eleven murders here and no convictions. Oliver Lee, McNew,
Tucker, and the balance of the gang are all deputies under the
present sheriff and several cold-blooded murders are credited up
to Oliver Lee and his friends, McNew, Tucker, and others. All
of these killings they claim were done in self defense, but in each
case Oliver Lee jumped the ranch of the man he killed."[33]

Because Fall was a suspect, Fraser traced his activities between
January 31 and February 2. It seemed that Fall left town on Fri-
day, about noon, the day before the disappearance of Colonel
Fountain, for his Sunol mining camp, which was shut down at the

31 *Ibid.*, March 6, 1896.
32 *Ibid.*
33 *Ibid.*, March 10, 1896.

time. On the same day, Llewellyn and a nephew of a Mrs. Mc-Cowan were in the yard of Mrs. McCowan's place at Organ, a mining camp in the Organ Mountains just off the main Las Cruces–Tularosa highway, about eighteen miles from Las Cruces. The nephew, a young man named Charlie, was unloading provisions from Llewellyn's buggy when Fall drove up. Fall saw the young man but could not identify him, and he asked very excitedly, "Who is that behind your buggy, who is that man?" Fall was "very white at the time." Llewellyn "laughed and said it was Charlie, Mrs McCowan's nephew." Fraser was curious about Fall's strange behavior.[34]

Fraser's informants told him that on Saturday, the day of the murder, Fall remained about the house all day at Sunol. During the afternoon he drove off with his team. Fall claimed he arrived at Las Cruces about six or a little after dark. Fraser reported "this is not so, as he was met by a rancher on the road from Sunol half past eight driving like the old Harry." The Santa Fe station agent swore that Fall did not arrive in town until daylight. Fraser was interested in the fact that Fall's Sunol camp was seven miles on a line from Chalk Hill; he was told "that you can see the clothes on the line . . . from Chalk Hill and also see people when they are moving about with the naked eye and with field glasses you can tell who they are."[35]

Joe Morgan was another character whose movements were studied by Fraser. He learned that Morgan was in Tularosa while Fountain was at Lincoln. The Pinkerton agent also learned that Fountain was followed from the minute he left Lincoln by watchers organized in relays. Jack Tucker tracked the Colonel for awhile. In and around La Luz and as far as Tularosa two bearded cowboys, one of them identified as a Lee rider, Bill Carr, known as "Good-eye" or "Tuerto," stalked the Colonel and his son. The final relay was Morgan. When Fountain turned down the Tularosa road toward Las Cruces, Morgan was seen racing from town in a broad circle to front the buckboard. Barela met Morgan on a

[34] *Ibid.*, March 7, 1896.
[35] *Ibid.*

lathered horse during the afternoon on February 1, forty miles from Las Cruces. Fraser speculated that while this eliminated Morgan from the actual murder, he probably had been the messenger carrying tidings to the waiting trio that Fountain would soon be along the road.[36]

An indication of the whereabouts of the prime suspects, Lee, Gilliland, and McNew, during the time of the Fountain murder came to Fraser by way of a letter from Mrs. S. E. Barber, of White Oaks, to Llewellyn. Mrs. Barber reported that a neighboring ranchman, Bud Smith, was a close friend of Oliver Lee. She suspected Smith and Lee of poaching on her herds. According to her letter, Bud Smith had a visitor named Jack Maxwell. She had talked with Maxwell, who claimed to have stopped at Lee's Dog Canyon ranch on the night of February 1 and to have found Lee, Gilliland, and McNew absent. When they returned late the next morning, their horses were fagged and the trio weary as if they had been in the saddle all night. Mrs. Barber reported that Maxwell had a large sum of money and had expressed an intention of going to Mexico. At the time, he appeared to be under the close surveillance of Smith.[37]

Fraser had to catch Van Patton and Brannigan on the run, since they were out on the trail most of the time heading search parties. In his brief interviews with these two old friends of Colonel Fountain, the Pinkerton agent learned more about the tracks the first posse had discovered. Van Patton later found an identical set of boot tracks on the dirt roof of one of Lee's adobe ranch buildings. Lee's big white horse, whose shod track Clausen had traced all along the original trail of destruction, was later found by Van Patton and Brannigan at the Las Cruces livery stable, and his hoof prints compared with those prints found on the trail. The scouts assured Fraser the tracks matched perfectly. Van Patton and Brannigan had watched for an opportunity to check the boot tracks of Lee, Gilliland, and McNew against the three sets of boot tracks found about the buckboard and campfire. Fraser was told

[36] *Ibid.*, March 5, 1896.
[37] *Ibid.*, March 10, 1896.

that McNew's right boot track matched perfectly the track with the run-over heel picked up on the Chalk Hill–Jarilla trail.

On the evening of March 7, Van Patton related to the Pinkerton man that during the day his scouting party had found a place where large objects had been buried and then taken up, and it was his opinion "that the bodies had been removed to some distant place by the people who did the killing." In this connection Fraser asked Van Patton if "he had seen or heard of the three men who were reported by the mail carrier as riding back and forth watching the road and the mail driver; he said they had run the men down and found they were Gilliland and two Lee Cowboys. When Van Patton and his two Mexicans rode up toward them they came on a run for him with rifles ready, but when they saw Garrett and the other men, eight in all, come up over the hill, they drew up and pulled in their horses; they claimed they were looking for cattle." Concerning this incident, Fraser added in his report to McParland: "Now to go back a few years, I wish to state that I am informed by Governor Thornton and others here that about 1882 Walter Goode was killed by Oliver Lee, Tom Tucker, and Bill Kellum, known as Cherokee Bill, and his body was buried in what is known as the White Sands and was watched for a long time in the same manner as the men have been watching the road in the vicinity of Lunas Wells."[38]

Of all the men working in the field on the Fountain case, Garrett was the hardest man to make contact with. Fraser did not meet the former sheriff of Lincoln County until March 10. After Fraser presented Thornton's letter of introduction, Garrett, according to the operative, said "that he knew me and knew from the Governor that I was coming to render him any possible assistance." After a brief introductory meeting in Garrett's room, Fraser and he agreed to meet later in the day at the Lindell Hotel in El Paso to avoid being seen by the Fall crowd. Fraser found Garrett evasive and grouchy, indifferent to the story of Gilliland and two Lee riders patrolling the Tularosa road after the murder and to about every other possible lead Fraser came up with. The

[38] *Ibid.*, March 7, 1896.

Pinkerton agent was eager to go to Tularosa and attempt to take statements from people in Oliver Lee's domain, fearful that if he waited too long all persons with knowledge of the case would be intimidated into silence. To this Garrett answered "that a trip to the Tularosa country would be very dangerous for me to make as Lee and his crowd would not hesitate to kill a man who openly went into that country to investigate this case. From further conversations with Mr. Garrett I saw plainly that he didn't want me to go out and cause a stir by an open investigation. He told me that what he wanted me to do was to try and pull everybody off the idea that Oliver Lee, Gilliland, and McNew are the men," and stop the Colonel's friends from talking so much. "He further stated that if he could be made sheriff . . . he would have things where he could start right in on this gang."[39]

Fraser and Garrett returned to Las Cruces on different trains to avoid suspicion. The two met a number of times during the next two weeks, always secretly and on Fraser's initiative. Garrett was an enigma for the Pinkerton agent; it appeared that he wanted to work alone on the case and resented outside help. Fraser wondered if Garrett feared competition for the $20,000 reward, but this should have been of no concern as it was generally known that Pinkerton agency rules forbade its operatives receiving "any reward which may have been offered in connection with any case nor any gratuity for any service performed."[40] Fraser observed after several conferences that "Garrett is a man who says very little, so anything I learn from him is through questions. . . . Garrett has never said one word to me about receiving an affidavit from any one, and any information I get from him is mostly obtained by questioning so it can be readily seen that I am working at a great disadvantage."[41]

Fraser faced other disadvantages at Las Cruces, most of them caused by the tense, fear-laden atmosphere that hung over the

[39] *Ibid.*, March 10, 1896.

[40] Pinkerton National Detective Agency Circular, Denver Office. Original in New Mexico State Records Center, Santa Fe.

[41] Pinkerton Reports, March 15, 1896.

town like a pall. He explained to McParland: "To show how things are being closely watched by some one, or several, everytime one of the citizens who is interested in this affair leaves town on the Tularosa road, they no sooner pass out of town than a shot is fired for each one in the party, and the same way when any person or party comes in. These shots are fired only at night and some other signal is supposed to be used in the daytime. Fires are also used . . . . I thought, owing to the condition of affairs here and the number of spies on the other side of this case, that it would be as well to keep under cover as long as possible. I am told by all who have been on the ground and with whom I have come in contact that I will get no information from any one in the vicinity of where Colonel Fountain was last seen as everybody is afraid to talk and the only way that information is to be had is through the sources now obtained, friends who communicate through friends only."[42]

On March 10, Judge Gideon Bantz in court at Silver City, at long last handed down a decision in the contest case in favor of the Republican candidate for sheriff of Doña Ana County, Numa Reymond, declaring that the Democratic sheriff, Ascarate, had been continued in office by fraudulent ballots. This was the case that Colonel Fountain had instigated against Fall's machine nearly two years before. But the Doña Ana County Democrats refused to give up. Fall wired Bantz that he had applied for a new trial and that if "this failed they would appeal their case to the higher court and ask for an order restraining Numa Reymond from acting." Fraser lamented "now if this is done and the case tied up in the higher court and Ascarate allowed to continue on as sheriff, the progress on the case is bound to be very slow. There seems to be an awful change in Fall and his gang since this decision of the court and they seem very much put out about it, and no doubt are when they employ Judge Warren to come here and assist them. Warren is said to be one of the best attorneys in the Territory."[43] By March 20, Fall had called in another capable

[42] *Ibid.*, March 6 and 7, 1896.
[43] *Ibid.*, March 11, 1896.

attorney, one who, like himself, was a leading Democrat in the territory, to assist in the contest case—Harvey B. Fergusson of Albuquerque. Fraser reported that Fergusson "is said to be a very clever man and an enemy to Fountain" for the Colonel "slapped his face in court during some case."[44]

Pinkerton operative Fraser made plans to go up the Tularosa road and continue his investigation in Oliver Lee's country despite Garrett's warning. There were three things he felt compelled to do before heading east. One was to check out the story of incompatibility and jealousy in the Fountain family. An earnest inquiry into the matter produced this succinct comment: "There is nothing in connection with Colonel Fountain's domestic affairs to cause him to disappear and there was never any trouble between his wife and him, and she was not jealous of him."[45]

The second matter Fraser took care of before his Tularosa trip was a recommendation to Governor Thornton concerning custody of Fountain case evidence—this became a most critical item subsequently. "I find that the various articles that will figure as evidence in this case such as the coins found, also the napkin and piece of boy's shirt waist, and other articles have not been kept together but are scattered all over; some articles in the hands of one and some in others. I would suggest that all the articles pertaining to the case be properly marked for identification by parties who found them and then turned over to one reliable person and locked safely away."[46]

The third matter Fraser hoped to arrange before leaving Las Cruces was a meeting with Fall and Lee for the purpose of taking their statements. By March 18 he was ready to tip his hand by throwing off his disguise as a mining machinery salesman. He watched Lee's and Fall's movements during the day, and when he was certain they were together, he made his call at Fall's office. First, Fraser showed his credentials and explained his position in the Fountain case. Fall agreed to supply an official statement

[44] *Ibid.*, March 20, 1896.
[45] *Ibid.*, March 7, 1896.
[46] *Ibid.*, March 12, 1896.

and "turned loose by first saying that he would state his position in the case; he did not like Colonel Fountain any more than he did a snake . . . . He is a man who has killed several men." Fall declared that "Jack Fountain had made some ugly talk about him and told on the street that the murder of his father was put up in his office and that he was at the head of the gang of murderers and thieves. Now I want to say to you . . . that I believe Fountain is dead; at first I thought he might have left and would turn up in Cuba as he was a Spanish scholar, and as he was inclined to be sensational, this would just suit him." Fraser then asked if he thought Fountain would have taken the boy with him, providing he had done as Fall suggested. Fall replied that "he may have had reasons for taking the boy as he was very much attached to the little fellow and there was a rumor," but before going any further, Fraser said the Judge stopped and said it was only a rumor and if advanced by him would be regarded as some plan to divert attention or a trick of his to lead the officers off the right track. Fraser asked him to continue. Fall proceeded to pass on a salacious account of alleged family indiscretions. Next he derided and belittled Fountain's work as a prosecutor, claiming he got his indictments and convictions on "manufactured evidence." Fall used this term several times during the interview. Lee "chimed in to agree with the judge." Fraser was alert to the fact that "both of these men occupied positions where they could watch each other and Lee kept his eyes on Judge Fall during the entire conversation." Fraser asked Fall "if he would explain where he was on Saturday, the day of the disappearance of Colonel Fountain. At this question both Judge Fall and Oliver Lee burst out laughing and Lee winked at Judge Fall." Fraser told Lee that "he need not laugh as I would soon reach him; this caused another laugh." Fall claimed he reached Las Cruces from Sunol at eight in the evening. He denied he had met any person on the road, this answer given several times. "As I had finished with Judge Fall I turned my attention to Oliver Lee and started to ask him what he knew about the matter when Judge Fall interrupted me and said he would like to explain Mr. Lee's position in this case, and then went on to say that Mr. Lee had been accused of being connected with the disappearance of Colonel Fountain; the warrants issued for Mr. Lee were proof enough of that in themselves and he, as Mr. Lee's attorney and friend, had advised him not to talk to any one as to where he was on that day or any other day, but when the time came he (Judge Fall) had the papers and witnesses to prove where Oliver Lee was, and added, pointing his right hand toward Lee, 'I have letters that you know nothing about' .... I noticed that Lee always watched Judge Fall and the Judge kept looking at him all the time; at one time he started to tell something, but Fall shook his head and Lee, who was looking straight at him stopped short and began talking about something else."[47]

Fraser checked and found that the only indictments against Lee were those which Sheriff Sena of Lincoln County brought down to Las Cruces on February 12. These were the same indictments, for cattle rustling only, which Fountain had gained with the help of the steer hide Les Dow had brought in from the Lee-McNew herd.[48] So two days later Fraser again met with Fall: "I asked him if he did not think it was a mistake not to allow Oliver Lee to make a statement explaining where he was at the time of the disappearance of Colonel Fountain. Judge Fall replied very promptly that he did not think it was a mistake and that he had carefully considered the matter before advising him to say nothing to any one. . . . I asked him if in the face of all the talk about the case he did not think it was poor judgment for him not to make a statement and again he said no. He then went on to tell me how this affair was all politics and that certain people only wanted a chance to kill Oliver Lee . . . . I broke in to say that Lee was not accused of any connection in this case and for this reason I thought he should make a statement. I further stated that I had noticed how bad it looked for him not to make a statement when I came to write up my report." Fall was adamant.[49]

In a few days Fraser was moving east toward Tularosa, recheck-

---

[47] *Ibid.*, March 18, 1896.
[48] *Rio Grande Republican*, February 14, 1896.
[49] Pinkerton Reports, March 20, 1896.

ing every spot which had yielded evidence to previous searchers and interviewing a long list of persons he had built up from his investigation at Las Cruces. Chalk Hill and other key spots had little to tell; weather, time, and the tracks of countless searching parties had erased the signs which had spoken so eloquently to Van Patton and Brannigan. And Fraser found the people along the way equally as mute as Chalk Hill, the red sand dunes at Jarilla canyon, or the taciturn Pat Garrett.

CHAPTER XVI

Justice Dethroned

PINKERTON AGENCY OPERATIVES continued their investigation of the Fountain murder case through the first half of 1896, chasing elusive, fast-fading clues. One of their biggest breaks came on a visit to the territorial penitentiary at Santa Fe. Slick Miller, the famous cattle thief Colonel Fountain had prosecuted and won a conviction on during the 1894 rustler roundup, was ready to talk. Governor Thornton encouraged Miller to talk freely, assuring that if his cell-block confession led to the arrest and conviction of the Fountain killers, he could expect a full pardon.

Miller's statement told that a ring of small cattlemen from Socorro, Lincoln, and Doña Ana counties, of which he was a member, had poached on the herds of the Southeastern New Mexico Stock Growers' Association, not only to build their own spreads, but also out of spite since they resented the syndicates appropriating the best water and grass in the region. To fight the big boys, they had joined hands in an informal association of their own, which included Ed Brown and Miller of the Socorro area and Bill Carr and Billy McNew from Doña Ana County. When Fountain's rustler investigation got too close for comfort, these small operators met at Brown's ranch and drew up an assassination plot. Carr and McNew reportedly said that "it would be of no use to try to do business in the country as long as those fellows [Miller explained they meant McDonald, president of the association, Cree, secretary, and Fountain, the chief investigator and prosecutor] were allowed to interfere."[1]

Miller claimed that he knew all about the 1894 plot to exterminate Fountain, Cree, and McDonald, for he "slept with the men

[1] Pinkerton Reports, April 1, 1896.

and they had no secrets before him, and they planned the assassination in his presence." McNew and Carr were certain they could get three or four men from their county to help out.[2]

The plan developed just before the term of court at Lincoln, 1894, went something like this: At the conclusion of Lincoln court it was expected that Fountain, McDonald, and Cree would travel directly to Socorro to try a docket of rustler cases in that court. If this were the case, an ambush site was decided upon; if the three marked men went their separate ways from Lincoln, squads of killers were assigned to intercept them before each reached his home. Miller said that the point chosen for Fountain was Chalk Hill. In either event, the "plan was to watch for a favorable opportunity and closely observe the locality selected for the execution of the deed, and it was further agreed and arranged upon by all the parties that McNew, Ed Brown, and Carr were to carry the dead body or bodies from the place of the murder to the San Andres mountains. It was the plan to throw the body or bodies over some of the high ridges, so as to lodge them on a shelving or projecting rock with which the country there is abundantly provided. In that part of the country there is very little stock, and being therefore very little or seldom visited by any one, it was chosen to prevent detection of the crime and the finding of the dead bodies."[3]

Miller related that after waylaying Fountain, Cree, and McDonald, the killers were "to disperse and leave in different directions, obliterate trails and tracks, and make pursuit and trailing a difficult matter." Participants were to return to their ranches and hold herds of cattle ready to drive across their back trail to "obliterate their tracks." Ed Brown proposed to hire professional killers to do the job, but one of the gang objected, saying "he would never trust such important work to hired men, but would do his share himself." Miller was expected to do his share of the killing, but he refused to have anything to do with the plot. Ed Brown offered him $500 and two horses and afterwards raised the offer

2 *Ibid.*
3 *Ibid.*

to $2,000. When Miller remained adamant, the gang threatened him saying "as I knew the whole plot, I had to take an active part in the undertaking or they would make me leave the country."[4]

Of course, Fountain's whirlwind drive against the rustlers blasted this assassination conspiracy. Miller and Brown were arrested on rustling charges; the general scare caused their confederates still at large to scatter into Arizona and Mexico. Brown jumped bond and became a fugitive, too. Miller was convicted and sentenced to a ten-year term in the territorial penitentiary.

Governor Thornton was anxious for the Pinkerton men to follow up the leads provided by Slick Miller's confession. Agent Fraser had lost his anonymity at Las Cruces in his attempt to get statements from Albert Fall and Oliver Lee. Thus, there were limitations on what he could accomplish. For this very important reason, and because the agency wished to assign him to a case in England, Fraser was taken off the Fountain case.

Before leaving New Mexico, he made a summary report to Thornton concerning the investigation he had made at Las Cruces. First, he stressed the importance of getting statements from "Oliver Lee and others if it is at all possible by having them away from their legal advisor Mr. Fall." And Fraser concluded: "I feel satisfied that this entire matter will come home to Oliver Lee, and that McNew, Tucker, Carr, and others are implicated in this matter. I am thoroughly satisfied that Judge Fall was not at Chalk Hill, but I am not satisfied that he was not a party to the conspiracy. There is certainly a master hand in the whole affair, and the great legal point would be the proper disposition or disposal of the bodies so that they could not be found. There is nothing to prevent Judge Fall from being able to see what was going on provided he used a pair of field glasses while at Sunol, for with the naked eye from Chalk Hill you can see Sunol and if Judge Fall was a party to this conspiracy there is nothing to have prevented him from knowing whether or not the plan had been carried out by the other people at Chalk Hill."[5]

4 *Ibid.*
5 *Ibid.*, April 4, 1896.

McParland sent W. B. Sayers down from Denver as a replacement for Fraser. He met with Thornton at the Governor's Palace on April 17, and after reading Fraser's reports on the Fountain investigation and discussing the case with the Governor, Sayers interviewed Slick Miller. The informer could add little beyond what he had reported in his confession to detective Fraser, except to recall that "McNew was completely under the control of Oliver Lee and anything that Lee told him to do he would do, believing that Lee could get him out of any trouble," but Miller suggested that if McNew "could be gotten away from Oliver Lee he would be easily broken down, as he was a very weak man in many ways, but in Miller's opinion nothing could be done with him so long as Lee was with him to advise."[6]

Miller recalled that McNew "always wore boots," and that "he used to run one of them over badly at the heel." The informer also told Sayers that "McNew was with Oliver Lee when Lee killed the Frenchman .... The Frenchman had some cattle and a ranch at Dog Canyon and he was a cranky old man and when Lee had cattle rounded up the Frenchman would go out and look through them and see if there were any stolen cattle belonging to him in the bunch; he also threatened to have Lee indicted for stealing stock, and Lee was afraid that he would and could furnish proof, and Miller heard Lee and McNew talking about it several times and Lee said he would kill him. Then the Frenchman sold his cattle to a man named Riley and still lived on his ranch doing a little farming; he had some dogs and when any of Lee's cattle came around would run them off with the dogs. Lee again threatened to kill him, and one day, Lee, McNew, and a man named Dan Davis went to the Frenchman's ranch on horseback; the Frenchman met them at the door with his gun and began cursing Lee and Lee shot him; he fired at him three times, only one bullet taking effect. There was nothing done about it, as the Frenchman had no relatives and no friends to take the matter up, so Oliver Lee jumped his ranch and the matter ended." Miller closed his interview with Sayers with a comment concern-

[6] *Ibid.*, April 22, 1896.

ing the Good killing. "Lee and Tom Tucker killed Good and there was a man named Cherokee Bill who was with them. Lee was afraid that Bill, who had no interest in the country would give it away, that he took him on a trip to Old Mexico to get some cattle and when he got to a convenient place on the other side of the line he killed Cherokee Bill and returned to his ranch."[7]

Sayers spent most of his time between April 15 and May 15, 1896, at Socorro working on Ed Brown. His purpose grew out of the belief that there was a link between the 1894 assassination plan, which failed, and the 1896 plot, which succeeded. Sayers felt that a statement from Brown was essential to the Fountain investigation for two reasons: first, Brown had been a ringleader in the 1894 plot; and second, on February 1, 1896, he had been traced down river to Rincon, reportedly heavily armed and hiding in the cottonwood groves. With the co-operation of local authorities, Sayers had Brown jailed at Socorro on a fresh cattle-theft charge. The prisoner was questioned daily by the Pinkerton agent. Brown was a willing informant, telling all he knew about the 1894 scheme and speculating on what probably happened at Chalk Hill the past February. The prisoner showed strong interest in the Fountain reward money and believed that he could crack the case, not only by locating the bodies, but also by getting a confession from one or more of the Fountain killers. But he made it clear that because of the danger involved he would have to be assured that once the plot had worked, Oliver Lee and his gang would be brought in promptly and placed behind bars, without bail. Brown seemed to be going on the assumption that the Fountain killers had followed the 1894 formula for disposing of the victims, in the San Andres, and he had a fairly certain notion of the exact spot. Brown's proposition, based on his claim that he had influence over Carr and McNew, was that he ride east of the San Andres to Carr's ranch, "and get Carr to steal a bunch of cattle and drive them to Brown's ranch" in Socorro County. Brown was to notify the local sheriff who "would be on hand to arrest Carr with the cattle, and also put Brown in at the same time: then Carr was

[7] *Ibid.*

to be confronted with the evidence against him on the conspiracy and Brown was to talk the whole thing over with Carr in jail and get him to make a full confession."[8]

Sayers did not "like this plan at all," and told the sheriff that he "did not see how we could possibly go into such a scheme as it would give Brown all the power he wanted on his side of the fence. We would be sending him out to commit a crime and induce another to do so." This, Sayers believed, would place great power in the hands of the defense attorneys when the Fountain killers came to trial.[9] As it turned out, nothing particularly significant came from Sayers' investigation at Socorro, and the Pinkerton agency discontinued its role in the Fountain case on May 16, 1896.

In Doña Ana County, Lee, Gilliland, and McNew walked the streets of Las Cruces, flaunting their pistols, intimidating Colonel Fountain's friends into silent acquiescence of their freedom. The public cry against them over the territory had waned to a tiny voice, now and then weakly protesting their being at large; besides the *Rio Grande Republican*, their most persistent critic was the Albuquerque *Citizen*, which from time to time reminded its readers of the shame they had brought to the territory and especially southern New Mexico—"The bloody hand of the Fall gang has about ruined Doña Ana County."[10]

Lee became a substantial civic leader. Joining Fall in the autumn of 1896 as a member of the Democratic Central Committee for Doña Ana County, he was selected as a delegate to the Territorial Democratic Convention for that year, and served on his party's nominating committee for county officers. In that same election the Republicans persuaded Pat Garrett to run for sheriff. The old Alabama-born peace officer, a lifelong Democrat, could not in good conscience accept the Republican nomination, so it was worked out for him to run on the Independent ticket.[11]

Garrett was looked upon by the Fountain party at Las Cruces

<hr>

8 *Ibid.*, May 7, 1896.
9 *Ibid.*
10 Albuquerque *Citizen*, October 14, 1896.
11 *Rio Grande Republican*, October 9, 1896.

as a panacea; yet Garrett won the election and nothing happened. Lee prospered. His herds increased, so did his range. He imported deep drilling equipment and installed steam pumps, which produced water on the plains and enabled him to extend his range.

Colonel Fountain's friends pushed Garrett to act, for, as they pointed out, every day, week, year of delay was an advantage to the side of the Colonel's killers. Les Dow, so important for the territory's case in establishing motive, was gunned down one dark night at Eddy. Certain prosecution witnesses became less willing to testify, or, as happened in several cases, they forgot everything they knew about the Fountain case. Many left the country.

Meanwhile, the Colonel's killers became more poised, more confident, and even arrogant on occasions. Garrett did nothing through 1896, 1897, and into 1898. His die-hard supporters began to grumble; some said he was afraid to tackle Lee. But Garrett had his reasons and his problems, too. His biggest obstacle to moving in was Fall. Like a steel screen, he shielded his cronies. The late sheriff's contest suit was evidence of his skill in delaying proceedings and thwarting justice. Garrett feared that Fall would control any grand jury called, thereby insuring that no indictments against Lee, Gilliland, and McNew would be issued. He could probably get bench warrants, but he would have to present persuasive evidence to convince the judge at the inevitable habeas corpus hearing Fall would manage immediately for his partisans. Garrett's star witness, Jack Maxwell, had ridden south for the healthier climate of Chihuahua. Brannigan's notes on the tracks from Chalk Hill and the marking sticks had been stolen. As a matter of fact, a good deal of the evidence collected by the early posses was missing.

Added to all of this was Garrett's suspicion that, despite all the assurances of support from the friends of Colonel Fountain, he was on his own, because Fall had bluffed the Anglos at Las Cruces. It would appear that, with his man out of the sheriff's office, Fall would no longer be all powerful at Las Cruces. But the inventive attorney had come up with a new weapon. Most of the Anglos at Las Cruces had a past; this was a rather common *raison d'être* for residence in New Mexico Territory. Fall's callous nature made him indifferent to his past; but his neighbors, many of them now prosperous, respected citizens, were sensitive about theirs, and Fall, who knew the scandal about most of them, made no bones about using it if it suited his purpose. This threat of exposure of an embarrassing past made people reluctant to cross Fall in any way—to file petitions, to serve on grand juries, or in any other way to set the wheels in motion which might produce justice in the Fountain case. For Garrett, there was something helpless and hopeless about the whole matter.[12]

Garrett's most cherished hope was that at some time he could get Gilliland or McNew away from Fall and Lee. Gilliland had talked to some already; McNew was considered vulnerable. The months passed. Garrett waited, watching Lee's side-kicks, tried to avoid as best he could the charges of procrastination and the demands for action by the Fountain party. All the while the old outlaw hunter became more taciturn, grouchy, and bitter.

Garrett's chance came during the spring of 1898. Jack Maxwell, his star witness, had returned to New Mexico. The Doña Ana County sheriff provided Maxwell with a bodyguard, and armed with bench warrants, he struck fast at the Sacramento crowd. His dragnet picked up McNew and Carr. Lee and Gilliland escaped. Disappointingly for Garrett, neither of his prisoners was as communicative as expected. Their defense counsel, Albert Fall, had coached them carefully on cell-block etiquette.[13]

The preliminary trial for McNew and Carr was held at Las Cruces in mid-April, 1898. Jack Maxwell, the territory's first witness, nearly collapsed on the stand under Fall's merciless harassment. In faltering tones he testified that he was at Lee's Dog Canyon ranch around February 1, 1896, but showed uncertainty as to the exact date. All he could remember was that Lee, Gilliland, and McNew came in while he was there. At Fall's urging, the witness admitted to having told conflicting stories to a number of people.

12 *Ibid.*, April 15, 1898.
13 *Ibid.*, April 8, 1898.

Saturnino Barela, the stage driver, told his story of meeting Colonel Fountain on the Tularosa road on that fateful afternoon, of the three mysterious horsemen following the Colonel, and of finding the suspicious sign at Chalk Hill and sounding the alarm at Las Cruces. Brannigan related his discoveries as a posseman, placing stress on McNew's run-over boot track. The Mescalero agency scout told of losing the killers' trail just three miles from Dog Canyon ranch when the herd of cattle was driven across the posse's line of march.

Carl Clausen detailed for the court his trip to Wildy Well ranch. He quoted Lee as saying when asked why he and his men were not out helping to search for the Fountains, "What do I care for that damned son of a bitch?" The witness identified McNew as one of the men at the ranch house. On Fall's cross-examination of Clausen, "several tilts occurred between him and witness," but was unable to shake Clausen's statement.

Eugene Van Patton took the stand to tell of the clues his posse had found on the initial search, the blood-soaked sand, a sample of which he had sent to Governor Thornton, and the two powder-burned coins and bloody handkerchief, which Van Patton exhibited in court. An important bit of testimony came from Kent Kearney, one of Garrett's deputies, who stated that Gilliland had visited his ranch in the Sacramentos and commented, "Don't you think the country better and quieter since the son of a bitch was killed?" Gilliland also told Kearney that "he thought it was a very slick job and that he had watched the searching parties at work."

Dr. J. H. Blazer testified that on Thursday, January 30, 1896, Fountain had stopped at his house overnight on his way home from Lincoln court. During their visit, Fountain explained to Blazer "how he had secured indictments against a gang of cattle thieves and said he had enough evidence to convict and send to the penitentiary the whole gang if they did not make away with him or the witnesses. He mentioned Lee, Gilliland, Carr, and McNew as members of the gang. He stated that he had seen some suspicious characters on the road . . . . He seemed to know them but mentioned no names." Blazer told of seeing two men pass his house that afternoon, but did not see their faces.

Next witness for the territory was James Gould, who was working at McNew's ranch on February 1, 1896. He swore that McNew was absent on February 1, and he recalled that about a week before, "Gilliland came to the ranch after cartridges and said if anyone asked for him to say he had gone to Roswell." Gould said that instead of turning toward Roswell, Gilliland rode in the direction of Dog Canyon. Gould did not see him again until four or five days after Fountain's disappearance. Some time later, while working on McNew's pasture fence, Gilliland told Gould that Lee, McNew, and he had watched the searching parties, and that the "old son of a bitch had left Texas in a chicken coop and raised hell everywhere he went, but he wouldn't raise any more."

Prosecution witness Riley Baker swore to a conversation he had with Gilliland in February, 1896, in which Gilliland pointed out the place where he had watched the posses search for Fountain. Baker remarked that the killing of the child was a horrible murder. Gilliland countered that Henry Fountain "was a half-breed, and he did not know that he was any better than a dog," and added "that if the body had to be found before anybody could be convicted, it would be a long time before anybody could be."

The final witness to appear in the preliminary trial was Jack Maxwell. This time he was more composed, and he swore that he was at Lee's Dog Canyon ranch on the day of the murder, February 1, 1896, and that Lee, Gilliland, and McNew were absent. The *Rio Grande Republican* reported that while Maxwell "was not so badly rattled as on his first examination, when he almost completely collapsed; many believe him to be holding something back and that he is afraid to tell all he knows." The prosecution was surprised that the defense offered no evidence at this preliminary trial. Fall's defense strategy during these proceedings had been to torment prosecution witnesses with rough, grueling cross-examination, which more often than not upset and confused them, and with harassment by bringing up references to their past.

As it turned out, virtually every territorial witness was a fugitive from some sort of crime committed in the neighboring states and territories. The court discharged Carr, declaring there was insufficient evidence against him, but bound McNew over, without bail, to appear before the next grand jury.[14]

Garrett was in better spirits after the McNew preliminary. Although Maxwell hadn't performed as effectively as the prosecution had hoped, several of its ·vitnesses had given telling testimony—notably Deputy Kent Kearney, and he had more to tell when the trial came up. With McNew festering in his hot jail cell, without hope of bail, there was a good chance that he would eventually break down and talk.

The sheriff got another break in the Fountain case later that spring. War with Spain galvanized New Mexico Territory. Companies formed and rushed off to join Colonel Roosevelt's Rough Riders in Cuba. Captain Albert Fall mustered Company D, New Mexico Volunteers and marched off to war. Without Fall around, Garrett calculated that if the war lasted long enough he could have the whole gang convicted and hanged by the time Fall got back home.

He had to capture Lee and Gilliland first, which proved to be more than he had bargained for. With Fall gone, the pair stayed away from town. They had plenty of friends over the country to warn them of posses. On July 10, Garrett received a tip which said the fugitives were camping just east of the Organs. He formed a quick posse of four riders, including Deputy Kearney, and raced for San Augustin Pass. By evening the fugitives' tracks pointed decisively toward Wildy Well, and Garrett's men, estimating they were about two hours behind, loped easily through the night over an old cattle trail toward Lee's southernmost ranch. Arriving just at daybreak, Garrett posted his men about the ranch house; then, seeing the fugitives' horses and saddles at the corral, he slipped into the house. Two men roused and at Garrett's questioning denied that Lee and Gilliland were around.

[14] *Ibid.*, April 15, 1898. The testimony taken in the McNew preliminary is found in this issue.

Rejoining his posse, Garrett led a search through the outbuildings. A ladder leading to the flat roof of the adobe house indicated that the fugitives were hiding behind the mud-brick parapet extending above the roof. Three possemen were positioned to cover the stalkers. Garrett and Kearney crawled atop some low outbuildings adjoining the house and slithered to the wall. Kearney reached the parapet first, raised up, and yelled for a surrender. He was met with a fusillade which blasted him off the shed with a shoulder wound. Garrett rushed for cover, Kearney rolled under the shed, and a lively exchange of gunfire took place. One of the possemen hid behind a large tank; three bullets punctured his hiding place, and the head of water that gushed out "nearly drowned him." One of the bullets from the roof ripped through the shed lean-to and hit Kearney, this time in the hip. At this, Garrett called a truce to get his deputy to a doctor; Lee and Gilliland agreed to hold their fire while Garrett and his posse withdrew.[15]

The withdrawal was a strange move on Garrett's part since, at the time, Kearney's wounds were not regarded as serious. While Lee and Gilliland were well placed defensively, they were vulnerable. The July heat would make their fortress an oven before evening, and as they had no water, it would have been expected for them, out of desperation, to attempt to fight their way out. Garrett could have sent one of his possemen for reinforcements had he regarded them essential to taking the fugitives. He had trailed this elusive pair for months, and now he had them cornered; all he had to do was wait. Under the circumstances, therefore, it is not surprising that Lee and Gilliland were more than willing to agree to a truce. The minute the posse was out of sight, they rushed to the corral, saddled their mounts, and rode into the rough mountain country at the head of Dog Canyon. After the fight at Wildy Well they faded so far back in the rough that Garrett was never closer than fifty miles to their trail. The only possible explanation to Garrett's handling of the situation at Wildy Well, aside from possible panic, concerned Kearney's value as a witness for the

15 *El Paso Times,* July 13, 1898.

Fountain murder trial which Garrett hoped to bring to fruition. Kearney had been a big help at the McNew preliminary; great things were expected of him as a future prosecution witness. It was possible that Garrett weighed the prospects of Kearney dying from his wounds against trapping Lee and Gilliland and decided to gamble that he would have a crack at them another day. As things worked out, Kearney's wounds became infected and he died.

Before Lee got too far back in the rough, he sent a letter, containing his version of the Wildy Well fight, to the editor of Captain Fall's paper in Las Cruces, the *Independent Democrat*. The letter, as published, claimed that Deputy Kearney had fired first and then demanded that Gilliland and Lee surrender. The fugitive averred that he would never surrender to Garrett, because he feared for his life as a prisoner of the Doña Ana County sheriff. Lee's letter had a lot to do with bringing the Fountain case to a climax. Before he died, Kent Kearney responded to the letter, declaring that Lee had lied in his statement of who shot first. Kearney claimed that as he reached the top of the outbuildings, he straightened up to peer over the parapet of the adobe house. At that moment he discovered Lee and Gilliland aiming their guns at him. He called to them to surrender and they both fired; then an exchange of fire took place.[16]

Several southwestern newspapers criticized the *Independent Democrat* for publishing Lee's letter, claiming it favored criminals. At El Paso, the *Tribune-Telegraph* indignantly demanded that Garrett "go after Oliver Lee and Gilliland with a posse and bring them in, dead or alive. They have at least to answer for the killing of Deputy Kearney, even if they can clear themselves of the Fountain murder. If he cannot arrest them with a posse of four, then take 40; or 400 if necessary. This open defiance on the part of the outlaws is most humiliating to the law and order element of the entire Southwest, and El Paso, its metropolis, hereby registers a protest." The San Marcial *Bee* exploded: "Of all the criminals that have passed and are passing, none have before presumed to assume the role of dictator as to just who the peace officer should

16 *Ibid.*, July 14, 1898.

be who would receive recognition at their hands. Lee and Gilliland have taken this course with Sheriff Pat Garrett. They boast they will never surrender to or be arrested by Garrett, but if the latter be removed by the governor or is defeated at the polls in the coming election, they (the outlaws) may decide to assume harmonious relationship with Mr. Garrett's successor. This grandstand of the outlaws is only for effect, and political effect at that . . . . The law will finally do business with Messrs. Lee and Gilliland, and not Messrs. Lee and Gilliland with the law, and no matter at what time or place the curtain is rung down on this drama of blood, the law's supremacy will be recorded."[17]

But it was an El Paso *Times* editorial on the Lee letter which precipitated action from the Governor's Palace at Santa Fe to end the matter once and for all. "New Mexico should be a perfect paradise for the yellow journalists of New York. In New Mexico outlaws and murders, upon whose heads a price has been set, are fond of being interviewed. . . . In the states an outlaw, dodging the officers of the law, would not think of writing letters to the press to excuse his crime . . . . But in New Mexico, Oliver Lee, after killing an officer of the law, armed with warrant for arrest . . . sends the papers a graphic description of the fight he made and tells why he will not be arrested by this or that officer. And still some people wonder why New Mexico is not admitted to statehood. It would be better for Uncle Sam to place that territory under martial law until its criminal element can learn that crime cannot override the law. Let Governor Otero lend Sheriff Garrett some aid and send enough men after Lee to capture him in short order."[18]

Miguel A. Otero, who succeeded Thornton as governor of New Mexico Territory in 1897, was just as earnest as his predecessor in desiring to bring the Fountain murderers to trial. Like Thornton, Otero was anxious to achieve statehood for New Mexico, and he was especially sensitive about the unfavorable effect the Fountain case was having on this cherished goal; thus, Sheriff Garrett re-

[17] San Marcial *Bee*, September 5, 1898.
[18] El Paso *Times*, August 29, 1898.

ceived every assistance from Santa Fe in his search for Lee and Gilliland. During January, 1899, Garrett's informants sent word that Lee had been seen at Bacerac, in Sonora, and that one of his riders had collected a string of horses at the Dog Canyon ranch to deliver to Lee's Mexican rendezvous.[19]

Governor Otero sent requisitions to the governors of Chihuahua and Sonora for the extradition of Lee and Gilliland; but the elusive pair was not to be found. Then Otero learned that a life-term prisoner at the Yuma penitentiary, Arizona Territory, had some information concerning the Fountain murders. Otero received permission from Arizona Governor N. O. Murphy to interview the prisoner, who told Otero that he was at Fall's Sunol mining camp on the day of the Fountain murders. After a lookout came in and reported that Fountain was on his way home from Lincoln, three men were sent on horseback up the road to intercept the Colonel.[20]

Otero passed the results of his interview on to Garrett, and the manhunt continued. The Governor was determined to bring the Fountain case to a climax, and his energy and interest made things happen. In the New Mexico legislature, a bill was introduced to create a new county, to be named Otero, from portions of Socorro, Lincoln, and Doña Ana counties. The bill's sponsors, who included Captain Albert B. Fall just home from the wars, claimed that the change was necessary since the El Paso and Northeastern Railroad, building through this section, required a new county for the more efficient conduct of its business. Since the new county was to be superimposed over the Fountain murder scene, the railroad plea was only a blind. The Otero County bill was tailor-made for Oliver Lee and Jim Gilliland—there was the old dictum that a defendant must be tried in the jurisdiction where the alleged offense occurred. No jury of Tularosans could ever be expected to convict their folk hero. Otero appointed Lee's friend, George Curry, sheriff of the new county. Word was sent along the New Mexico underworld; on March 13, 1899, Lee and Gilliland came

19 Las Vegas *Optic*, January 28, 1899.
20 Miguel A. Otero, *My Nine Years as Governor of the Territory of New Mexico*, 92–93.

in and surrendered to Curry. Since the new county as yet had no
jail, the prisoners were taken to Socorro jail. Three days later,
Lee and Gilliland were brought to Las Cruces and arraigned on
indictments charging them with the murder of Kearney and
Henry Fountain.[21]

Defense attorney Fall appealed to the court on the question of
jurisdiction, arguing that the new Otero County by right had
jurisdiction in the case. Presiding Judge Frank Parker dismissed
Fall's claim, and declared Doña Ana County had jurisdiction in
the case; but on Fall's plea that Lee and Gilliland could not expect
a fair trial at Las Cruces because of the bitter feeling against them
there, the prisoners were granted a change of venue to Hillsboro
in Sierra County.[22]

Parker set the trial for the last week in May. Both sides went
to work on strategy. Richmond P. Barnes, district attorney, assisted by William B. Childers (retained by the Masonic Order)
and Thomas B. Catron (special counsel appointed by Governor
Otero) comprised the prosecution. Almost immediately they
faced a problem. McNew, still in jail on the charge of murdering
Colonel Fountain, had, through Fall's efforts, obtained a change
of venue to Silver City; his trial came up in April. This time the
prosecution asked for a continuance, which was denied. Proceed-
ing against McNew at this time would require the presentation
of evidence they planned to use in the upcoming Lee-Gilliland
trial. Rather than tip their hand to Fall, they decided to enter
nolle prosequi in the Colonel Fountain murder charge against
McNew; and after the prisoner supplied a $5,000 bond in the
Henry Fountain murder case, he was released.[23]

While preparing their case, the prosecution attorneys received
two big breaks, which seemed to clinch the territory's case against
Lee and Gilliland. One was a letter from Larimore, North Dakota, addressed to the district attorney, Santa Fe, and written by
one T. J. Daily: "For the past three years I have watched the outcome of the case that I am in possession of facts that will bring

21 El Paso *Herald*, March 16, 1899.
22 Las Vegas *Optic*, March 28, 1899.   23 El Paso *Herald*, April 28, 1899.

about justice and to find the bodies that have been murdered and hid away. I was there at the time when attorney Fountain disappeared with the child. I was employed by Oliver Lee and on the above occasion I by chance came into possession of facts and was ordered out of the country by certain parties and being green or not much acquainted, I thought it best to keep still as I have heard of such cases before and knew my life was not safe. So I will be willing to aid justice all I can providing I am assured protection and if you think you need me I will go at once."[24]

The other big break was Garrett's discovery of additional witnesses, indicated in a letter from Barnes to Catron: "I believe we can safely announce ready for trial with excellent chances for conviction . . . . There is new evidence . . . that is now almost a certainty and which will bring Garrett the evidence of three Mexican residents here who had a dead beef in an arroyo near the road about two miles east of Chalk Hill and who saw the murderers pass with Fountain and his son. These witnesses have been afraid to speak before this on account of their own crime—they were stealing Cox's cattle. But we have worked it all out through an old Indian to whom they had confessed and who was on the ground in Van Patton's searching party and saw suspicious things, and I shall know before the train leaves today if they can testify as is hoped. The Indian story is a clincher, and we are prepared to force the truth out of the Mexicans."[25]

Fall's defensive strategy was apparent several weeks before the Hillsboro trial. He packed the papers with stories on the so-called politics of the Lee-Gilliland case. He pointed to Tom Catron and R. P. Barnes, leading Republicans, and charged that the prosecution lawyers were a renascence of the old, corrupt Republican cabal, the Santa Fe Ring, and that the Ring had mounted a partisan conspiracy to crucify two Democrats, Oliver Lee and Jim Gilliland. It was evident that Fall had carefully coached Lee and Gilliland. Judge Parker had committed them to Socorro jail with strict

[24] Daily to District Attorney, Santa Fe, Larimore, North Dakota, May 14, 1899. Catron Papers, University of New Mexico Library.

[25] Barnes to Catron, Las Cruces, May 31, 1899. Catron Papers, University of New Mexico Library.

orders of no bail, but they were out most of the time, traveling by train to the various towns, clean shaven, neatly dressed, polite, always willing to be interviewed, and becoming celebrities of sorts. When the pair turned up in El Paso, the *Herald* had a reporter follow them about town, and he wrote that "everywhere that Lee and Gilliland went yesterday in this city they attracted a crowd which trooped at their heels as small boys behind a circus clown. They both appear to be very affable gentlemen and not at all inclined to be ill-tempered. When asked about the case Oliver Lee said 'the Prosecution must prove that he is dead and that we killed him. And that cannot be proved. It will be utterly impossible for them to secure a conviction.' "[26]

Fall contrived some additional pre-trial staging to buttress his claims that the whole proceedings were political; that he would produce evidence to prove that the trial was persecution of Democrats by Republicans; and that not only Lee and Gilliland but he himself as well had been marked for assassination by the Republicans. Fall made a grandstand play in this direction just after he arrived at Hillsboro. Jack Fountain, one of the Colonel's sons, was in town as a prosecution witness. Fall rushed to Judge Parker and pleaded that Fountain be placed under a peace bond, since his presence made Lee, Gilliland, and Fall fear for their lives. Parker asked Fountain if there was any reason why the bond should not be imposed, and Jack answered: "Your honor, I am just a young boy, and haven't had much experience, but I will say that I never said I intended to kill any of these men, and don't say so now, though they deserve killing. If the court pleases to hear me I will state what I did say." Parker directed him to make his statement, and Jack continued, "I said if my father's bones were ever found and identified (and I think I know how to identify them positively), there is one man I would kill first, if I were not killed first." Parker asked, "Who is that man?" and Jack, pointing, said, "Albert Bacon Fall!" Fountain recalled that Fall squirmed. The court placed the Colonel's son under a $500 peace bond.[27]

[26] El Paso *Herald*, April 28, 1899.
[27] Jack Fountain Memoir. Fountain Papers, University of Oklahoma Library.

Because of Colonel Fountain's prominence, the gruesome character of the Chalk Hill murders, and the bizarre occurrences in the three-year period between the ambush and the trial, the trial at Hillsboro would have attracted wide attention in its own right. But the Fall-Lee histrionics added to the drama and made the newspaper copy even more exciting. Leading papers over the country sent correspondents to cover the trial. Workmen ran a telephone line to Hillsboro from Lake Valley. Western Union Telegraph leased the line, and its operator kept the wires busy with Hillsboro news.[28]

Fall's melodramatic handling of both the preliminaries and the actual trial won the reporters' fancy. Colonel Fountain and little Henry were almost forgotten, as readers over the Southwest and the nation were treated to a steady diet of character sketches of Fall, Lee, and Gilliland. These stories metamorphosed the accused killers from hard-bitten gunmen to abused, misunderstood young Robin Hoods. Even the crowds at Hillsboro, which doubled, trebled, the village's two hundred population, were caught up as the image of the Fall crowd was transformed by a friendly press. Thus complete credence was given to Fall's request to the court that extra deputies be scattered about the courtroom to protect him and the prisoners; Lee and Gilliland were "hurried to their cells and at their own request not taken on the streets at any time. They are with a heavy guard which they have asked since the trial opened as a result of feared assassination."[29] Another story that evoked great concern among their steadily growing supporters was: "Lee and Gilliland are in the little jail across the street tonight. They are guarded by two of their friends, who are heavily armed. This was brought about by Lee, who complained to Judge Parker this morning that he feared assassination by unknown parties, and the Judge consented that two of Lee's friends could guard him tonight."[30]

[28] Santa Fe New Mexican, May 26, 1899.
[29] El Paso Times, June 3, 1899.
[30] El Paso Herald, May 28, 1899.

The historic Fountain murder trial got under way on May 25; the attorneys took three days to form a jury. The prosecution strategy was torpedoed at the beginning. First, the key witness from North Dakota lost his nerve and failed to arrive. The cow-stealing Mexicans whom Garrett was going to bring in had run off to Chihuahua. And Jack Maxwell was missing again. There was even dissatisfaction among the lawyers. Childers had become disenchanted with the Fountain case because the Masonic Order, which had pledged to pay for his services in prosecuting the Fountain killers, was slow in paying. Just before the trial he wrote Catron that certain lodges in the territory had declined to put up any money whatsoever. He pointed out to Catron that "the court fund is less than a thousand dollars. Mr. Barnes and the Judge will go to Las Cruces and try to get the people there to advance money to the court fund for the purpose of trying these cases. If these decline to do this, I shall simply announce that I will have nothing more to do with the case. In fact the utter indifference that they display inclines me to take this course anyway."[31]

Enough money was raised in Las Cruces to assure Childers' services; but Maxwell continued to be a problem. Garrett left with a posse to search for him. He was only one of fifteen prosecution witnesses who had failed to appear. As a matter of fact, the only people in town whose lives were in danger were the prosecution witnesses who dared come for the trial, several of whom were Lee and Gilliland relatives or former friends. The El Paso *Herald* reported that "feeling over the case on trial is great and the deadliest enmity exists between some of the staunch friends of Lee and Gilliland and as they are constantly brushing one anothers' elbows on the sidewalks, an outbreak may occur at any moment. The tension is great and a sort of ominous silence pervades the town, like a calm before a storm."[32]

While the court waited for Maxwell, District Attorney Barnes

[31] Childers to Catron, Albuquerque, April 29, 1899. Catron Papers, University of New Mexico Library.
[32] El Paso *Herald*, May 27, 1899.

outlined the points to be established and then called former Governor Thornton as first witness. He related his efforts to solve the murders and told of receiving samples of blood-soaked sand and of blood-stained horse hair.[33] Albert Fountain, Saturnino Barela, and other witnesses followed, each briefly telling the court of his role in the discovery of the ambush and in the initial search. Theodore Heman, foreman of the Lincoln County grand jury which indicted Lee and McNew for cattle stealing, swore that these indictments were obtained primarily through the efforts of Colonel Fountain. The defense objected strenuously to this, claiming it showed motive, but Parker overruled the plea. On May 29, Garrett tracked down Maxwell and brought him in; the reluctant witness claimed that he had been ill.[34]

Maxwell took the stand on May 30. He swore that on February 1, 1896, he was at Lee's Dog Canyon ranch, where he spent the night. Lee, Gilliland, and McNew were absent. Next morning, Sunday, after breakfast he walked down to the corral. At midmorning he saw four persons ride in from the northeast toward the house. Maxwell recalled that the riders came up within two hundred yards of him and dismounted. He recognized three of them to be Lee, Gilliland, and McNew. Maxwell stayed at Dog Canyon Sunday night and remembered that McNew slept in the house with him; Lee and Gilliland took their arms and bedding and slept outside. The witness reportedly "broke down on cross-examination in the hands of Judge Fall and confessed that he had lived at various places under aliases, and that Pat Garrett gave him a contract to pay him $2,000 of the reward money for evidence leading to the conviction of the Fountain murderers."[35]

Much of the prosecution testimony thereafter was a repeat of the McNew preliminary; Riley Baker told the court that Gilliland had said that "killing the child was no better than killing a dog, and that the bodies would never be found and no one ever con-

[33] El Paso *Herald,* May 29, 1899.
[34] Socorro *Chieftain,* June 2, 1899.
[35] El Paso *Herald,* May 31, 1899.

victed for the murder." James Gould reiterated his story that just before the Chalk Hill ambush, Gilliland had picked up a supply of cartridges and told him to tell inquirers that he had gone to Roswell; instead he had gone toward Dog Canyon ranch. About a week later McNew and Gilliland returned together and told Gould they had watched search parties and remarked "that son of a bitch came up from Texas in a chicken coop and raised hell everywhere but he would not do so again. I remarked that he might have needed killing, but not his son. Gilliland then said the boy was a halfbreed and it was no more than killing a dog." One new witness, a cowboy named Frank Wayne, testified that he had stopped at Dog Canyon ranch the day before the murder, looking for a horse. Lee had cautioned him not to say anything about what he had seen "as it might interfere with our plans."[36]

Fall, with Harry Daugherty and Harvey B. Fergusson, his defense colleagues, placed their reliance on an alibi and corpus delicti. A battery of defense witnesses trooped up to swear that Lee, Gilliland, and McNew were at Dog Canyon ranch on February 1, 1896, setting out grapevines. Since the prosecution had not produced the bodies, Fall urged the jury that no murder could be proved. Fall won the gallery and the jury with his harassment of prosecution witnesses, some of whom on several occasions nearly collapsed on the stand under his vicious railing, his resurrection—for the world to see—of an embarrassing past, and his asides, like "Garrett was ousted from the sheriff's office because he refused to murder Lee and Gilliland,"[37] and "besides the witness Maxwell have you heard of any other witnesses having been offered money to testify falsely?"[38]

Fall's emphasis on the so-called politics of the case had its effect too. The *New Mexican* noted that "the political phases of the Fountain murder case developed with today's testimony. Evidence today has been fraught with political feeling against Lee

36 *Rio Grande Republican*, June 2, 1899.

37 El Paso *Times*, June 3, 1899.

38 *Rio Grande Republican*, June 6, 1899.

and Gilliland rather than tending to show them guilty of the Fountain murder."[39] After telling the jury of a plot by Las Cruces Republicans to have Lee and himself assassinated, Fall placed Lee on the stand; he told of letters to Fall he had seen written by gunmen who had been approached by Llewellyn and Reymond, offering them money to kill Lee and Fall. The prosecution objected on the grounds that the letters were not in evidence; Parker sustained the objection unless the letters could be accounted for in some way. Thereupon, Fall took the stand and swore that he had recently searched for the letters but could not find them. Surprisingly, Parker allowed Fall to proceed. Lee returned, and when Fall asked him who had put up the money, Lee replied that he understood it was Numa Reymond.[40]

As could be expected, the Fountain murder case was tried in the newspapers, too. The reporters at Hillsboro took note of every little instance that showed favorably for the defendants. When defense witnesses told of a plot by the Fountain party to blow up Lee's ranch house, "the spectators almost burst forth in cheers" that this alleged plot should be exposed to the world. Following this development, the El Paso *Times* reported that "the sympathy of the local community, particularly the ladies, is now with the defendants."[41] As the trial developed, items appeared such as "the ladies of Hillsboro set a bouquet of flowers in front of the defendants this afternoon."[42]

The press colored its reports on the trial in favor of Fall and Lee. Words uttered by Fall, Daugherty, and Fergusson were treated as great gems of oratory; the prosecution was represented as obtuse and unimaginative, their efforts and persons heaped with derision that, at times, approached ridicule. One instance of this favoritism by the press grew out of Catron's attempt to induce Judge Parker to instruct Fall to cease bullying prosecution witnesses. The papers reported that Fall's response to this was that

[39] Santa Fe *New Mexican*, June 2, 1899.
[40] *Rio Grande Republican*, June 6, 1899.
[41] El Paso *Times*, June 10, 1899.
[42] *Ibid.*, June 6, 1899.

"he would interrogate the witnesses to suit himself and advised the heavyweight attorney to sit down." The prosecution became so irritated at the slanted coverage of the Hillsboro trial that they published the following notice in the *New Mexican, Rio Grande Republican,* and the few other papers friendly to them: "All newspaper reports including the Associated Press sent from here about the trial of Lee and Gilliland are gross misrepresentations of evidence and facts generally. We ask you to publish this daily until the trial is over or we notify you that misrepresentations have ceased."[43]

On the eighteenth day of the Fountain murder trial, District Attorney Barnes opened final arguments for the prosecution. He declared that the prosecution had presented a chain of circumstantial evidence, and "the whole chain was only to be explained on the one hypothesis, that the defendants murdered the Fountain child." The press reported that his speech "was rather flowery, and the figures of speech and quotations from Pickwick Papers probably went over the heads of the jury. The interpretor had a hard time to translate some of the fancy work, and sometimes the advocate had to repeat his expressions."[44]

Childers followed and made a point to deride Lee's claim that "he was afraid to come in because Garrett would kill him. These men had no reason to resist arrest. They need not be afraid of the sheriff . . . they would have been safe in his hands. Lee went in and out of Las Cruces without fear until March, 1898. He was not afraid. McNew was in the custody of Sheriff Garrett for many months and he was not killed, or mobbed, or threatened. . . . It is a wonderful thing that the most important letters in the case of the defense are missing. . . . The defense laid much stress on the fact that it was only after the Governor by permission of the court had agreed to protect them from violence and permitted them to surrender outside Doña Ana County that the defendants felt willing to surrender themselves for trial. On the contrary, the Governor arranged with these fugitives from justice in another county simply

---

43 Santa Fe *New Mexican,* June 7, 1899.
44 El Paso *Herald,* June 15, 1899.

to take away their last excuse for resisting arrest. The Maxwell contract was not unusual. It is all right to pay a man money as a detective to secure evidence in a case or to put in shape to use that which is in his possession. When the Governor offers a reward for a fugitive it is the same thing. Shall a man's hands be tied? It would be offering positive protection to criminals if money could not be used by the proper authorities to secure the criminals or evidence leading to the conviction of criminals."[45]

Childers closed with a comment on one of the props of the defense—corpus delicti. "To hold that you cannot convict of murder because the body cannot be found is to condone murder, to put a premium on crime. You cannot so hold. It is so easy in this country to waylay a man and conceal his body where it cannot be found. There is every evidence that these three men were the perpetrators of this crime. The men have wholly failed to explain any of the incriminating circumstances that form a web we have woven so tightly around them but instead of refuting our evidence, they have resorted to politics and raised the cry of politics. Is there any politics in this case? Was that then a political murder? We never heard of politics in this case until the term was injected by the defense."[46]

Fall closed the defense with a biting harangue on the politics of Doña Ana County. He derided each prosecution witness and wound up with the dramatic declaration, "Jack Maxwell is a liar," which provoked "considerable applause" from the gallery.[47]

Tom Catron closed for the prosecution. "We have endeavored on the behalf of the prosecution to present before you evidence to satisfy you as to the true state of facts. We have made no effort to bring into this case anything that might be calculated to appeal to your prejudice or passion and complicate this case with matters that are entirely irrelevant. They have striven by every means in their power to prejudice you, gentlemen of the jury, against not only the witnesses for the prosecution but against the counsel on

[45] *Ibid.*
[46] *Ibid.*
[47] *Ibid.*

this side as well. I care nothing about the slurs and insinuations that may be thrown out against myself. I have been in this country too long and I am too old a man to take notice of such things. . . . But I do not like to have matters brought up before a jury in order to influence them that are not connected with the case on trial in any possible way.[48]

"They say there could have been no motive for the killing of the little boy, even admitting that there was one for the murder of his father. No motive? Suppose the boy was alive at the camp fire, did not that little fellow know who killed his father? The murderers had to do away with the boy. He would have them without doubt. They could not conceal him with any safety to themselves. They had to kill. They were determined to finish their work . . . . They talk about the *corpus delicti*. Texas is the only state requiring the production of the dead body in order to prove the commission of murder. But these men are from Texas. They knew the law there and used all possible means to conceal the body."[49]

It was nearly midnight when Catron finished. Parker sent the jurymen to their rooms for the night; then Fall demanded that they be recalled and a verdict considered at once. Parker acquiesced to Fall in this request as he had on so many instances during the past furious eighteen days. In seven minutes the twelve returned and presented their decision to the drama-charged courtroom—Not Guilty! The gallery cheered wildly, "Lee and Gilliland were the recipients of hearty congratulations for half an hour after the announcement"[50] and the merrymaking at Hillsboro sent up a noise such as would have caused the Fountain ghosts to stir in their graves.

[48] *Ibid.*
[49] *Ibid.*
[50] Santa Fe *New Mexican*, June 13, 1899.

CHAPTER XVII

Epilogue

To THIS DAY some people call it the Fountain mystery. But what is the nature of the mystery? Then, only those who supported Fall and, now, only a few persons consider the identity of the murderers to be a mystery. There is, however, an element of mystery in the disposition of the bodies of Henry and Colonel Fountain. Even this can be explained without too much difficulty. Fall's gunmen could shoot down Rhodius, Coffelt, Rochas, and others with impunity, largely because these unfortunates were more or less insignificant in the community and had no friends with the courage to fight the Fall-Lee crowd. The assassination of Fountain was another matter. As a civic, political, military leader, he was well known throughout the territory and the Southwest. His prominence and the public outcry that could be expected at his murder had to be reckoned with, and the plot demanded that the bodies be disposed of so that they would never be found.

Many of Fountain's friends believed that Fountain and his son were buried in some secret, unmarked grave in the White Sands. This is doubtful, for a lesson had been learned from burying Walter Good there. In no time at all the shifting gypsum shroud revealed his remains to searchers. No such risk could be taken with the Fountains. Slick Miller's confession revealed the scheme for hiding Fountain's body in the 1894 plot, but too many persons knew of it for the plan to be used in 1896.

The emphasis by the defense on corpus delicti was significant. Lee, Gilliland, and McNew were extremely confident and poised in the public statements, in which they declared that no murders could be proved. Gilliland boasted several times to friends and relatives "what a slick job it was" and that "if the bodies had to be found before a murder could be proved, no one would ever be convicted." While the Fountain murder case may be the first in which this principle was ever applied in the courts of New Mexico Territory, it was not unknown, being relied upon heavily in Texas courts. Several of the Fall-Lee gang were fugitives from murder warrants in Texas, and even the most simple-minded criminal could be expected to learn the loopholes in the law. Most of Fall's practice consisted of defending Texas and New Mexico criminals; he was much in demand at El Paso as a defense attorney, and shrewd and keen-minded lawyer that he was, he could be expected to know every facet of Texas criminal law.

Thus, corpus delicti would have been a well-known fact to him, and as the mastermind behind the Fountain tragedy it is reasonable to believe that he shaped the scheme to remove all trace of the bodies and thereby provided himself with the basis for defense should the matter ever come to trial. Lee was in the process of installing steam pumps at the wells scattered over his range. Each pump required a boiler and a firebox to produce the steam power. As Gilliland and others talked, word got out that the victims had been cremated in one of these fireboxes. During 1900, an unmarked grave was discovered high in the Sacramentos; its contents included burned human bones and a Winchester with a charred stock. Near the grave, searchers found a Masonic pin.

Although Fall did not pull the trigger, he inflamed the Sacramento gunmen filled with fear of the consequences of Colonel Fountain's stock-theft investigations. The fact that Fall had been successful in keeping them out of prison in earlier escapades as their defense attorney undoubtedly provided them with the daring to make their attack on Colonel Fountain. One story of the period was that when he was told of Fountain's success before the Lincoln County grand jury in obtaining indictments against Lee and Mc-New, Fall was reported to have ordered Lee and McNew "to get those [the indictment] papers at any cost."

Fountain's vigorous prosecution of the rustler indictments he had obtained at Lincoln court provided Lee, Gilliland, and Mc-New with a motive for murder. They had before them the prospects of a ten-year prison term such as Slick Miller had received. They were desperate. But Fall had a motive too. The enduring obstacle to his achieving Democratic pre-eminence in Doña Ana County and New Mexico generally was the Fountain-led Republican opposition; and he "hated Fountain like a snake" for old scores and scars, such as the Colonel's role in his removal as Third District judge. Pinkerton operatives Fraser and Sayers had observed that Fall was the mastermind of this conspiracy and that Lee was completely under his control. Similarly, Slick Miller reported that Carr, Gilliland, and McNew were completely under the control of Lee.

The murder of Henry Fountain suggests that the slayers were local men. This precocious eight-year-old boy had seen the Fall crowd many times at Las Cruces; he knew them. The killers were compelled to do away with the child to eliminate the possibility of future identification. This killing was important, too, in ruling out the claim made by Fall that killers were imported for the job. Gunmen brought in from Texas or Arizona Territory need not have feared recognition by the child and could have been expected to spare him. The Slick Miller confession was relevant to this point, too. In 1894, when it was proposed to import killers to do away with Fountain, McDonald, and Cree, one of the conspirators dismissed it with the statement that "he would never trust such important work to outsiders."

Another curious angle to the Fountain case was the difficulty in obtaining witnesses. Joe Morgan bullied leading Las Cruceans into discontinuing any discussion of the case. Witnesses left the country. Jack Maxwell went to Mexico, and even after returning he was so frightened by the anticipated consequences of his testimony that Garrett had to search for him with a posse and force him to attend the Hillsboro trial. Many witnesses forgot all that they knew, and key witnesses died; Les Dow, important to the prosecution for establishing motive, was gunned down at Eddy before the Hillsboro trial, and Deputy Kearney died from wounds received at the Wildy Well fight.

Fall and his cohorts used remarkable ingenuity in destroying clues; obliterating the trail to the Dog Canyon ranch by driving a herd of cattle across it just as the Las Cruces posse closed in is a case in point. Not only were clues destroyed, but evidence disappeared. Brannigan's notes on the tracks and his marking sticks vanished. The Pinkerton reports were stolen from the Governor's Palace at Santa Fe, indicating the far-reaching nature of the conspiracy. At the time of the Fountain murders Tom Tucker, a Fall-Lee partisan, held a commission as deputy sheriff at Santa Fe. When Pinkerton operative Fraser was relieved by Sayers, the former warned his colleague that he would be watched. Sayers noted that after he arrived at Santa Fe his every movement was under surveillance; his stalker was identified as Tom Tucker. Governor Thornton told Sayers that several letters concerning the Fountain case, including the one advising of Sayers' assignment to the case, were missing from his desk. Thus, Fall was informed that the detectives were still investigating the Fountain murders. Then, shortly after the Pinkerton agency was called off the case, according to a story in the Las Vegas *Optic* dated May 16, 1896, the entire file of their reports on the Fountain case was stolen from the Governor's office. Fraser and Sayers made their reports directly to McParland at the Pinkerton regional office in Denver, who, in turn, sent them to Governor Thornton. The Pinkerton file contained detailed information and statements on all phases of the investigation, including witnesses and evidence; thus Fall fairly well knew what to expect of the prosecution and which witnesses and evidence to do away with. In recent years the Pinkerton reports have turned up in private hands in the Tularosa country.

Considering the sensational nature of the case and the vast interest in it, one would expect that someone would have talked. Gilliland talked too freely after the Chalk Hill ambush, and was warned and watched. When Carr got religion, Lee and McNew watched him closely, for they feared that an emotional testimonial by him during revival services might give them away. For the most part, those who knew kept their secrets to the grave out of fear of Oliver Lee. One is reminded of the story told by the irrepressible Alfalfa Bill Murray: "One night during church services, the preacher was exhorting his flock on brother love, urging them to love even their enemies. Admitting that this was difficult at times since even he had unloved enemies, the preacher ventured there was not a member present who had no enemies. At this, an old fellow seated near the pulpit jumped up and shouted that he for one could swear that he had no enemies in this world. The preacher doubted this and asked 'how come?' to which the old fellow responded 'because I've outlived all the bastards.' " This was the case for the Fountain killers. They outlived most of those who could supply information of who and how.

Those few who did talk, did so surreptitiously, or on their deathbeds. One story told by several, confirming the cremation account, recalled that killing Colonel Fountain was no problem; doing away with the child was difficult, however, so straws (grass stems) were drawn. One account said McNew drew the short straw; another that Carr was with the party and that he drew the short straw; and yet another was that Lee drew it and paid the others to do his job. It was said that Gilliland carried a handsome gold watch until he became embarrassed by an inscription on the case, "From the grateful citizens of Western Texas to Senator Fountain."

One of the saddest stories told by old-timers concerned Gilliland's sister, who at the time of the murders was a young girl working at Dog Canyon ranch for her keep. Going to slop the hogs early one morning, she found them rooting up from a shallow grave near the fence the remains of Henry Fountain; as the swine tore at the boy, she went into shock. Later, her husband was killed by McNew in a range argument. A sensitive, brave, and fair-minded woman, she corresponded with the Fountain family at Las Cruces; her letters showed sympathy and regret. One, written in 1916, read in part: "I write this in great fear. One of the men who killed your father and little brother has just killed my husband. If I had done my duty on the stand (although it would have ruined my brother), it is possible my husband would still be alive. There is great danger here as long as the three [Lee,

Gilliland, and McNew] live. I have missed not corresponding with you folks."[1]

Another tragic figure in the Fountain story was Pat Garrett. The old bounty hunter was wrecked by the verdict at Hillsboro; all the time and effort he had put into the Fountain investigation was for naught. President Theodore Roosevelt appointed him collector of customs at the Pass in 1901, but, after a boresome stint as a federal official at El Paso, the mystical attraction of the Fountain case pulled him back to the Tularosa country.

Garrett settled on a spread in the San Andres just off the road that led into Oliver Lee's domain. While he did some ranching, it was no secret that he had returned to southern New Mexico to complete a job he had begun in 1896. The fact that the Fountain case reward money was still available no doubt was a strong inducement; added to this was Garrett's determination to vindicate himself—he still rankled at the public ridicule and shame which his failure to bring in the Fountain killers had stirred up.

Garrett's tenacity, his waiting for someone to crack and talk, must have been irritating to the Fall gang. Thus, it is not surprising that on a spring day in 1908, as Garrett drove his buckboard along the Las Cruces road, he was shot in the back. Nor is it surprising that the man alleged to be Garrett's killer, Wayne Brazle, was defended by Albert Fall, who, using the old reliable self-defense plea, won an acquittal for his client.

The principal figure in the Fountain case, Albert Bacon Fall, was stalked by shame and tragedy. Always the opportunist, he came to realize that Colonel Fountain, Catron, and other territorial Republicans had built well, for it seemed that the only way a man could win election to important public office and really get ahead in New Mexico was to be a Republican. So in 1902, believing statehood was near, he abandoned the party he had fought so hard to develop and became a Republican. Fall held various territorial offices as a Republican, and when statehood was

[1] Lucy Raley to Albert J. Fountain, Jr., Orogrande, New Mexico, October 27, 1915. Fountain Papers, University of Oklahoma Library.

finally achieved in 1912, he was elected, along with Tom Catron, to the United States Senate.

Fall's service as senator was conspicuous for promoting his own and other private interests in New Mexico, notably his extended but unsuccessful attempt to take the Mescalero reservation from the Apaches and open it to Anglo exploitation. In 1921 he was appointed to President Harding's cabinet as secretary of the interior; in this high post he brought shame to his state and the nation.

If the infamy of Teapot Dome is Albert Fall's monument, epitomizing his role as a destroyer, by dramatic contrast, Albert J. Fountain's many enduring monuments attest to his role as a builder. Edgar Beecher Bronson, Fountain's personal friend, esteemed the Colonel's role as a builder so highly that he gave him first position in his *Red Blooded Heroes of the Frontier*. His appraisal of Colonel Fountain supplies a fitting epitaph for that anonymous grave in the rock-ribbed Sacramentos: "Whenever the history of the Territory of New Mexico comes to be written, the name of Colonel Albert J. Fountain deserves and should have first place in it. Throughout the formative epoch of her evolution from semi-savagery to civilization, an epoch spanning the years from 1866 to 1896, Colonel Fountain was far and away her most distinguished and most useful citizen. As soldier, scholar, dramatist, lawyer, prosecutor, Indian fighter, and desperado hunter, his was the most picturesque personality I have ever known. Gentle and kind-hearted as a woman, a lover of his books and his ease, he nevertheless was always as quick to take up arms and undergo any hazard and hardship in pursuit of murderous rustlers. . . . He despised wrong, and hated the criminal, and spent his whole life trying to right the one and suppress or exterminate the other."[2]

[2] Bronson, *The Red Blooded Heroes of the Frontier*, 98–99.

Bibliography

I. Manuscripts

Thomas B. Catron Papers, University of New Mexico Library, Albuquerque.

Hiram Dow Manuscript, University of Oklahoma Library, Norman.

Albert J. Fountain Papers (Typescripts), University of Oklahoma Library, Norman.

National Archives, Washington, D.C.

Records Concerning Albert Bacon Fall. Record Group No. 60, Department of Justice.

Records of the Office of Adjutant General Concerning Albert J. Fountain. Record Group No. 94.

Records Relating to Service of Albert J. Fountain in New Mexico. Record Group No. 60. Department of Justice.

Service Record of Albert J. Fountain (1861–66), War Department Files, Record Group No. 94.

New Mexico State Records Center, Santa Fe

General Orders File, Adjutant General's Office.

Governor's Letter Books. New Mexico Territory, 1879–96.

Reports of the Adjutant General for New Mexico Territory, 1879–96.

Reports of Albert J. Fountain to the Adjutant General's Office, 1879–90.

Pinkerton National Detective Agency Reports, 1896.

II. Published Documents

United States Congress. 45 Cong., 2 sess., *House Exec. Doc.* 93.

———. 38 Cong., 1 sess., *House Exec. Doc.* 1.

New Mexico Constitutional Convention. *Proceedings.* Santa Fe, 1890.

———. *Address to the People.* Santa Fe, 1890.

New Mexico Legislature. *House Journal* (1889–90).

Report of the Commissioner of Indian Affairs, 1861–90.
Report of the Secretary of War, 1875–86.
Richardson, James D. A *Compilation of the Messages and Papers of the Presidents (1789–1908)*, Vol. VIII, Washington, 1908.
Texas Legislature, *Journal of the Texas Senate*, (1870–74).
War of Rebellion, Official Records of Union and Confederate Armies.

III. Books

Alsberg, Henry G., ed. *New Mexico—A Guide to the Colorful State*. New York, 1953.
Bailey, Harry H. *When New Mexico Was Young*. Las Cruces, 1946.
Bancroft, Hubert H. *History of Arizona and New Mexico (1530–1888)* (Vol. XVII of *Works*). San Francisco, 1889.
———. *History of California (1860–1890)* (Vol. XXIV of *Works*). San Francisco, 1890.
Bronson, Edgar B. *The Red Blooded Heroes of the Frontier*. New York, 1910.
Calvin, Ross. *Sky Determines*. New York, 1934.
Casey, Robert J. *The Texas Border and Some Borderliners*. Indianapolis, 1950.
Charles, Mrs. Tom. *Tales of the Tularosa*. Ed. by Francis L. Fugate. Alamogordo, 1953.
Cleaveland, Agnes M. *Satan's Paradise*. Boston, 1952.
Coan, Charles F. *A History of New Mexico*. 3 vols. Chicago, 1925.
Conkling, Roscoe P. and Margaret B. *The Butterfield Overland Mail, 1857–1869*. 3 vols. Glendale, 1947.
Cremony, John C. *Life Among the Apaches*. Tucson, 1954.
Crichton, Kyle S. *Law and Order Ltd*. Santa Fe, 1928.
Davis, Ellis A., ed. *Historical Encyclopedia of New Mexico*. Albuquerque, 1945.
Donnelley, Thomas C. *Rocky Mountain Politics*. Albuquerque, 1940.
———. *The Government of New Mexico*. Albuquerque, 1947.
Douglas, C. L. *Famous Texas Feuds*. Dallas, 1936.
Fergusson, Erna. *Murder and Mystery in New Mexico*. Albuquerque, 1948.
———. *New Mexico—A Pageant of Three Peoples*. New York, 1951.
Fountain, Albert J. *Dona Ana County—Her People and Resources*. Las Cruces, 1885.

Gillett, James B. *Six Years with the Texas Rangers*. New Haven, 1925.

Griggs, George. *History of Mesilla Valley or the Gadsden Purchase*. Mesilla, 1930.

Harkey, Dee. *Mean as Hell*. Albuquerque, 1948.

Harrison, Nan H. *George W. Coe—Frontier Fighter*. Albuquerque, 1951.

Hening, H. B., ed. *George Curry (1861-1947)—An Autobiography*. Albuquerque, 1958.

History of New Mexico—Its Resources and People. 2 vols. Los Angeles, 1907.

Hunt, Aurora. *Major General James Henry Carleton*. Glendale, 1958.

———. *The Army of the Pacific*. Glendale, 1951.

Jones, Fayette A. *New Mexico Mines and Minerals*. Santa Fe, 1904.

Keleher, William A. *The Fabulous Frontier*. Santa Fe, 1945.

———. *Turmoil in New Mexico, 1846-1868*. Santa Fe, 1952.

Kelly, Florence F. *With Hoops of Steel*. Indianapolis, 1900.

Kerby, Robert L. *The Confederate Invasion of New Mexico and Arizona*. Los Angeles, 1958.

Lewis, Oscar. *The War in the Far West, 1861-1865*. New York, 1961.

MacCallum, Esther D. *The History of St. Clement's Church*. El Paso, 1925.

Mills, W. W. *El Paso—A Glance at Its Men and Conflicts . . . Fountain the Infamous*. Austin, 1871.

———. *Forty Years at El Paso, 1858-1898*. El Paso, 1901.

Nicholl, Edith M. *Observations of a Ranchwoman in New Mexico*. London, 1898.

O'Connor, Richard. *Pat Garrett—A Biography of the Famous Marshal*. New York, 1960.

O'Neil, James B. *They Die but Once—The Story of a Tejano*. New York, 1935.

Orton, Richard H. *Records of California Men in the War of the Rebellion*. Sacramento, 1890.

Otero, Miguel A. *My Life on the Frontier*. New York, 1935.

———. *My Nine Years as Governor of New Mexico Territory*. Albuquerque, 1940.

Prince, L. Bradford. *A Concise History of New Mexico*. Cedar Rapids, 1912.

———. *New Mexico's Struggle for Statehood*. Santa Fe, 1910.

Ramsdell, Charles W. *Reconstruction in Texas*. New York, 1910.

Raynor, Ted. *Old Timers Talk in Southwestern New Mexico.* El Paso, 1960.

Richter, Conrad. *The Lady.* New York, 1957.

Sacramento, California, Directory for 1859.

Siringo, Charles A. *A Lone Star Cowboy.* Santa Fe, 1919.

Sonnichsen, C. L. *The El Paso Salt War.* El Paso, 1961.

————. *The Mescalero Apaches.* Norman, 1958.

————. *Tularosa, Last of the Frontier West.* New York, 1961.

Stanley, F. *Desperadoes of New Mexico.* Denver, 1953.

————. *The Civil War in New Mexico.* Denver, 1960.

Twitchell, Ralph E. *The Leading Facts of New Mexican History.* Vol. V. Cedar Rapids, 1917.

Webb, Walter P. *The Texas Rangers.* Boston, 1935.

White, Owen. *Out of the Desert—The Historical Romance of El Paso.* El Paso, 1923.

Wooten, E. O. *The Range Problem in New Mexico.* Albuquerque, 1908.

IV. Articles

Ayers, John. "A Soldier's Experience in New Mexico," *New Mexico Historical Review,* Vol. XXIV (October, 1949), 259–66.

Crimmons, Martin L. "Colonel Buell's Expedition into New Mexico in 1880," *New Mexico Historical Review,* Vol. X (April, 1935), 133–42.

Murray, Richard Y. "Apache Pass—Most Formidable of Gorges," *Corral Dust,* Vol. VI (June, 1961), 17–19.

Pettis, George H. "History of Company K, First Infantry, California Volunteers," *Personal Narratives of Events in the War of Rebellion.* Providence, 1885.

————. "The California Column," *Publications of the New Mexico Historical Society,* Vol. XI, (1908).

Russell, Carl P. "The White Sands of Alamogordo," *National Geographic Magazine,* Vol. LXVIII (August, 1935), 250–64.

Stratton, David H. "New Mexico Machiavellian? The Story of Albert B. Fall," *Montana—the Magazine of Western History,* Vol. VII (October, 1957), 2–14.

"The Old Lincoln Courthouse," *El Palacio,* Vol. XLVI (January, 1939).

Waldrip, William I. "New Mexico During the Civil War," *New Mexico Historical Review*, Vol. XXVIII (October, 1953), 251–90.

V. *Newspapers*

Albuquerque *Citizen*.
Albuquerque *Journal*.
Austin *Republican*.
Austin *State Journal*.
Dallas *Herald*.
Denver *News*.
Doña Ana *Republican*.
Eddy *Argus*.
El Paso *Herald*.
El Paso *Times*.
Flake's Bulletin.
Galveston *News*.
Galveston *Tri-Weekly News*.
Houston *Times*.
Independent Democrat.
Las Vegas *Examiner*.
Las Vegas *Optic*.
Lone Star.
Mesilla *Independent*.
Mesilla *News*.
Mesilla Valley Independent.
Roswell *Record*.
Rio Grande Republican.
San Marcial *Bee*.
Santa Fe *New Mexican*.
Santa Fe *New Mexican Review*.
Silver City *Enterprise*.
Socorro *Chieftain*.
Springer *Stockman*.
Thirty-four.

VI. *Interviews*

Albert Fountain. Mesilla, New Mexico, August 12, 1961.
Elizabeth Fountain Armendariz. Mesilla, New Mexico, July 10, 1960, and August 13, 1961.
Henry Fountain. Mesilla, New Mexico, August 10–12, 1961.

INDEX

294

Index

Bunting, George: 226
Butterfield Overland Mail: 10, 11, 16, 22, 46, 48, 75, 96

Caballero, Jose: 118
Caballo Range (New Mexico): 31, 40, 131
Caffrey, William: 186
Caldwell, Charles: 80
Caldwell-Blacker-Fountain Law Firm: 89
California Column: 14, 15, 21, 23, 24, 26, 27, 32, 34, 96, 168; Company E, 9ff., 15, 21, 23, 24, 26, 27; Second California Cavalry, 14, 16, 112; Fifth California Infantry, 14; First California Volunteers, 14, 15; Third United States Artillery, 14; Company G, 28, 29, 32
California Column Veterans: 92, 166
Campbell, Don: 63, 70, 79, 81
Canby, Edward R. S.: 21
Candelario Mountains (Mexico): 107
Canutillo, New Mexico: 118
Cardis, Luis: 48, 75, 76, 84
Carleton, James H.: 10, 14, 15, 20, 24, 25, 27, 28, 35, 37, 103
Carpenter District (New Mexico): 136
Carr, Bill: 214, 247, 256, 257, 260, 264, 266
Carson, Kit: 24, 168
Casad, Thomas: 81, 96, 97, 102
Catron, Thomas B.: 93, 138, 156, 179, 185, 186, 191, 199, 204, 215, 271, 275, 280, 281, 288
Cernillos, New Mexico: 162
Chalk Hill (New Mexico): 3, 4, 228, 230ff., 247, 249, 255, 257, 258, 262, 264, 272, 274, 277, 285
Chamberino, New Mexico: 170
Chaves, Andreas: 207
Chaves, J. Francisco: 175, 183, 187
Chaves County, New Mexico: 222
Chihuahua, Mexico: 22, 46, 51, 107, 110, 114, 154, 172, 262
Childers, William B.: 185, 191, 201, 271, 275, 279
Chilili, New Mexico: 37
Clancy, Frank W.: 201
Clark, Amos: 50
Clarke, Gaylord: 48, 49, 52, 55, 71, 72, 74, 77ff.
Clausen, Carl: 161, 236, 264
Cloudcroft, New Mexico: 214
Cochise (Apache): 17
Coffelt, Mat: 217, 282
Cohen, Bart: 205
Colorado, New Mexico: 170, 177
Colorado River (Arizona): 11
Colville, Jim: 123
Concordia, Texas: 114, 118
Contrecio, New Mexico: 150
Cooke's Range (New Mexico): 131
Corpus Christi, Texas: 55
Coyn, Tom: 122
Cree, James: 220, 221, 223, 224, 225, 245, 256, 284
Cremony, John C.: 14, 16, 19
Crook, George: 131
Crouch, John S.: 96, 97, 102, 105
Cubero, Mariano: 116
Cubero, Nestor: 118
Cunliffe, Henry: 48
Curry, George: 270
Curtis, N. Greene: 8, 23, 48, 190

Daily, T. J.: 271
Daugherty, Harry: 277, 278
Davis, Edmund J.: 53, 55, 56, 58, 60ff., 64, 68, 74, 80, 81, 83, 84
Davis, Jefferson: 87
Davis Reconstruction Program: see Texas Reconstruction
Dawson, Sue: 147
Deming, New Mexico: 120, 142, 143, 154
Denver and Río Grande Railroad: 169
Denver Exposition (1889): 170
Dickey, Fred: 32
Dog Canyon (New Mexico): 24, 214, 217, 234, 236, 237, 259, 265, 267, 270, 276, 277, 285, 286

295

Index

Index

UNIVERSITY OF OKLAHOMA PRESS

Norman